A Single Rose

A Single Rose

Louis S. LaCava

VANTAGE PRESS
New York

Published by Vantage Press, Inc.
419 Park Ave. South, New York, NY 10016

Manufactured in the United States of America
ISBN: 0-533-15290-9

Library of Congress Catalog Card No.: 2005906454

0 9 8 7 6 5 4 3 2 1

In honor of Ma and Pa for their untiring faith in the Almighty and the knowledge that with Him all things are possible—through perseverance in doing His Will for the Glory of God. Without having had their example and their words, my own travels over the rough and unknown waters of life could never have been survived.

In setting out to write their saga, **Egidio—Ora et Labora**—I discovered my own story, *A Single Rose*; without the exemplary faith in God of Egidio and Anna Maria LaCava, there would have been no stories to write. . . .

Contents

Author's Note

Originally these pages were detailed to be a primer, telling what enkindled such motivation and enthusiasm to write the epic *Egidio—Ora et Labora*. But somewhere in the process of gathering information, making the outline, and finally writing, the "primer" took on a life of its own.

Initially, material was gathered and collated solely to touch on a theme, to scratch the curiosity of the reader, helping to define the book *Egidio*'s purpose, and the effort that was put forth in writing it. Essentially, the biography of the great Egidio would humbly be told through the eyes of one of his offspring; herein lies the problem in construction of a primer. In order to tell the story of Egidio the pages had to include something of the son . . . but because of tragedy, struggle, and abundant human drama in his own life the written page quickly formed an image, whereby a story emerged to stand alone.

Although *A Single Rose* opens avenues of enlightenment about the inspiration and birth of such a daunting task as writing an epic, it actually is, to a minor degree, a complement to *Egidio—Ora et Labora*—an affirmation that without a shadow of a doubt, hope is eternal, and one should never, never, never give in or give up, for through prayer and faith when one seems lost, the joy and peace nestled in your rainbow is just beyond the horizon!

A Time to Learn

Graduation was over, diplomas awarded. All the fun and frivolities were finished. It was time to settle down to work and save enough money to buy a car. College was always in the back of my mind; I was confident I would either attend night classes or register at a community college after a year or two, but first I had to make some serious money. Nothing has changed—even today, with all the opportunities for higher education, many kids still fall into the same trap of working a year to make money, with every intention of returning to school. Yet never doing so I had a wide range of interests, with a million things to my schedule and so many irons in the fire all I could see was smoke—they called it type-A personality.

There were many definitions for type-A. Some said it was having many hobbies and talents but proficiency in none of them. Today it's called type A-1; I don't know what the 1 stands for, but I suspect it has something to do with what's been learned through the advanced science of psychology. Coincidentally, no one could give me any advice—using the old cliché: I had to do what I had to do. It would be several years before the colloquial saying "I've got to do my thing" became famous, but I never equated enthusiasm and energy with "my thing." I was just young, healthy and excited—determined to live life to its fullest potential.

As I recall, jobs were scarce in 1952, but if you were willing to work you could find employment. The previous year I had held three jobs while attending school: construction worker, ice cream man, and custodian, where I worked nights helping the head janitor in one of three Wethersfield schools. Sometimes I was alone late, and there were moments, I must admit, when it was very creepy. But I survived, and it was a meaningful experience—I was supporting myself and learning many skills. At the same

1

time I was experiencing "the rigors of life." Having three jobs may have appeared ambitious, but it wasn't of my own choosing; it was out of necessity. I was one of fourteen children, and such a big family required many hands, cooperation, and love to make it work. A huge household took an abundance of milk and bread to feed a hungry lot—everyone contributed.

My senior year was a busy but exciting one. Nat King Cole had some big hits, and top on the charts was Kay Starr's "Wheel of Fortune." It never entered anyone's mind what a strong connection that song would have to the Class of '52. The omen was so very remote. The 50's also brought a new and great artist on the horizon by the name of Mario Lanza. He had a natural and tremendously big voice that came out of a fifty-inch chest supporting strong and healthy lungs.

The most popular car was a Studebaker, its design rather weird compared to today's aerodynamic engineering feats. It had the appearance of a fish, as I recall, and was very low to the ground with a pointy front and a back slightly tapered down. It might have been ahead of its time in design, for who would ever dream that in the late twentieth century cars would require a passenger to nearly fold their body in half upon entering? Keeping this in mind, one looks back with a smirk recalling a ludicrous claim by the Soviet Union at the time of Nikita Khrushchev's visit in 1957, that all the lots filled with cars were staged for propaganda purposes!

It would be less than frank to give the impression that my high school years, especially the last, were always stressful. I can look back today with nostalgia, remembering joys and wholesome fun spiced with bits of humor. One incident that occurred in the spring of 1952 gave me first-hand insight into how our judiciary system worked. It was my first, and may I add only, experience with the courts, and all started one balmy night at a gas station where I used to work or help out. I had several friends who were gun enthusiasts, and on this fateful night a car carrying three of them pulled into the station. One friend, the leader, John Schmidt (names have been changed) came inside and said to the attendant, Frank Tocascio, "Close up early and come with us."

2

His answer was typically 50's: "What's happenin'?"

With a big grin on his face, John said, "We're going to the dump to shoot rats." Frank's eyebrows rose, with no other facial expression and without reply, so John looked at me and said, "Lou, come on. You'll be the driver and spotter for our safari." Alan Chooney, the third guy, drove a dazzling Chevy equipped with spotlights, and a spotter's job was to stay in the car and simply turn the handle so the light would sweep in a 180-degree arc, causing huge rats to scatter in all directions.

While John was asking me to be the spotter, Frank—a big, muscular but gentle and reserved guy, who spoke in soft monotones—was pumping gas and broke into a funny cackle laugh before he answered, "Give me five minutes to finish with this guy and I'll close up." Well, "this guy" wanted everything under the hood checked, so instead of five minutes it took twenty. In those days all stations were totally full service, so this was the normal practice, although only about one in four indicated they wanted the service. But this particular night the last customer had to be that one!!

The author took over pumping the gas and Frank was checking under the hood. Excited in anticipation of our trip to the dump, I inadvertently pumped a couple of tenths more than the three gallons that had been ordered. Back in the 50's most customers ordered gas in gallons, not dollars, and this man almost had a conniption about my error. After some embarrassment, I apologized and offered to pay for the two-tenths (about three cents worth); he just grunted "Be more careful next time," put a cigar back in his mouth, got in his car and left. The time was about eight P.M., and it was dark. Frank tallied up the register while the author hauled the various outside racks—tire cabinet, wiper blade rack, windshield washer pail, etc.—under cover for security. The other three guys waited quietly and patiently, standing against the car while eyeing a pretty girl waiting for the bus, hoping to get a glimpse of her legs when she stepped up to enter.

As Frank was having some trouble locking the door, Alan suddenly yelled over, "Gees!" A police car drove in, as was customary around that time of closing, just to verify the attendant

3

had secured the premises before his departure. They gave special attention to this corner, for it was a busy intersection and traffic could come through from two main highways and a boulevard. In addition, an overpass spanned two concrete pillar abutments holding gigantic steel I-beams; they supported the massive deck structure that moved cars diagonally over the huge intersection. This was 40's structural engineering, and brief deck spans required huge connecting supports. A tragic collapse causing death during this construction would catapult Hartford and the state of Connecticut into national news.

This overpass produced continuous noise, and as I laid awake on hot summer nights—we lived two blocks from the area—I could hear the resounding pound of trucks in the still of the night as they transported their wares to Boston and New York. The din, din, din often helped me fall into a sound hypnotic sleep masking weird dreams. In contrast to the cacophony above the deck (the four-lane bridge was the longest continuous plate-girder bridge in the country at that time) the overpass cast long, dark shadows below. Here was an ideal corner and creepy inner sanctum for thievery, so it was no surprise the gas station had been broken into several times. This corner and intersection received more than average police coverage in Wethersfield; additionally, the location was only three blocks from the City of Hartford.

The policeman got out of his car and asked if the door was locked. Frank said it was, but the sergeant checked it anyway. Little did I fathom that in approximately three hours this same lawman and the author would meet again!

I got into the car and left the door open for Frank, and as he got in with the money satchel he said he had to drop the day's receipts off to the owner, Mr. Mall. In the meantime the guys were getting a little anxious, to say the least. Everyone was starting to talk at once, when I came out with something original like, "Hey, guys, shush, or you'll wake the dead." They all got the hint, and the conversation went on to the subject of guns, which was extremely boring to me. I didn't know anything about them and had no desire to learn. I was just being a good friend, willing to be a spotter and happy that we were finally on our way.

4

Alan turned his car around and headed up Jordan Lane to Mr. Mall's. As we were heading up the hill Alan had to slam on his brakes to avoid hitting a black cat running across our path. The sudden reaction saved one of the cat's lives but jolted us, which moved John to say, "That's a bad sign. Maybe you should have hit it." Then he emitted a laugh, for there wasn't a superstitious bone in his body. The satchel of money and receipts was quickly delivered, and as Frank hurriedly approached the car, Alan slowly crept forward, and every time Frank caught up, trying to get into the car, Alan sped up again—slower, then a little faster. Finally, Frank just stopped running and started to walk in the other direction when someone said, "Oh, oh, I think he's going home." Frank didn't live a block or two away, so that's when Jim said to turn around quickly. A tire-screeching U-turn brought displeasure from an approaching motorist, who had to jam on his brakes, and, sounding his horn, he shook a clenched fist in obvious annoyance. (It was uncouth and a rarity in the 50's for an irate driver to flash his IQ in anger or disgust as is so common today.)

Now, the trip to the dump was only a short ride—less than three miles. During the ride there was great camaraderie, loud discussion and arguing about the effectiveness of certain firearms and about guns in general—again; 30/30's, shotguns, sawed-offs, even muzzle loaders. My forbearance, running thin, brought me to the point of exasperation. That's when I started to sing "Be My Love" (the theme from the hit motion picture *Toast of New Orleans*, starring Mario Lanza) at the top of my mighty lungs. Pandemonium ensued. Someone yelled, "Shove a handkerchief in his mouth," while others were not as charitable. Jim, who was sitting next to me, took a blanket folded on the ledge behind the back seat and wrapped it around my head, causing hysterical laughter.

We were on Main Street in Old Wethersfield, ready to turn onto Marsh Street, where we would pass the ancient historic cemetery and burial grounds. The group became spooked when the author started to tell of Wethersfield's sad history of witches.

"Did you know that nearly half of the fifty-one men and women that suffered from accusations, slander, trial or execution for witchcraft came from Wethersfield, Hartford, and Windsor?" I asked in a pedagogical tone.

"Ahhhh . . . come on, Lou, let's not talk about cemeteries," one guy yelled out. I retorted that it was better than guns, and continued, remembering the story of a woman named Mary Johnson, Wethersfield's first witchcraft case. I described how she was in bad stead with the town around 1646, publicly whipped for stealing, and actually hung two years later for collusion with the devil. One gravestone in the burial grounds is bizarre. It depicts in vivid, gruesome detail the savage murders of Mrs. Lydia Beadle and her five children by her husband, William, in 1782. In conjunction with the persecution of "witches" from around 1648 to 1670, and the slaves (Wethersfield had fifty-nine in 1790), these murders were a horrific blight to the community, and were an unfortunate part of Wethersfield's otherwise uniquely long and colorful history. One other interesting tidbit about the ancient resting place is that many bodies of convicts and inmates from the state prison that used to be on State Street were buried there.

To get to the dump we had to negotiate a sharp curve; then an opposite bend down a steep grade would bring us to the entrance. It's fascinating for me to think that there used to be huge fields of onion groves on the flat fertile land along the river and the future location of the town dump. Wethersfield was a thriving agricultural haven, primarily because of its productively rich soil. It exported to all parts of the world: wheat, rye, barley, peas, seeds, garlic, flax, and a huge amount of onions, with the basic markets being the West Indies, England, and the Mediterranean, and on this continent along the coast from Nova Scotia to Louisiana.

Wethersfield, from 1730 to 1838, was the center for the cultivation of onions. It was a gigantic industry, a boon to a community that employed many people, including young girls, (mentioned because women were never working out of their houses). But it would fade away in 1838 after growing competition from other areas, several consecutive severe winters, rainy springs that stripped the minerals from the soil, and the ubiquitous worm blight put a damper on the industry.

6

Inside the car was now absolutely quiet. I couldn't help thinking maybe my friends were introspectively respectful of the dead—or was it just anticipation of the moment to come, intertwined with slight apprehension and perhaps thoughts that maybe this was not the right thing to do. I never found out what they were thinking, but it was unlike this bunch to be this reticent! As I looked over at the First Church of Christ my mind again wandered back, and I was overwhelmed by the history of one of the oldest established towns in the country. The first meetinghouses in 1645, where public gatherings for elections and other purposes were held, must have been spirited places.

History lessons had told us about John Oldham, who with ten others settled in Wethersfield in 1634. We also knew about who inhabited the land for 8,000 years prior, from the Nomadic Paleo and Archaic Indians to the Woodland Indians, who were truly great people. Native Americans were naturally skilled, and dexterous in many ways; they were blessed with an abundance of gifts that eventually "found the shoes" they would wear, having made them responsible for and credited with many industrious revelations. One skill was agricultural techniques that would be passed on to the "settlers"; also, their ingenuity and talent for crafting bowls, plates and spoons from stone and wood made way for the first tools—crude and ancient in scope, out of necessity, but certainly genius. This set the engineering stage that evolved to make it possible for future manufacturing of textiles; also, the Indians initiated bartering that eventually brought commerce into the area on a large scale, making the flat sand beds along the Connecticut River a thriving developed expanse, and eventually leading to increased settlement.

We started down the steep muddy road that led us to the dump area, known as the "plains," where the "infamous safari" took place one brazen moonlit night in April of 1952. It was certainly possible that wild herbs used to grow and were harvested by Indians on the road we now traveled; the Indians, the Algonquins, were tribesmen of the Woodland period, and one of the tribes was the Wongunks of Wethersfield. In 1633 they invited English settlers to Wethersfield and showered them with food, friendship, and amenities in hopes they would settle and help protect them from other tribes. The Pequots, in particular, had threatened to wipe them out. John Oldham came to Wethersfield in 1634 and settled permanently with 10 others; that is why it is considered the first town in Connecticut. The Connecticut Colony's General Court in the Code of 1650 and 1672 Revision stated, "The most ancient towne for the river is determined by the Courte to bee Weathersfeild."

Halfway down the grade, Alan cut the car speed to almost a crawl to save undo stress on the shocks, for the road was riddled with ruts as a result of recent heavy rains. He slowed to a dead stop when we came upon a huge washout on the right side of the road. Gingerly, he maneuvered the vehicle slowly to the left; surprisingly, the car went down in the hole and came out easily, but branches from a hedge row on the left brushed the car and slapped through the back window, hitting my hand that was on the door. Then it whipped back to my shoulder until I grabbed it, bending it back and out the window. This interruption would turn out to be the least of our troubles as the night progressed.

It was pitch black when we finally arrived at the plains. Richie, who was sitting in the front seat, snapped on the spotlight, reflecting a weird iridescent smattering of colors and hues. The strange variegation must have been an omen and should have been a warning of what was to come. The phenomenon was due to the simultaneous position of the car, angle of the spotlight, speed with which John turned the light, and reflection off a red and blue clamshell crane parked a distance from our approach.

Jim, one of the other guys, yelled, "What the hell is that?" and I assured him it was just an optical illusion caused by the spotlight passing over the reflector light on the crane. Alan turned the car to face the depth of the dump area, where most of the common rubbish was buried, turned on the other spotlight, and shut off the engine. The four anxious hunters left the car and got their guns out of the trunk. The author followed.

There was a brief discussion about the advisability of using the 30/30, for it made the loudest noise at discharge, and supposedly we didn't want to disturb the "town fathers." But it was no more than jovial camaraderie . . . the "hunters" knew it was going to be used. Richie said, "Lou, get in the car, back it up, and rotate the spotlights." I immediately jumped in and started turning the handle around and up, which directed the light close to the ground. The guys started yelling, and I couldn't believe my eyes: there were hundreds and hundreds, maybe thousands of big, fat healthy rats scattering in all directions. Lined up about five or six feet apart, the guys began to shoot; Boom! Boom! Boom! An army of rats was immediately blown up on the plain. I thought for such small targets, most of "the hunters" had impeccable accuracy, and then it occurred to me that although they were all excellent shooters, the location and volume of rats made it quite easy to zero in the scope—even I could have hit the target!

The shooting continued for nearly two hours. During this time I wondered why the blinding spotlights didn't freeze rats' motion and out them in a mesmerized state like other rodents and carnivorous animals. Also, I'll admit I wondered more than once, not whether this noise could be heard on Main Street, but rather if someone would become curious and call the police. The hour was close to 11 P.M. and I was getting anxious to wrap it up. But I didn't want to disturb my friends' fun. Several big rats, confused about the direction for freedom, and in belligerent jingoistic fashion, headed in counterattack straight at the garrison. Jim let out a howl. Richie screamed, "Take them out! Take them out!" Boom! Boom! Boom! The cordon was split and, to my delight, the enemy escaped in the dank, dark, eerie plains.

The hunters gathered their composure and resumed shooting, but as I rotated the spotlight to the right side of the arc I was startled that the left side was emblazoned. Turning my head, I said to myself, "Murphy's Law never fails." For up the hill, descending the rutted dirt road, was a car, certain by its style to be a cop! In fright, I yelled, "Hey, cop's car!" Immediately the four of them jumped in the back seat of the car, tucking the guns in behind their feet.

Awkward and strange as it seemed, we all tried to appear as nonchalant as possible without looking suspicious. I started the engine and slowly rolled in the direction of the hill. By that time the police car was past the potholes and ruts and now approaching at a faster speed. When he was about fifty feet from us he blinked his high beams on and off as a signal to stop. He pulled his car almost parallel to ours but left about ten feet in between; this, I found out later, was part of procedure to give him space to react if the officer encountered "undesirables." As he slowly emerged from the car with a large flashlight in his left hand, his right hand loose at his side, I recognized the face. It was the same sergeant who was at the station three hours prior. Turning to the back seat with a sense of foreboding, I said to the guys, "Everyone be quiet. Let me do all the talking." Tall and handsome, his demeanor impressed me as a cop who would be congenial and understanding—in that assessment I was accurate. But, eventualities being what they are and human nature not always being able to grasp the importance of silence, we created much grief and fear, time and money—loss, in reality, of the taxpayers' money!

Slowly he walked to our car. The grade had a slight elevation, giving him an excellent vantage point; peering down on us he could easily detect any sudden movement from our vehicle. His silhouette, projected by the lights, made it obvious this intimidating man was there for a reason. He gingerly came toward us with his hands by his side, and recognized me from the gas station and for another reason which had nothing to do with the law. He approached the car with fast long strides. I cranked the window down and he pointed the light in my face, momentarily blinding me. "LaCava?"

I nervously answered, "Yes, sir." He was familiar with my face, for my dad was building in Wethersfield, and when there was pilfering this sergeant often came to the job to fill out a report. There were times after school he would see "my group" working at the site; plus, it was commonly stated that all LaCavas looked alike.

He continued, "This is not your car."

"No, sir."

"Do you know what time it is, LaCava?"

"No, sir."

"Does your father know you're out this late on a school night?"

"No, sir."

"What are you doing down here, LaCava?"

"Oh, just taking a ride, sir." At this time I was confident that he would just tell us to get home, so I was rather calm. It wasn't a lie; I just didn't tell the good officer the full story.

"Taking a ride in the dump at eleven o'clock at night, with four people sitting in the back seat?"

"Well, some got out to relieve themselves. When I noticed your car they got nervous and jumped in the back seat." (That was sure stretching it!)

"LaCava, four in the back seems unusual."

"Yes, sir."

In contrast to my respectful attitude, what transpired next made the decision between me sleeping that night or lying wide awake tracing every hairline crack in the plastered ceiling above my bed. Alan Chooney laconically chimed in from the back seat with a gruff voice, "Officer, is it against the law to sit four in the back seat?"

"All right, everyone out of the car but you, LaCava." The sergeant, in addition to being familiar with my family and me, also had a brother who was the building inspector in town. These things were sifting through my head like a Ferris wheel in full motion. That's when my conscience suddenly became a reservoir of fear in a sieve of terror. At this point I had lived a million years in my head! I lamented about the embarrassment to the family, especially because we were in business; also, the ramifications that would come from this experience. I mused, "I'll be plagued with this stigma the rest of my life. This will be my curse. I'll never live it down." I felt a sick feeling in the pit of my stomach and thought: if only one of the other guys had gagged Alan before the sergeant came to the car—if only . . . If only's were for children and that is what I felt like at the moment—a small, innocent, vulnerable child!

There was a different perspective back then. This was the 50's in a closed society; post war brought rectitude, valor, and dignity, with many new role models. Standards were set for the youth and they were to be strictly adhered to. The culture was predicated on wholesomeness and righteousness. Little things were extremely important. Neglecting to address an adult as Sir or Ma'am, not tipping your hat as you passed a lady, not rising to give a girl or a pregnant woman a seat on a bus or trolley, was rare and unforgivable. And God forbid you ever talked back to or hit a teacher—it was more than a disgrace—you weren't praised or machismo to your peers. You were a zero—a nothing. There was no Rambo or macho, rather you were despised and ostracized, ignominiously routed and expelled from school. If a girl had the misfortune of having a baby out of wedlock she was shamed and labeled promiscuous; the birth would be quietly celebrated, the sinner excoriated, and she was forced to move to another town. The sexual revolution (with its Woodstocks) of the 60's was still a decade away. It was Johnny Ray, Frankie Laine, Lionel Hampton, Duke Ellington, Earl Bostic, Count Basie, Patty Page, Rosemary Clooney, Perry Como . . . a slow measured calm—time in our history when there was still the "good guy" and the "bad guy," the victim had rights, and the majority of parents would not tolerate disrespect from their children or anyone else's. Thank You and Please were still in Webster's, and with its impersonal advantage, e-mail was not the way of communication—-I was I, and You were You and together it was We, for and with each other. When someone talked to you, you were expected to look in their eyes, not over their shoulders thinking of what to say. When you were with someone, you were taught to be with them totally, not remote or wishing to be somewhere else. Sincerity was still vogue.

It was a time in our history when the youth looked up to, respected, got guidance from, and took pride in lionized adults. Indeed, there were many role models. Our representatives in Washington were wholesomely dedicated individuals, who took tremendous pride in and felt responsibility for service to their constituents. They were proud of the challenge to uphold their duties conscientiously, with dignity and class, that they were entrusted with. There were very few who would obsequiously cast their vote against the moral conscience of America in terms of human rights. To have legalized abortion was unthinkable; to force people to pay for it would have meant revolution. I remember when one of our senators came to school to address the assembly of senior students, we had a feeling of awe—not that he was some god of a higher deity, rather that what was told, we could believe. There was seldom a credibility gap! When an answer was sought you didn't get some vague, ambiguous, high falutin' gobbledygook response that left you with a weird feeling—what did he say? Our country was evolving politically, economically, and socially into a more diverse culture—nevertheless, slowly measured—where care and simplicity were not cast aside for greed and convenience at the expense of mores.

The sergeant took all four of my friends over to the cruiser and said in a very authoritative tone, "Line up." It was near the back of the cruiser, a distance of about fifteen feet from where I remained. One of the boys was slow in moving into the exact position where the policeman wanted him, which brought an angry look onto his face—the author interpreted this as a bad omen. These fears would soon be justified decisively! He walked over to the car, where I was still inside. The back door on the left side was open and he glanced perfunctorily in that direction as he said to me, "LaCava, you should know better." Meanwhile, I was silently praying that he would not look inside the car and see the guns. As he walked around the door with his flashlight directed into the vehicle, he noticed and confiscated the firearms; it quickly became apparent my prayers had not been effectively or sincerely offered. He slowly returned to his cruiser and put the guns inside the trunk, which he then slammed shut—he was not very happy!

A high decibel combination of static and garbled words came from his car radio, which I couldn't make out. He hurriedly got into his car, closed the door, and called back to headquarters. I was nervous and curious about what he was saying but could only detect a few words at best. The rest seemed to be in code, but I was sure it was about us. And very shortly I knew my fate was sealed. Abruptly he emerged from the car and arrested the four with dispatch. There was little reaction from my friends; only John Schimdt informed him that "we were doing the town a favor, ridding it of the rats." The sergeant didn't think too kindly of the remarks as he filled out reports very quickly, obtaining names and addresses and all pertinent information. There were no Miranda rights read back then, and I believe in many ways a cop's life was less complicated.

It took about ten minutes for the officer to get all necessary information. The moon waned slightly though still was bright enough to illuminate the dump—a location not at all compatible with the intrigue and ecstasy of the tragic love story of Romeo and Juliet. We had worked in depth with Shakespeare in our second year literature class, and I still remember my teacher, Mrs. Humphrey, an extremely skilled and dynamic pedagogue. She would yell and scream and was inspirationally gifted. When you finished a semester under her tutelage, you knew literature and could recite long passages from great writers and poets. As the sergeant approached, my appearance changed from fright to ambivalence and I remember reciting to myself; "The stag at eve had drunk its fill where danced the moon on Monans rill." He was upon me, and I was back to reality, now into *Macbeth*: "Can all the oceans of the sea wash this blood from these hands?" He looked at me, and for a moment I saw a look of compassion on his face when he said, "LaCava, I've got to arrest you, too."

I answered with a stutter, "Yes, sir, I know you have to do your job, but if you arrest me you're going to have a murder on your hands."

With a quizzical look on his face, he said, "What does that mean?"

I responded, "My father's going to kill me!"

He softly said, "LaCava, I wasn't going to arrest anyone until your friend sarcastically asked if it was against the law to have four people in the back seat."

My father always advised his children to admit to a mistake and under no circumstances to taint the truth. Great civilizations have crumbled through deceit. He would end his counsel with "be up front, then go on from there; mistakes bring growth and wisdom." Later that night I wondered if admitting from the get-go that we were shooting rats would have made things different.

It had been almost two weeks since our dump rendezvous and subsequent arrest, and I still hadn't told my father. I was hoping in the dark crevices of my mind that the whole thing

14

would vanish by osmosis. Sunday morning was a bright, exhilarating day packed with energy from a strong southwesterly breeze. The day alone could instill well-being—a rare day in meteorological history in which the barometric pressure and related conditions were optimum for stabilizing a person's biorhythms. I had just finished breakfast and was reading the comics when the doorbell rang. My brother, Joe, went to answer it and was surprised to see a big, burly policeman standing there in full uniform. He hesitated a moment, and then in a clear voice said, "Is your father home?" Joe told him that my mother and father were not back from church. "All right, listen. Your father will have to appear in court with your brother, Louis—he is your brother, I assume?" Joe nodded in the affirmative. The cop continued: "On Thursday the . . . You make sure you give him this citation, okay?" Joe assured him he would, looking a little apprehensive. With that message the officer said "thank you" and softly tapped Joe's stomach with his nightstick in a friendly gesture; with a wink and a smile, he turned and left.

I went into the dining room when my name was mentioned, and as the officer gave Joe the citation, a flashback engulfed me with the same fears as the night of the arrest. Joe, who was gregarious and full of fun, always equipped with a joke when the occasion allowed it, blurted out, "What's the charge? Oh, Your Honor, shooting rats," then heartily let out a series of laughs, briefly relieving some tensions. Then the author declared, "Yeah, wait until Pa reads that; he's going to kill me." Soon the "black sheep" would be singled out when the shepherd returned; there would be no preparation of the fatted calf for the prodigal son, rather everything that had transpired would come home to roost—all Hell would break loose!

Wethersfield, being ancient in scope, maintained its own "cute" wood-framed Courthouse of Common Pleas, providing a quaint, rather provincial setting with a colonial architectural style. It was most likely of post and beam construction with interior walls covered over in later years. Full pitch gables, wood roofs, and cladding shingles, six inches to the weather, embellished traditional culture, although were replaced by clapboard over time. Most original dwellings were colonial, yet some gothic detailed cornices reflected the distinct ambiance of this unique neighborhood. The area was surrounded by a group of 110 structures built before 1840 that depicted the sage pioneering Yankee grit and spirit. Some of these houses, dating back to the seventeenth and eighteenth centuries, are constantly maintained, with their preservation in good stead even today. These treasures that historically identified that period were not far from the old courthouse.

There was the Standish House, built in 1787, which served as a general store in the mid-1800's and later as the ticket office for the Hartford-Middletown stagecoach. With smooth colonial lines it was equipped with two fireplaces, and double hung windows of nine-over-nine glass that gave it depth and its own identity. Nearby stood the Hurlbut-Dunham House, built in 1804, presumably for John Hurlbut, captain of the Neptune, the first ship from Connecticut to sail around the world. This structure had a widow's walk on top, a legend that told of the sailors' wives who spent hours standing up there to watch the river as they awaited the return of their husbands on the whale boats. Not too far away was the Joseph Webb House built in 1751, the site of a meeting between General George Washington and the French to plan the battle which won the Revolutionary War; it still echoed the gallantry of that period when he rode into town. And about a third of a mile from what was the old courthouse is the Broad Street Green, steeped in history, as this was where the original settlers built their homes in the 1630's. The common area was used to protect animals from wolves and as a military training ground from the 1650's through the Civil War. It was within this area, valued for its history, that the rat boys would make their infamous debut.

The little old courthouse, built to accommodate a limited number of cases, didn't look like a court of law. It was a small, simple colonial structure with gables. If the roof lines had been extended it would have presented a salt box image. The walls were painted a bland green, and in the back a big portrait of the Governor and the Chief Justice of the Supreme Court hung at eye level. The judge's bench in the front sat on an elevated two-foot riser platform made accessible by three steps cut in from the left side. Two large mahogany doors were inside an entrance alcove accommodating cork bulletin boards for display of important official notices. The worn pine wood floors resounded with loud creaking, usually causing heads to turn when being trod upon by hard leather-bottom shoes.

The time surrounding my arrest was a period in the country's history that perhaps we will never see again. Comparatively, the crime rate was tremendously lower than the latter years of the century. Drug-related offenses were almost negligible; moreover, there were very few frivolous lawsuits, fewer lawyers, and consequently a more efficient court system.

My days prior to "Wethersfield's famous trial" were filled with reprimand and lecture; my father's philosophy about courts was not unlike others who emigrated from Europe. Survivors of strife and prejudice, they lived through years of economic depression practicing strong faith, sacrifice, sheer determination and grit. He would often say to his kids, "Remember courts—you only see from the outside. You don't win inside—keep away." I am sure the foundation for his view and opinions was partially shaped by the lynching of 11 innocent Italians in Louisiana in 1913, plus the Sacco and Vanzetti "trials" and subsequent executions.

Cases were heard every Thursday night in the little courthouse in Wethersfield, and occasionally we would sit in on a particular case that was of interest, usually in conjunction with a business law class. I don't remember ever getting extra credit for this effort, although it made a good impression on the teacher.

The night of my case (incidentally, all five of us were tried together) was quite chilly. It had rained the day before and a cold front had moved in. I was wearing just a light jacket when I left the house with Pa, got into the car, then asked him if I could go get my topcoat. The lectures continued throughout the ten-minute drive to the courthouse, and when we got there my four friends were standing outside with their fathers; all had a serious, tense demeanor, save one. We exchanged glances, but my father's anger was evident in his terse reply to one father who offered sympathy, in which he stated the police should have more important responsibilities than to arrest kids shooting

17

rats. My father answered, "They should have been home studying," and walked inside. I followed after him to the building while my friends filed behind me with their fathers.

The courthouse was packed with as many people as allowed by law, and most of them were students from Wethersfield High School. The five of us sat together, with our fathers directly behind each offspring. A classmate sitting nearby said in an audible voice, "You guys look like gangsters with those topcoats." At that moment the bailiff boomed, "All stand." Judge Gordon entered, the general oath was read, and the judge sat down, followed by the visitors.

"What's the first case?" Judge Gordon asked, although I'm sure he must have known what was on the docket that night.

"Your Honor, the Town of Wethersfield vs. Louis LaCava, Richard Schmid. . . ."

"What's the charge?" he asked.

"Your Honor, these five boys were arrested for shooting rats at the town dump on . . ." And before he could finish, the courthouse exploded in a roar of laughter. I looked over at my father, who by this time was utterly awash with contempt; the judge banged his gavel incessantly.

"If I hear another sound from anyone of you students I will clear the courthouse! Now please continue."

"Your Honor, these boys were shooting within town limits; also, it was close to eleven P.M., clearly in violation of statutes."

"Do these gentlemen have any previous record?"

"No, Your Honor, they are decent boys with clean records, from good families, and have never been involved in any trouble. For this reason, Your Honor, we would like to recommend the case be nolled."

The author doesn't remember the immediate reply from Judge Gordon after the prosecutor finished. I only knew it was in the affirmative, but loud and clear he continued warning that he didn't want to see us in his courtroom again. I was elated, and with an enormous feeling of relief I was just thinking about food, as apprehension had stripped me of any appetite. So I almost died when my father stood up and said in a serious voice, "Your Honor, in all due respect, I think you made a mistake—you

18

should have given them all thirty days to teach them a lesson." The Judge looked over with resignation and said something to the effect of "if I see them here again . . ."

At that point we were walking out and most of the court-house spectators had already left. I was embarrassed when my father stood up to speak, but the noise of the people leaving was a comfort, and I was hopeful that many of my friends had not heard him. But he was probably right. My father lectured me all the way home. It was the same theme with variations. A lesson was learned, and the story of the rat-shooting "safari" in 1952 was told for many years to come.

Model—Mentor—Menace

Graduation was less then thirty days away. Preparations for that week had begun, rehearsal for various senior activities was already underway, and the class of '52 was briefed on the format and protocol for the night diplomas would be awarded.

But I had an abundance of make-up work in math, history, business law and English, as well as architectural drawings to complete. I had worked on all of this while convalescing from a very scary medical episode experienced at the end of this year, my senior year. I also had to familiarize myself with music the choir would be performing for graduation, and during this process I flashed back to previous months.

There is a mentor in everyone's life, I believe, and more times than not this person did or said something—or perhaps many things—that proved to be instrumental in changing the direction one might have otherwise gone in. My mentor was an English teacher. She was a person without unusual or extraordinary teaching skills, and perhaps never won any awards for her work. She merely performed her duties faithfully every day; yet she instilled a certain confidence in me that has never left. Her gestures took no great preparation or energy on her part. She thoughtfully observed and pointed out the strong characteristics in her students. They weren't necessarily monumental—most were small things done well, like a certain gift, skill, or talent; but they would accumulate, and when strung together side by side by side usually made some difference in a person's being. She was very perceptive to recognize particular traits and act on them. Most likely she was never aware of this special gift of hers; I'm convinced to this day it was born out of love for her job and her students.

If a student was good in interpreting Shakespeare, she would make it a point to tell him or her in class. If someone had good skills in spelling, the class would listen as she pointed that out. I was gifted in diagramming sentences and had above average reading and memorizing skills, but if she didn't tell me I might never have known. I thought everyone could diagram sentences with aplomb, or surely at an equal pace—if not faster—than I. One day after the completion of a diagram test, I tidied my desk and looked up while everyone else still diligently concentrated on the exam. This teacher quietly walked up to me and in a soft voice said, "Louis, are you finished?" When I nodded my head in the affirmative, not to disturb my fellow students, she picked up my test paper, browsed casually at it and returned it to me. After the allotted test time elapsed, she told the class of my unusual diagramming prowess; all sentences were correct. And when it came to literature interpretation she let me know that this area needed more of my time but that I had the ability to get the "hang" of it.

A teacher that can energize and motivate the student to do his or her very best, by expounding on his strong gifts while working extra with him in weak areas, should be commended. Apropos to this skilled teacher, I recall a story told by Dr. Leo Buscaglia in one of his television lectures—when little Johnny got nineteen out of twenty wrong on a test, the teacher exclaimed with great enthusiasm, "Johnny, you got one right! That's great! Next time we'll work to get two right, and up and up until you get all twenty right!" Then he went on to point out that in this way little Johnny had been given some hope for success.

The teacher I speak of was Mrs. Doris Armstead. The author always liked to write poetry. It started in elementary school when I experienced great pleasure crafting ideas into abstract concocted phrases with rhythm, meter, and sometimes with rhyme. I really never knew what I was doing, and it would be years before I would learn some semblance of basic poetic structure. I only knew it was exhilarating and challenging, so when I look back in retrospect I can define my poetic style as "blank verse with rhyme"—some poems had meaning, others were drivel. One day Mrs. Armstead surprised me by creeping up behind me and asking what I was writing. Shyly, I covered my pa-

21

per with my hand and said I was just scribbling. She picked up the paper and mused over it, smiled, passed it back, and left.

I was an average student who made honor roll a few times, and had an abundance of curiosity plus a plethora of enthusiasm. If I applied myself, I seldom had a problem raising a grade—conversely, if the subject bored me, time lingered and the grade dropped. One incident in my second year of high school enlightened me about this. The assignment was to do an essay on a poem, and a biography on the author. I went to the library and picked out a book by Dante. Well, when the teacher in this class noticed the book I had chosen she went ballistic! She asked if I knew who he was. I admitted I know little about him, except that he was a genius with fables; yet, I told her, I was anxious to learn, adding that I had older siblings and heard discussions many times about Dante while they were doing papers on him. Also, my dad was from Italy, and I was interested to find out where this important writer was born, schooled, and did most of his writing. The teacher emphatically informed me that the book and author were "over my head" and intimated, "Italians don't know when to come out of the rain." I quickly perceived contradiction in her remarks (for wasn't the brilliant Dante an Italian?) She selected a book for me that I had absolutely no interest in, and consequently did poorly with the report—maybe out of spite.

I was very quiet, always respected my teachers, and in many ways was naive to prejudice and discrimination. At that time, I was well aware that a person with a name ending in a vowel would have a more difficult time integrating with the so-called "norm." Hearing blatant remarks by those in authority, made for the sake of humiliation and discouragement, was something I was neither frequently aware of nor would dwell on. We were taught to always be kind and respectful of those in authority, especially teachers, and above all to mind our own business and study hard.

The author had a perfect attendance record all through high school until the last year, one month before graduation. I was athletic, relatively healthy, robust, and rarely suffered from colds or throat infections. I felt to some degree my good health could be attributed to skating. I was a figure skater; jumping and spinning are an integral part of the sport. It was this weekly workout that gave me power and stamina. However, in a period when too many activities surpassed my body's abilities to recoup from lost rest, thus weakening my immune system, a physical transformation took place. It happened one night while bowling with my buddies: I just didn't feel like my energetic self. We were using the small ten-pin lanes in a nearby town. Bowling was a clean-cut sport that required very little money, and it didn't keep us out late. We usually scheduled an alley for five-thirty or six P.M., had our fill of bowling, ordered pizza, and were home by eight-thirty, with plenty of time to complete homework.

I clearly remember my arrival home that night, suffering with a little, though rare, headache (Some of my close friends used to facetiously say that I gave them but never got them). I took a glass of ginger ale and went straight to bed, where I fell into a stupor, awoke around eleven P.M., and didn't sleep again for over forty hours. The next day's experience was something you hear about but think can never happen to you. By 3 P.M., after Mom gave me aspirin powdered in ginger ale, with no sign of improvement, she decided to call Dr. Girardi.

Although his office was only ten minutes away, the doctor would not arrive until six o'clock in the evening. Upon his arrival, I was lying on a sofa in the living room. Now you know I was really sick if I was in the living room! Traffic in the living or dining rooms was forbidden. Why? Because it had to be kept clean and neat for company! There was much sympathy for me from my older sisters; consequently, no umbrage was taken for disregarding this house rule. Upon his arrival, the doctor asked my mother for all the specifics pertaining to my illness and greeted me with a big grin. Dr. Girardi was a very tall, handsome man with an infectious smile, and an optimistic and comforting personality. He approached and asked me immediately to open my mouth, stuck a tongue depressor in it, looked down my throat with the flashlight he had fished out of his little black bag (doctors once actually carried them), and informed my mother that I had a sore throat. With all due respect, I didn't need any smiles or anyone to tell me I had a sore throat at that point. The throat was obviously sore, and all I wanted was some medicine to make me feel better. Pain and suffering were part of life, we were taught, but what bothered me was the time lost.

My extremely high temperature didn't concern the doctor, but he informed my mother a culture was necessary to rule out a strep infection, although he felt sure it was only a classic case of a hidden virus making its rounds throughout the area. Was it bacteria or a virus? He reached into that black bag, pulled out a long syringe, and proceeded to inject me with penicillin, suggesting it should quiet me down; in addition, this was just a "precautionary measure" if, by chance, I had strep. The antibiotic started to absorb through the tissue, causing a mild burning sensation around the center of my chest. I never had penicillin before and didn't say anything to my mother, thinking this was the normal reaction after a shot. But by eight P.M. the pain in my chest intensified as if someone was inside me with a blowtorch. The glands in my throat started to swell to the point where it became increasingly more difficult to breathe, and then my whole body started shaking violently with chills. At this point Mother became calmly concerned, for she had never experienced me being that sick before, particularly hearing me moan. Calling the doctor again, she indicated she would like an immediate call back, and ten minutes later Dr. Girardi was on the phone, advising her to give me aspirin and plenty of liquids.

The next twenty-four hours were filled with continued burning pains in the upper half of my body, chills—hot to cold intervals similar to extreme fire followed by frigid ice currents—violent headaches with difficulty breathing, complicated by itching all over my body that could not be assuaged. The doctor returned again the following day and explained that this might be an allergic reaction to penicillin and to continue feeding me aspirin and plenty of liquids. I stopped taking the aspirin on the third day, suspicious it was causing the itching, and on the fourth day all the itching vanished. That was the last time I would ever take aspirin or penicillin in my life. The irony of the story was that the only relief from this nightmare came from the Malva herbal tea my mother gave me continuously from the first night. I attribute her heroic deeds, combined with mother's intuition, to my rescue from suffering. The only positive aspect of this experience was the discovery that I was allergic to penicillin and aspirin. But what an expensive price to pay!

On my first day back to school I learned what the make-up entailed, and to my surprise found only one subject that I felt would be a problem to complete. Three days before the end of classes for seniors, from what the author can recall, I submitted all of my English make-up work, which included approximately eight pages of poetry in lieu of some essays. I had taken the literature tests previously and was pleasantly surprised, under the circumstances, when the marks were a B and C. It behooved me to think that this teacher may have been a smidgen generous, but perhaps not. I certainly wasn't going to question the grading criteria, rationalizing to ease my conscience that maybe the tests were graded on the curve.

On the last full day of classes I was walking toward my homeroom when Mrs. Armstead approached from the opposite direction. "Louis, I want to talk to you before class, so please come directly to the classroom as soon as the bell rings." The building had three floors, without elevators, and there was an allotment of six minutes to navigate between classes. When the rooms were adjacent to one another we often would dilly-dally with our friends until the last second, or we waited until the bell rang and then made a mad dash for the room. Dodging and bumping others while crossing over to the opposite side of the corridor made it like a combat zone, thus her reasoning for asking me to come directly to class.

My natural inclination was to fear rejection of at least part of my make-up work—the anthology of poems. The poems were in text form, and were not specifically about the reading assignment, but rather what I felt poetically—what the poets call today a "poetic experience." Since homeroom I had prepared myself for periods when I would be burning the midnight oil, writing make-up essays. As I walked into the empty classroom, somber, ashen, and nervous, she was standing in front of her desk. My right hand was in my pocket holding tight to a small escutcheon the size of a silver dollar of Blessed Martin that I always carried. (Blessed Martin was under the scrutiny of canonization. The church was in the process of investigating the authenticity of miracles attributed to him, but my oldest sister had told me many times that he was, among other things, the helper of students in need, and to make devotions to him. It always worked for me.)

Mrs. Armstead motioned for me to sit down. In front of her was a folder containing my total assignments for the semester. While quickly thumbing through the papers, she complimented and praised my attentiveness, punctuality, and enthusiasm to learn. The author said to himself, "What a gentle way to lower the boom on a guy!"

She continued, "I was very pleased by the results of your make-up tests, Louis." I disliked being addressed as Louis, but an exception was made for her; anything she called me was permissible. Maybe she didn't grade on the curve, I wondered with a barb of bravado.

"And the poems—the poems that you wrote have me convinced that you thoroughly read and understood your assignment—they're quite good!" (I had skimmed through the pages and integrated some interesting areas that I could understand into my poetry.) With the sincerity and genuine tone of her remarks I felt my heart start to palpitate! I looked over cautiously, noticing a pleasant, albeit rare, smile on her face, and for a moment she wasn't my teacher, but an attractive woman. Students started to file into the room. She rolled back her chair, and I stood up in anticipation of her ending the talk—I was right. She thanked ME as I turned to go to my desk. Elated, pleased, but above all, very humble, I whispered to thank Blessed Martin.

This experience was the first time in four years of high school that anyone aside from one of my sisters or my mother had favorably commented on my writing—and a teacher, besides! It left a good feeling. In contrast to this, I tried in vain to conjure up logical reasons for how two English teachers could have such diverse opinions of my ability to write, one even intimating, albeit subtle, defamation of my heritage.

The acceptance of my poems as an adjunct to the required make-up instilled a fresh incentive to write and confidence in my total being. I continued to write poems, but not with any regularity or passionate desire to be a writer, rather as a hobby and pas-

26

time. Also, I was starting to write lyrics to songs and sloppily creating music to fit the theme and "texture" of the words I wanted to project. This was many years before I had any formal training in song writing theory. Everything I wrote was predicated on what was self-taught. Anyway, I loved music with a passion; it was fun and a highly enjoyable challenge. The only detriment to teaching myself was creating some bad habits that had to be undone years later.

In addition to my poems and so-called composing, I was also writing a story for publication. The name was *The Love Story*. In synopsis, it told of a very tender relationship between a boy and a girl as they experienced love at first sight, married, and planned to live their lives vowing complete devotion and affection to one another. The bond was ultimately broken when she fell victim to an incurable disease and died. My sister edited, typed, and forwarded the manuscript to *The Saturday Evening Post*. She thought it was excellent (with prejudice, of course). Two months later I received a "do not misconstrue" letter. It was later sent to *Collier's*, but I never received a reply. I wasn't disappointed or overwhelmed to any degree by the declination until years later, when a movie was made entitled *The Love Story*—my *Love Story*, same premise, same plot, same climax, same drama; the only differences were the names and descriptions of characters and the author. I was convinced that the time sequence was a formidable defense for me yet accepted "coincidence" and continued on my humble way. How frightening and foreboding that the reality of the plot would be dramatically played out in my own life! The author still has the yellow-paged manuscript written in the 50's!

In the post-high school days, when I was working two jobs, writing, singing, and skating, I was always enthusiastic and with a schedule. On Saturday afternoon I was either down in the family room working the piano or in the study—which I built in the cellar—with an old L.C. Smith typewriter, pounding away. On this particular day I happened to be working in my study on *The Love Story* when my mother called down, and I can still hear the words, "Louie, you have some mail from the U.S. Army."

I answered, "I'll be right up, Ma!"

My heart sank momentarily, for I already knew what the

letter was. The Korean War was on and my brother Frank, only one year older, was on his way; now I knew I'd be there within six months myself. I was interested in going into the Army, for it would be a change and give me time to sort out a few things in my life, like everyone else, but I abhorred war—war in all its horrendous acts of violence, barbarity, and carnage; war steeped in hate, power, and ego that motivates to satisfy the oppressor but abandons the masses; war where often the participants don't know, forget, or don't care about the reasons it started, which is the most dangerous element of strife. No, war I was not fond of, but like so many of my brothers I was willing to serve.

"Be informed . . . You are to report to the US Army Headquarters . . . On the twelfth of . . . New Haven, Connecticut . . ."

I read with trepidation and some relief, for anticipation of this "greeting" for many prior weeks had finally brought closure to the fact that I would be in Korea quickly after basic training. Paradoxically, there was a feeling of delight in the outside chance—although remote—of meeting up with Frank. I pulled my paper from the typewriter and went upstairs again, for the mind was adrift, far removed from the pen. As I walked into the kitchen my mother was preparing dinner and I shared the contents of the letter with her. She looked at me in silence, but I could read by the serious expression on her face, wonderment—when will it [war] and the departures of her sons end? Though she had seven letters of greeting come into her house, including to those who volunteered, she never got accustomed to the disruption the government brought upon her family.

Singing was one of my passionate desires and great ambitions. I wanted to make it big with my voice—with a burning intensity. I possessed a strong tenor voice, but used it ill-advisedly to impersonate other artists. I had studied briefly with the lead tenor of the Hartford Symphony, Brad Mason, who cautioned me on several occasions to use my own voice, but in my youth I wanted to do my Al Jolson, Mario Lanza, Bing Crosby, Dean Martin, Frankie Laine—(you name him)—impersonations and save my voice for last. I didn't fathom that an unnatural continued misuse of the voice could harm the vocal cords as well as inhibit one's true vocal identity.

Friday, Saturday, and Sunday nights were used for frequenting nightclubs or dance halls—in Ocean Beach, Lake Compounce, Crystal Lake, Savin Rock, places along the shore—to dance and acquaint myself with the bandleader in the hope that I could sneak in a song. I naively dreamt some agent who just happened to be in the place that night would hear me and offer a contract, and I would be thrust to stardom! The dreams of youth took precedence over reality, for some of these places were featuring big names like Duke Ellington, Lionel Hampton, Tommy Dorsey, Les Elgard, Count Basie, Sammy Kaye, etc. To have the audacity to imagine that I would be allowed to sing, that they would take a chance with a young neophyte, was ludicrous—but there would be times . . .

More often than not they would graciously decline, citing union rules as the usual excuse. I was anxious to illustrate my gift. And I had a strategy: during intermission I approached the leader for an impromptu audition and casually belted out a high note. The reaction was mixed. One looked at me, smiled, and patted my back in encouragement; another said, "You have powerful pipes, son, keep it up." Still, one walked away. . . . "See me later," which was his way out. I was astute enough to know that immediately following the show he would be on a bus to his next gig.

But on a few rare occasions I did have the opportunity to sing. And one Sunday night at the Gay 90's Club in New Haven (which had an open front to the street and continuous entertainment), I made my debut. This night would become fateful in my life. Upon my return, after bringing a friend home, I was hit broadside by an eighty-year-old man from New Jersey, driving a BIG Buick (the largest they made). He had been following his son, who was hauling a trailer, and had lost him. In his confusion, he ran a stop sign on White Street in Hartford and met me as I had just moved across the center of the intersection. The investigating officer estimated his speed, by the skid marks, and as incredible as it may seem in this area, it was between sixty-five and seventy miles per hour!

Unfortunately, the accident occurred before mandatory use of seat belts. I suffered a severely bruised left lung, a cracked rib, several lacerations and abrasions to my forehead and left shoulder, and severe whiplash that affected my lower back and left sciatic nerve. Despite the fact that it took approximately six months to recover, doctors attributed the minor extent of injuries to my superb physical condition, which came from figure skating—the jumping and spinning and continual lifting of a partner over my head in pair skating. My 1949 Pontiac convertible car ended up 150 feet from impact; it had been hit at the center post that hinged the back door. The investigating officer commented, "Somebody up there likes you," then explained that if impact was just a foot closer to the front of the car I would have been killed. He said the strong post and frame system in that model took the brunt of the blow.

Army headquarters was abuzz with recruits; as one doctor examined me he asked about the accident, which I downplayed, saying it was nothing. He didn't respond to my answer but directed me to another part of the hall, adjacent but separated by large screens from the other men being examined. I sat down until another doctor came over and gave me some papers to fill out, which took five minutes; when he saw I was finished he returned and advised me to go home.

Surprised, saddened, and disappointed, I nearly fell rising from my chair. My back injury was too much liability for the Army to gamble with. When I started to question the doctor he turned and walked away. As I began to leave, another recruit directed to the same area asked me what to expect. I just walked away, muttering, "Keep the faith." In my angry state, the harsh tone to my answer didn't bother me until I got home, when I felt regret at the possibility my uncharitable reply may have caused him undue anxiety.

A while after my brief experience with the Army, I decided to start night classes at the University of Hartford, formerly Hillyer College, which was undergoing expansion. The school had received generous gifts from philanthropists, opened an endowment, and formed a Board of Regents and Trustees to oversee the strategy needed for diversification.

My courses were elective: Math, English, and Psychology. The first night in English Literature class was one of happy anticipation, for this was something that motivated and inspired me; I was enthusiastic about the prospect of expanding my knowledge in many areas as well as improving my writing skills. Walking into the classroom that night I was surprised to find not only the number registered was huge, but beyond that, all seats were taken in this gigantic room, except for a few in the front row. Now if there was one thing the author disliked more than being addressed as Louis, it was sitting in the front row. I believe it all stemmed from my upbringing. At an early age we were taught to be at the end of the line, and sit removed from the front, which was ordinarily reserved for others—leaders or those in authority. It was not only respectful, but just plain good manners to stay in the background. The philosophy, I am sure, was connected to some extent with Scripture: "First shall be last and last shall be first." In most cases throughout my life, I found the benefit outweighed the inconvenience of being last.

I stood in the back musing over the situation, when a short, middle-aged woman came bounding into the room, and in a booming staccato voice said, "The four of you standing in back—come down in the front. There are enough desks," and with a smidgen of sarcasm she added, "If you dislike sitting in front rows you'll have to make an effort to get to class on time." Walking toward the front I remembered thinking to myself what an intelligent way it was for her to preface a new semester. Besides, the people standing were on time; she was the late one.

"I trust all you have purchased your books; those of you who have not, please do [so] before the next class, or it is fruitless to continue. Open up to the table of contents—run your finger down to the five; before you come back be sure you read one through five. I have little patience for those who have difficulty in this class if they don't do the assignments." She then, with a stern expression, handed a "whack" of paper to the person next to me, at the end desk, who was told to pass it around. While passing the paper I couldn't help but think that for a college professor her use of slang set a poor example.

My thought was interrupted when the guy on the end, while passing the paper, prematurely let go, thereupon "the whack" feathered outward, then butterflied in several directions. As paper scattered onto the floor, several of us near to the *faux pas* re-

31

acted with grins, a natural reaction—but the grins were short-lived when the professor walked in our direction and glared. She then grimaced grotesquely while yelling directions to the class for a pop quiz, purposely leering at those of us who had smiled.

"Write an essay on any writer or poet of the nineteenth or twentieth century—English or American. It can be recent, contemporary or you can pick a favorite. You'll have forty-five minutes. If you can't think of one, then write about yourself." Several in the back of the class laughed loudly, which caused her to respond, "It wasn't meant to be funny!"

I wondered at that point how many in the class were thinking perhaps they'd take her suggestion. She then mentioned Edgar Allen Poe. Discussing this later, two of us in the front surmised Poe must be one of her favorites. The only knowledge I had of Poe was parts of a poem we had to memorize in eleventh grade, called *The Bells*:

Leeping time, time, time,
In a sort of Runic rhyme,
To throbbing of the bells:
Of the bells, bells, bells . . .

Despite the assumption Poe was her favorite I knew I wouldn't pick him from the get-go because of the lack of possibilities with this guy. She did not throw into the mix Longfellow, Edna St. Vincent Millay, or Emily Dickinson, none of whom was a favorite, nor did I remember enough to inspire me to write an essay about them in forty-five minutes. I knew that Longfellow and Millay were from Maine, and I was vaguely familiar with *The Sound Of The Sea*; I could recite parts of *Paul Revere's Ride* by Longfellow; but I was ignorant on specific poems they identified with; moreover, I lacked knowledge of interesting highlights of their lives. And at that time Dickinson was a bore to me; however, after many years of poetic discipline and maturity, I've come to understand and love her work, and now appreciate her brilliance—alas, belatedly! The only poets I felt comfortable writing about were Rudyard Kipling—several of his works interested me, especially, *If*—and Robert Frost, who, with G. K. Chesterton, were two of my literary mentors.

I finally settled on Kipling, for what reason I can't recall, only that we had studied his work in the last year of high school, and I remembered *If* and *Gung-a-Din*. I also knew he was born in India and was awarded the Nobel Prize in literature. I liked his work and thought he was a fine English "chap." I started slowly, but soon the wheels spit out information in all directions.

Upon finishing, I checked my spelling, phrases and syntax, and felt I had put together a decent essay for the first class. What a surprise waited for me! I'll quantify the previous statement by adding that over half the class had a rude awakening. Teachers used red pencils of two shades to mark papers back then—today they use highlighters. One was the ordinary red, used to mark average or minor literary transgressions; the other was a sharp purplish red to desecrate the paper that had serious mistakes and aberrations. My paper was marked with the purplish red pencil, from top to bottom, on both sides, with such "corrective animosity" I couldn't distinguish my own handwriting! Spewed along the outside margins and on the tops and bottoms were messages—frank, candid, leaving no doubt as to the point she wanted to convey: much too lengthy, be more careful with spelling, paragraphs running, sentences should be reversed, gerund not applicable, watch the use of compound/complex sentences, etc., etc. She must have stayed up all night just to correct my paper. And when I conferred with others in my class, I learned few were spared of her dire inclination to demand clarity, sub-creativity, and perfection.

I had entered Hillyer College from the beginning with a mindset that it was going to be temporary, considering eventually going out of state to school, though I had no idea how temporary. The boring psychology professor I was able to adjust to somewhat; regardless, the tyrant for English literature and my easy-going temperament were, alas, not compatible by any stretch of the imagination. It was a course transfer or *adios*; and it was *adios*. Subsequently, I learned that an unbelievably high percentage of students dropped her class; if the numbers were accurate this was a sad commentary on education.

Formidable Years

My years from age twenty through twenty-five were serious and busy. Not unlike my peers, I was searching for a pattern to shape the future; yet as I compare our characteristics and other factors, I realize we were distinctly different. One dynamic was that the unusual size of my family hampered me from choosing what I wanted to do to earn a living; and for the same reason I was unable to focus on my first loves, whatever gifts and talents I may have possessed. Secondly, available opportunities were very limited then, compared to the diversity in today's technological age. Options were basically in three categories: sciences, construction, and engineering. The ancillary trades like writing and the arts were usually reserved for those truly gifted, backed by wealth, or with a burning passion for that field. A large family came with many advantages and joys, but there were also hardships. Such unique circumstances required sacrifice from every family member. Selfishness was *persona non grata*. My father was a leader with certain unspoken rules stated primarily by example, and we instinctively abided by his covenants. That was the essence, the bond that kept the family intact, strong, and close. While our thinking was limited in one sense to specific daily needs—like eating—there was never a lack of love, respect, or affection. The air around our domain always breathed with excitement and frivolity, even in times of great deprivation. And this gift was the dominating factor and catalyst for sustaining basic rudiments for the path to family success and survival.

I never fully realized while growing up the tremendous vision my parents had about life in general. They had the wisdom to understand that suffering was inexorably linked to daily living, and when it was accepted on these terms, great rewards were bestowed. It was a philosophy neither taught nor learned through books, but rather revealed through the gifts of grace and faith. This distinguished me from most of my peers.

A period of de-Italianization had started in the late 20's and reached its zenith in the middle 50's. Many immigrants of Italian descent deemed it extremely important that their children disassociate themselves from the European culture (sometimes encouraged by social agencies) and to Americanize as part of the country's "melting pot." These parents felt it essential if their children were to have the same chance in society as others in getting jobs and fitting in with societal "norms." Discrimination against Italians was rampant—so flagrant, in fact, that in desperation some parents went to the extreme of changing their last name so their children could function in a "homogeneous" society. They desperately wanted to provide them with a level playing field when applying for jobs, unencumbered by harangue and insults. But when officials got wind of this, if you even looked Italian you were often relegated to the bottom of the list. But I must also add with emphasis that there were many decent and compassionate citizens—an overwhelming majority—who had empathy and took the rap in support of the "guinea" and the "wop." The few who organized in the name of discrimination sadly set the tone of the debate and thus were the main cause of strife and horrible acts of violence that plagued the country for many years. That mark of coercion, bias and aggression is indelibly recorded as a terrible blight in our country's history, and some of those responsible for condoning—thus prolonging—the hatred were political figures and others with power, who should have known better; i.e. some our of most "respected journalists"!

The next three years of my life were spent managing the paint and decorating department of my father's building business, having replaced a brother who had been drafted. I continued with skating and singing lessons and learned to play the guitar in addition to dabbling with semi-abstract oil painting on canvas. I also had a great interest in opera, which led me to see some of the greatest tenors in the world.

These were years of limbo. Although I had skills in management and the construction trade, they would certainly not have been my first choices, and yet we were bred to always approach a

35

task with energy, enthusiasm, and an ambition to accomplish it. I was good at what I did, well liked, and kept the job moving to meet all schedules with time to spare, reaping monetary rewards. But these were also formidable years for me—I was young, robust, and anxious to break out into the world on my own. It never occurred to me then that there were thousands of others just like me, with a burning desire to earn a living singing—to make the "big time."

Praise for my singing was never lacking, which fueled my confidence; but still my teacher warned me, when I appeared anxious to break out, that although I had a pleasant voice with strong timbre I had a long way to go. He cautioned me to learn to craft phrases smoothly with adequate breath control, and improve on enunciation, and although he was delighted with my success in reaching the high notes effortlessly, he was concerned with my overextension in the high registers. He warned that it was necessary to be extremely conscious of "reining in" so I didn't become boisterous and overrule the composer's intent. He also stressed the importance of a singer's diction for his success, a fetish of his that almost drove me nuts!

Impatience is a gift of the young, and I was blessed with this gift, especially when it came to promoting my singing. I had learned lyrics to over 150 songs, was loquacious, gregarious, and enthusiastic. So I decided to try something novel, in the form of sending an unsolicited demo to Columbia Records, thinking the least that could come from this would be an audition and the worst an interview with someone in the general office. It was imperative an effort was made, as I knew it was essential for them to meet me if an avenue of opportunity in the singing business was ever to bear fruit.

First, I had to rent a recording studio. But upon inquiry I found the cost was prohibitive, and when an accompanist was added, I estimated I'd be put in hock for over a year. So I devised the next best strategy: construct my own in-house studio. We had a finished recreation room in the basement, part of which could be retrofit to acoustically accommodate recordings. My brother Frank and I were absolutely sure that good sound and favorable decibel readings could be achieved. We would strive to get a good tone quality and let the vibratory action of the author's voice do the rest.

Now to record, of course one must have a recording device. After months of checking catalogs and doing lots of research, I was surprised to find that there were very few recorders out there, especially ones that could put down clear, concise tones without residuals, like a humming sound from the machine itself, or, let's say, the furnace. A technician from one source recommended a device called Bell. It was a big (humongous by today's standards) cumbersome apparatus, measuring about fourteen inches high by twenty square, and was it heavy! The expert assured me that Bell provided the most advanced technology on the market, and I had no reason to doubt him, for the store sold other brands that were equally expensive.

I decided to purchase the Bell, but upon hearing the price, my heart sank. The conversation went something like this:

"What does one of these things set a guy back?"

"Wait a minute, I'll get the book and figure it out." It was very busy, and close to half an hour elapsed before he returned to say, "It comes with its own hand mike. Did you want the high-voice mike stand, also?" I told him to please cost it out separately. Another ten minutes elapsed. "The Bell will cost $349 and the high-voice mike is another $150." In a quiet and dejected tone I told him I'd have to think it over. That was a lot of money, and I had to figure out how to swing it!

For the next few days I tried reason, then rationalization, to justify such a purchase. Using deduction as a source of logic, I found it supported my intention to have the Bell in my "studio" before the end of the week. Listing the advantages and disadvantages of owning my own recorder versus leasing a studio showed me the purchase would be cheaper and make it always available for practice and critique. Added to that, recording in my own house was more convenient, and without a recorder there could be no studio, and without a studio there would be no demo, and without a demo there would be no record contract, and without a record contract there would be no big time, and without big time there would be no name in lights, and without my name in lights there would be no money . . .

I devised a way to pay for the Bell. By discontinuing lessons in singing and skating, by refraining from impulse buying and strictly curtailing social activity—but still making my monthly car loan and insurance payments, room and board (only $15 per week, including food and laundry!) I would be able to swing it!

We constructed a studio in the rec room by using portable, lightweight partitions, strung over with white cotton sheets, which would allow the sound to penetrate slowly to the ceiling. This was supposed to prevent tones from escaping too fast, thus causing distortion and echo. The texture of the voice, as well as the piano, would be enhanced, as well as the end quality of the recording. Our theory was shot full of holes after the first take. Instead of a resounding, vibratory, compressing effect, the sound bounced around in the ten-foot square cubicle like a pinball set into motion, absorbing everything in its way and causing a cacophony of weird noises that wouldn't win a prize from a Cracker Jack box. The sound was comparable to a Spike Jones recording in an electrical storm on a bad day!

A week of experiments in every corner of the lower level proved fruitless. Then I had a preposterous theory that the problem of poor quality recordings was not caused by the ceiling, but rather by the floor. So we took newspapers and covered every square inch of asphalt tile in the recording cubicle, which we had now moved into the center of the room; we were elated when the next take had improved by about twenty five percent.

Next we pondered, if the newspaper-covered tile softened the bounce of the voice off the ceiling tile by its cushioning effect, would removing the sheets from atop the cubicle increase the total quality of the recording? Wouldn't that allow more room for voice and piano sounds to travel before finding the direction of least resistance? Our best hope was a proportional success that wouldn't sacrifice the vibratory quality of the tone. This adjustment decreased some distortion, but we were still experiencing an annoying echo.

But now we were on a roll! We tried newspapering one side of the flat, smooth, portable partition, hoping the print would act as a blemished surface to move the decibel out and away, and we were elated when very little echo remained in the next take. The only obstacle in the way of producing a first-rate professional recording was a distant tunnel chamber aftereffect, which was not all bad. But inconsistency plagued us—recordings were mediocre to horrendous! Yet we would not be deterred, for things were starting to come together. It was truly a marvel that we, lacking any engineering background in this field, could achieve favorable results through elementary trial and error school.

Three weeks went by without a solution to the increasing tunnel clamor. One strange thing that had us perplexed was its variation from day to day. Some takes had less chamber timbre than on other days. I thought about it constantly, and very early one morning I lay awake wondering what the weather had been on the days we were getting varied results. I jumped from bed down to the porch, where all the old newspapers were stored, and shuffled through to the weather page for each of the days over this three-week period. With great interest I learned that there had been either very humid or extremely dry days. And by checking through the dates I found that the tunnel effect appeared on the very dry days. I yelled, "That's it!" I figured that on the dry days the air is lighter and the sound would bounce around more than on humid days. Now this was a theory that deserved to be tested by increasing the humidity in the cubicle! But how to accomplish that?

In the basement, my dad had built a shower. There was a small window in it, but that wouldn't hinder our operation. In the final scheme of things this was ideal, because the shower room was elevated about ten inches, and that could intercept any floor vibrations that made their way toward our studio. Only one obstacle stood in our path—this small water closet was adjacent to the furnace room, and every time the oil-fired furnace went on, the area shook with noise that resounded to unmanageable heights on the recording. But we would not be deterred—this was the place where the demo was going to be produced! We would just have to shut down the burner when we needed it quiet. Naturally, we didn't tell Pa about this!

The first recording day was bright and sunny. Because it was impossible to get a piano into the small water closet, the demo would have to be done *a cappella*. I had learned by then that life was a continuum of compromises and trade-offs; therefore, a good recording was the reward for giving up an accompanist. Inasmuch as my pitch and phrasing were excellent, thanks to the prodding lesson after lesson from my teacher, I had little problem singing without an accompanist. We turned the hot shower on for about twenty minutes until the room was saturated with steam. Then we took the high mike stand, set it in front of the toilet, and crimped the wire under the door outside the utility room into the outer hallway, where the recorder was set up. Frank took a foam rubber mat and stuck it under the door to stifle noise. In addition, we took a four-foot lamp stand and tied a square of cardboard underneath, taping it to the bottom at a sixty-degree angle, then placed it close to my right. The reason for this shield was to direct my voice immediately away from me, toward the window, in hopes it would eliminate errant tones. I went inside the small bathroom, closed the door, and waited for the signal, whereupon the recording session began. After listening to the practice run, we knew we had the solution. The practice number (*Thine Alone*) was so good we agreed it would be the first song on the tape.

The analog demo, which was recorded on a six-inch reel using Scotch brand tape, was comprised of ten songs, including popular, semi-classical, Neapolitan, and operatic arias. We were ecstatic with the outcome, only having to retake three songs! The voice was clear and expansive; diction was superb and emotional, and the phrasing even surprised the author himself! I was very excited and anxious to deliver the tape to Columbia Records, as surely now with this tape they would at least consider me for an interview. I typed out a short letter, including all the pertinent information and niceties—who I was, what I did, my training, what was on the tape, etc.; signed it, placed the folded biographical information into the box with the tape, and delivered it in person.

Three weeks had passed when I received a small package. The box had large, bold lettering—Columbia Artists. I nervously unwrapped it to find that inside was my tape, as sent—it was never taken from the sealed box—and under the tape was an envelope, holding a letter addressed to Mr. Louie Val:

Dear Sir:

Please do not misconstrue the return of this demo as prejudgment of your talent. At this time, Columbia Records is under contract with the maximum number of artists our schedule permits. We encourage you to continue your quest and forward the tape to another recording company. Our good wishes for success,

General Manager, Recording Artists

The letter was unsigned. To say I was disappointed would be less than candid. In a few short years I had been rejected twice—*The Love Story* and "The Demo." But my spirit was not broken. This was incidental compared to tragedy that would befall me in the years ahead. I picked up the pieces, and did what our dad taught us at a young and tender age. "Hold your head up high in strife, let the wind and rain hit you in the face, and smile, for greatness is born of faith."

The next year I settled down at work while continuing singing and skating lessons. Having been matched with a partner, I was now part of a pairs skating team. In anticipation of entering competition, we worked diligently for eight months, until illness of her mother necessitated curbing our practice time. This left us at a terrible disadvantage, eventually leading to dissolution of the partnership. Later, I took another partner but skated for enjoyment only.

In the 50's and 60's, figure skating was a challenge. It wasn't trumped-up as a glamorous sport, and it carried a quiet stereotypical stigma of being "sissified," which was mostly due to ignorance. Additionally, it was very expensive. Unlike today, indoor rinks were few and far between; more often than not, we practiced on "outside ice" whenever weather permitted. Travel time to the few indoor venues was costly in time and gas expense. Payments for ice time, professional teachers, custom-made boots—this was a lot of money; you really had to love the sport before daring to think about your participation. There is a world of difference today; figure skating has fewer burdens, and consequently it is much easier to "make it" if you have the talent and the desire. Not only is it more popular, but there is more outside support, as well as an abundance of indoor rinks countrywide.

Today figure skating is a sport of convenience, like tennis and golf, so even those who make lackadaisical efforts can reap great enjoyment and rewards.

I had always wanted to go to college to get a degree in business, and by this time I was getting "antsy." Having spent much time reflecting on my future, I decided that if I ever wanted to get to and finish college it should be done now. Time was sneaking up on me, becoming my adversary. It had been three years since Hillyer/University of Hartford and Manchester Community College—six years since high school. I had always liked the University of Alabama, with my second choice being the University of Tallahassee—Alabama for the courses they offered—but frankly, the 'Bama football team was also a draw. Ultimately, the University of Tallahassee posed no problem with admission, and the thought of Florida's warm climate was very attractive!

The Fiasco

I arrived at a decision in July of 1958 to leave work and enter the University of Tallahassee for the fall semester. My parents were pleased. I had saved enough money to take me through two years, and by working summer jobs I could earn enough to underwrite the last two. In August I left work to tend to some unfinished business and meet with Felix Babel, head of Wethersfield High School's Guidance Department, to discuss my acceptance into U of T. He assured me that he saw no circumstances that would prevent my admission, despite lacking certain math requirements for my major. I had always performed well in my WHS math courses, which he said should satisfy their admissions department. And when we completed our business, he looked me straight in the eye and, smiling, added a "bye" line: "Louis, don't misbehave."

I often thought his advice of "don't misbehave" came from an episode in my senior year. I always loved to sing; I sang all the time and was blessed with a photographic memory for remembering lyrics. On our class graduation trip to Ocean Beach, about an hour drive, I sang one song after another until we reached our destination. The people near me at first sat back and enjoyed the performance, but by the time we arrived, they were ready to leave that bus!

It never made any difference to me where I was; if the mood hit me I would start to belt out a song—anywhere, anytime. A "mood" came over me one day as I walked to homeroom; excerpts from an aria in *Aida* boomed from within—to be heard over the cacophony of rushing students, from one end of the corridor to the other. I was feeling quite pleased, for the high registers were resounding effortlessly. Then, as I happened to pass the homeroom of a younger brother, his teacher came racing out, and in a voice of authority said, "LaCava, if you don't put that voice in

43

pianissimo you'll be auditioning that aria for the principal!" At the same time, Felix Babel walked out of his office and looked over at me, then back at the teacher with a puzzled look on his face, though he never said a word. I had no doubt he had heard my *Aida,* yet he had his own unique way of handling situations—an easy approach—"Let's talk." Mr. Babel was a one-of-a-kind great guy, and always a help to the students. This story has been told many times by my brother, while always explicitly dramatizing his reaction of embarrassment by slouching down in his chair, trying to disappear from his peers' sight.

My preparations to go to college were underway, having cleaned out my room and sorted clothes I would need. Next I would make the rounds of my friends, who were unaware I was going such a distance. There were three girls I was fond of; their names are still vivid in my mind. Terrie was a girl I skated with at the Loomis School in Windsor, where our skating club leased ice time. Our beautiful, short-lived friendship had started one night as I was coming out of a jump, and as my momentum carried me too far, I knocked into her, spilling her onto the ice. Fortunately, she was not hurt, but I felt terrible—I might add that was the last time I would ever bump another skater for forty years. The last day that I saw Terrie I gave her a dozen long-stem roses, and I still remember the note she sent to me in appreciation:

"Dear Lou, Thank you so much for the beautiful roses. They grace my piano, and every time I look at them they add warmth to my heart. You were so nice to think of me. Fondly, Terrie."

Elaine was quiet but vivacious; she liked fun times. I met her at one of my nightclub appearances, hoping to get an opportunity to sing. She was sitting alone when I approached her for a dance, but seeing she was quite shy, I sat down and started a conversation. It was a pleasant acquaintance. She was reserved, but intelligent, and we really hit it off. After a little while she told me she'd like to dance. Later I asked her why she was hesitant at first, and she replied, "Because of the way you were dressed; but now I can tell you're a nice guy." Well, the compliment made my night.

44

I always liked the latest fashion in clothes, prompting a few male friends to label me "the sartorial kid." I shopped at Summer's and Udolf's, as both carried the latest styles, often ahead of the "curve." And for a few years after Summer's left, some of my clothes were tailor-made by Anthony Sergi, a man blessed with special genius who understood my taste. I was grateful to have found such a talented person; he was continental, cultured, and knew his opera. Many interesting conversations and debates transpired between us regarding composers, plots, and the general theme of opera, plus great artists the likes of Tito Gobbi, Anna Moffo, Franco Corelli, Mario Lanza, and James McCracken. We attended operas together as critics, and these evenings were never without spirited banter, especially comparing the artist who sang the principal role that particular performance to others we had seen present the same role.

I remember how I was dressed the night I met Elaine because of the style—slim-jim tie, white shirt with either a Billy Eckstine collar or a narrow oval collar tied together with a gold or silver pin, semi-severe peg pants, jacket with wide lapels, and French toe shoes. Purple was the "in" color, as much as black is today. This frightened her. She thought I was a "zoot suiter," or what was called a "be-bopper." We had some fun times together, and when the time came for me to bid her good-bye, she wept. I never saw Elaine again.

I met Kim at an alumnus club party. We were drawn to one another initially by our drinking (rather, lack of drinking) habits. And when I said a few things to her she asked if she knew me. When I replied that maybe she did, I hoped she might then ask me some questions but found she was instead on the defense. She later admitted that my non-aggressive approach was very charming, eventually discovering this was the real me and not an act to, as they say today, "hit on her."

We sat down and started to converse. She was talkative and eloquent, well read and interesting; sometimes I found it difficult to get a word in—a big admission coming from me. This girl, blessed by looks which made her the splitting image of Sophia Loren, was a school teacher working on her master's degree. Our conversation was mesmerizing, smattered with limericks, poetic ditties, and original verses of our own. Amid this process of getting acquainted I told Kim I felt like I had known her all my life—now, there's nothing original about the assertion, except that's how I sincerely felt. I was going to continue with, "Where have you been . . ." but was interrupted (thank goodness, for that would have been close to commitment language) with, "I feel the same way, Lou."

I had the pleasure of driving her home that night, and we happily continued dating. Kim was a sweet girl and very cultured; I was thrilled to find she was knowledgeable about music and loved opera. It was the opera house we enjoyed most. She asked me to write when I got settled in Florida; I sincerely pledged to do so. But I never did. In later years, as I attempted to make contact with her, I was told she had married.

These three girls in my life were fine and wholesome, and I often think of them. I have always been proud that my actions were chivalrous, despite societal pressures and daily temptations. I carried myself with decorum and probity, adhering to the principles set forth by my parents as they raised me; the first duty is self respect, and as important, respect for others, then dedication to your family, to your neighbor and, most importantly, to God!

My plan was to leave for Tallahassee on the fourth of October but I changed it to the eighth, giving me extra time to rest and put things together. I hadn't even finished packing basic essentials to set up housekeeping in an apartment. The eighth of October was a typical autumn day—a cool morning with dew-laden grass. The sun was still hidden on the horizon, struggling to break through a haze. Early mornings, once light, now were dark. The leaves were late turning color due to a lack of rain, with only a smattering of flame here and there. On this morning at about six thirty, as I was loading my big blue and white 1958 Bonneville, there was this chaw-chaw-chawing and screeching echo resounding overhead. I looked up to see several regiments of geese, practicing formation drills for their anticipated trip to warmer climes. I wondered whose trip would be easier.

Once the car was loaded I confirmed the valuables in my jacket, especially the $100 in traveler's checks purchased the day

46

before, making sure they were in a secure pocket. Taking a towel from under the seat, I wiped dew that had formed on the windshield since leaving the garage. Would I encounter fog at the start of my journey? Mom and Dad were outside waiting to wish me well, and while rechecking to make sure nothing had been forgotten, I noticed Pa pulling out some huge sunflowers the previous night's frost had blackened. An unexpected awareness of fall descending upon New England enveloped me; my favorite season suddenly brought a wave of nostalgia and sense of regret for leaving at the most beautiful time of the year.

Rummaging through my clothes hanging in back of the driver's seat, I suddenly realized I had left my skates on the porch and ran inside to get them. Forgetting them would have been catastrophic! My mother asked me "Louie, what did you forget?" When I told her I had almost left my skates, my father lifted his head out from behind the sunflower plants and said, "O Jesu," a lovable, sarcastic Italian gesture applicable to anything in life that seemed trivial. I grabbed the bag and a half dozen Golden Delicious apples that were in the basket close to the door, stuffed them in my windbreaker, and hurried out to the car. As my parents stood waiting, I squeezed the skates into the trunk among duffel bags, suitcases, and sundry paraphernalia. After slamming the trunk shut, I kissed Mom and Dad goodbye, and as I walked toward my door I overheard my father say to my mother in Italian, "I can tell by his eyes it is not in his heart." I gingerly slid into my car, not realizing how prophetic my father's words would be!

The first couple of hours were peacefully quiet, with very little traffic but some ground fog. My first stop was well into New Jersey, when I stopped to use the restroom and get a cup of black coffee. On the turnpike entry ramp, a trim, nice-looking Afro-American soldier dressed in khaki with a private's stripe on the shirt was thumbing a ride. I eased my car over and yelled out, asking his destination.

"I have to get back to Fort Benning, Georgia. I've been out on furlough and I'm late—I'm due back by morning." I told him I was only going as far as Washington but to throw his bag in back and jump in if he thought that distance would help—an offer he happily accepted. Throwing his bag on top of my guitar case, he quickly got into the passenger's seat. This young man had visited friends in New York and reluctantly attended a ball game yesterday, knowing he would have little time to return to base. Having stood on that ramp for two hours, he was getting nervous before I came along. A born-again Christian, he felt this had been a test of his faith and had just asked the Lord to help him—before the words were completed, along came my blue car! We had a very nice conversation about Army life and other subjects, and on our long drive to Washington I came to appreciate this young soldier's intelligence. We covered everything from the weather to sports to entertainment, to his hopes and dreams. He was from Alabama, and his mother, whom he idolized, had raised him and his three siblings alone, sacrificing and working day and night. As we discussed family values, a loud buzzer sounded inside the car, which really startled him. He was not aware that a feature existed on the Pontiac Bonneville to warn the driver he had exceeded the speed limit or any other pre-set speed; we had a good laugh over this big-time reminder that my foot had gotten heavy! That little gauge saved me many a speeding ticket in my younger days.

As we neared Washington, we weighed this young man's options for arriving at Fort Benning on time. The train would be boring and less tiring than hitching but it might not get him there before his furlough ended. Rationalizing his superiors would "understand," I thought he had arrived at a decision; but then he asked me to stop on the turnpike so he could continue hitching—he couldn't chance being late. So I pulled the big Bonneville into the last rest area, where we exchanged names and addresses, agreeing to continue our friendship. Ours had been a comfortable encounter, although brief, where two people immediately found themselves on the same wavelength. Unfortunately that would be our last contact. I tried to reach him without success but never knew if he tried to do the same.

Tired, but happy, I arrived in Washington at four P.M.; the traffic was unreal! I had a reservation to stay at a brand new hotel across the Potomac River, which had an indoor skating rink. Traffic was stopped in one area for at least ten minutes, and when it finally started to move I thought I was pressing the accelerator—but the car didn't move! I looked down; my foot was on the brake. In those days the cars had a huge elongated brake set very close to the gas pedal—a big complaint of mine. But the cars were designed lower, and the universal shaft had no place to go but be humped up in the center of the floorboard, leaving very little space for the pedals. This mix-up had happened before, but I wasn't amused this time. I just wanted to get to the hotel, take a nap, grab a "bite," and get in an hour of skating.

A restaurant surrounded the hotel's glass-enclosed skating rink. Someone had told me that the Skating Club of Washington used this rink on certain nights. If that was true, I hoped this was their session night, for being nationally affiliated through the New Haven Figure Skating Club, I could use the ice as a guest. I wouldn't skate otherwise, as general skating would be crowded and jumping and spinning would not be allowed.

That night may easily have shaped the direction my life would take. I got up to my room around five-forty-five P.M., and as I was more tired than hungry, flopped down on the bed to take a nap. Almost immediately there was a knock on the door and the fumbling noise of a key. I slipped on a robe and was about to open the door when a young maid came prancing in.

"Oh! I'm sorry. I didn't think anyone was here because the room wasn't cleared yet with the desk." I told her everything was all right and I was hoping to take a nap after my long drive. As she pointed out that my room didn't have towels, an ashtray or basket, I told her there wasn't a need to fuss further and to just hand me the towels. Apologizing, she left.

Just into a ten-minute sleep, there was a knock on the door. Startled and in a daze, I hit a glass of water on the nightstand, and as it fell to the floor I realized my wonderful gift of forbearance was being severely tested. As I stumbled to the door, a man stuck his head in, identified himself as a "checker" and was just wondering if the room was satisfactorily cleaned. After assuring him everything was just fine, he gave me his card with instructions to call his extension if any needs arose. At this point, I decided it was fruitless attempting to nap and thought I'd take a shower, then go for dinner. Just as I was about to enter the shower the phone rang. "Sir, this is the desk. We're just confirming your one night visit—is that correct?" I was about to say that if these interruptions continued it might not even be one night! But I said a quick "Hail Mary" and answered, "Yes, Madam, that is correct." I returned to my shower and belted out a song!

Anxious to get a good look at the rink, I dressed quickly and went down to the restaurant. The rink was small but adequate. I decided to inquire about the possibilities of skating, and went out, down a short ramp, through a door, and into a small locker room. A girl greeted me and asked if I wanted to skate, inquiring about my membership—admission was reduced if you were a member. I informed her that I was from the New Haven Figure Skating Club.

An instructor we called Ed O, who had been with the Ice Follies for a number of years, was my first skating teacher. He was very encouraging to young skaters, and after first seeing me skate remarked that with the right kind of instruction I could be the next Dick Button. When this got back to me via a friend who had overheard his comment, I can't tell you what it did for my self-esteem. At the time I was very young and reticent, out of the loop, and Italian to boot—all the things that worked against an aspiring skater. His remarks, I learned, were inspired by his observation of the height and distance of my jumps, achieved with little effort. After the first few lessons he advised me to join the New Haven Skating Club because the instructors and coaches there could bring me along at a faster pace. Then he added something that I knew was true but was naive enough not to dwell on. He intimated that it was an "elitist" club, and because I was young, and Italian, besides, a professional would have to sanction me before I could become a member. When I got home, I looked up the word in a dictionary; a month later I was a member of the New Haven Figure Skating Club.

Now in the hotel rink a greeter quickly directed my attention to a sign on the wall listing rules for the privilege of skating there. Rule #1, etched in bold black letters, was: "There is no jumping and spinning allowed, not even in the center." This displeased me, and upon asking her if I had not already seen someone do a flip in the center, she answered in a perturbed voice, "Well, they shouldn't be. The manager is very strict about these rules!" Inquiring about the local skating club, I learned they met on Wednesday nights.

Upon my return to the restaurant, I ordered a double cheeseburger, fries, and a vanilla milkshake, then pondered whether to bother to skate or just go up to read and rest in anticipation of tomorrow's drive. As I was finishing my dinner a group of kids about my age came in and were seated adjacent to me. Their boisterous and spirited conversation, containing "axles" and "double loops" and details about how a certain individual performed last night, and facetiously describing how one in their group was out of rhythm in the opening line told me they were skaters with a troupe performing in the vicinity. Their decibel level made them extremely conspicuous and annoying to many diners. One girl looked around with a concerned look I interpreted to mean she was sorry if they were disturbing me, but I smiled, reassuring her that it was okay to laugh and have fun; it sure beats a grouchy, irascible bunch. I thought for a moment about introducing myself, for we had a common interest, but the shy side of me came through, and the probability of still getting an hour of skating, sans jumps and spins, made me decide to move on.

As I tried to squeeze through the maze of tables this group had created, I overheard one of the skaters say something in answer to a question, to the effect that "the Follies don't do things like that." I left, assuming they were from the Ice Follies, but they could very easily have been from the Ice Capades or some other show. Both troops were on U.S. and Canadian tours, the latter starring Donna Atwood and Ronnie Robertson—two great skaters whom I had the utmost respect for. Donna Atwood had natural talent and was very graceful; Ronnie Robertson was the greatest spinner—in my opinion—in the twentieth century. I actually had the opportunity to see the show in Springfield, and as part of Donna Atwood's act she would pick someone in the front (on-ice seats), sit on their lap, and hug them. The selection was spontaneous, tasteful, and brief, all in sync with the rhythm to her musical backdrop. It was extremely effective and thrilling, and I will candidly admit this with prejudice, for I admired her very much, and also because mine was the lap she sat on, and I was the person she hugged!

51

The Call

I left the restaurant to take another look at the rink and found it crowded—enough for me to opt not to skate. Back in my room I decided to call home, as I had a four A.M. departure time the next day. I figured chances of making contact with the LaCava compound in the next four or five days would be remote, so it seemed wise to check on things before I got back on the road. The call had nothing to do with what transpired in the next twenty-four hours, and it would be fair to say that the seed for my decision not to continue to Tallahassee had been planted in me when I first saw the ice rink.

I always wanted to travel with an ice show, just for the experience, and here was an opportune moment to hook up with a show. A year before a skating girlfriend and I had talked about joining a troop; she went with the Ice Capades, but something came into my life at the time of New England auditions and I was unable to get there. The next opportunity was two months away in Los Angeles, which also came at the wrong time. Now, in a period of my life when there was some uncertainty about the direction I was going, I felt the time was right to venture into the world of professional skating. We were told at the club, and we discussed frequently, how these companies were always seeking good skaters; the turnover rate was high. In addition to the frequency of skaters' fatigue and sickness, we rationalized that even if the line was full, a standby status was not something to reject. I was a fast study at this young, tender age, meaning I could master steps and rhythms in rapid fashion. Moreover, there were never any qualms about making the line, for a while back, when inquiring about the Ice Capades—when they were in Hartford—I was guaranteed by my coach that they would welcome skaters "like you with open arms." But he discouraged me to the nth degree, mainly because he thought I had promise, but as an individual performer—this would not be my Camelot!

I talked to Mom briefly and told her I would be leaving very early in the morning but would call again in a few days. She was happy to hear from me and like any good mother cautioned me to drive carefully. She also wished me good luck with enrollment. Before saying goodbye, she told me that the Pope was very ill, or the way the Vatican spokesman described it, "was in the ecstasy of repose." I hung the receiver up sullenly as a strange feeling engulfed me. The Roman Curia usually holds off a few hours so as to get the mechanics working for a Pope's successor, or to at least first notify the Sacred College before general promulgation. This was the first knowledge I had that the Pope was so sick, and yet I was convinced he was already dead. I was saddened.

Pope Pius XII was one of my favorite popes. There was so much about this man that I admired. His election in 1939 was predictable. Precocious, he showed very early signs of spirituality and religious fervor. His keen mind and intelligence, in addition to his religious convictions, were steadfast and complemented his strong faith. To this extent, he once challenged a professor to a debate after the teacher made some inane reference, contrary to fact, which provoked the young Eugenio Maria Giuseppe Giovanni Pacelli. It was fortunate for the good professor that he refused the challenge! Pope Pius XII's brilliance transcended time; he was convincing and invincible in debate yet had a way that was gentle—holiness discernible even at a tender age. And although frail, he was one of the most active and energized popes in church history. Extremely pious, he spent many hours in prayer and meditation, and his spiritual gifts were translated unselfishly with great latitude unto his flock. His brilliance encompassed a phenomenal range of interests with which he attacked church problems with aplomb, dedication, and love.

This Pope's tireless efforts to avert World War II, by negotiating with several European governments, desperately continued even after the war began. His prayer and energy were totally directed toward seeking peace, indefatigable at every juncture of hope. The war and its inhumane elements were Pius XII's main

53

concern; this caused him much pain and deep sorrow. He is credited with saving at least one million Jews from the Nazis through secret arrangements, and he continually pleaded in quiet negotiations that the [axis] powers stop the unnecessary, indiscriminate bombing of densely populated and historic cities, thus saving thousands of lives. In retrospect, the post-war criticism heaped upon this great pope was so inaccurate (and the play *The Deputy* prejudicially slanted), without fact, and unfair that it rendered a sacrilege and unspeakable injustice.

For well over an hour I reflected on the life of this great man, remembering 1950, when he proclaimed the Assumption of the Blessed Virgin Mary into heaven; it was time for great celebrations. But added to my despondency was the fact I had just finished reading a book entitled *The Vatican and the War*, by Camille M. Cianfarra, the son of an American correspondent in Rome for the *New York Times* from 1935 to 1942. Educated in Italy, he had witnessed every phase of Mussolini's tyrannical (what turned out to be imperialistic) policy. With great knowledge, Cianfarra was an expert at Vatican news reporting. Reading this book brought great insight into the workings of the Vatican and what transpired there during the war. Since then I have reread that book several times and never cease to be amazed at history's leaders' incredible failures. Besides discussing the working diplomacy of the Vatican, this book also detailed the politics of Italy, which spread far beyond the confines of the country, touching on problems of moral and spiritual values.

Many things were going through my mind that evening. It was comforting to know that throughout history tyrants and repressive totalitarian governments, the expansionist regimes with huge armies whose goals could only be accomplished by eradicating religion and God, have failed so miserably! But with the cost—tragically so—of millions of lives! I vaguely remembered from the book an article in the French newspaper *Figaro,* attributed to Mussolini. In the history of Western civilization, from the time of the Roman Empire, it has been shown that when the State clashes with religion, the State is always defeated. Mr. Cianfarra wrote that Napoleon had to discover this by the process of trial and error. Napoleon harbored a profound dislike for

Cardinal Consalvi, who was a great Papal Secretary of State. His eminence possessed great talent, undoing all that the French Emperor had obtained from Pope Pius VII, who dutifully bowed to the Emperor's rule. He continued: "One day Consalvi was summoned by the Emperor. 'Do you know that I am capable of destroying your Church?' shouted the exasperated Corsican. 'Your Majesty,' was Consalvi's humble reply, 'not even we priests have achieved that in eighteen centuries!' "

My thoughts were momentarily broken by a commotion outside my door. It was then that I decided to go down to see if the rink was still crowded. Walking to turn off my radio I hesitated, for the news commentator was talking about the Pope. I shut it off, picked up my skates, and left. But I had taken them with no intention of using them. Peering through the glass, I saw only a few figure skaters left at the rink; they were not only spinning but also jumping. My mood altered; if they're allowed to jump, this was a good sign. So I entered and skated vigorously for one hour. The hour. I sifted through eons of decision making; everyone has an hour of personal historic significance, which sends one's life in a certain direction, and this was mine. While leaving the rink it appeared to me quite clearly that not only would the trip to Tallahassee be aborted, but I would not be joining the ice show.

Two weeks later I was back in Connecticut working, writing, singing, and skating; and although my education would continue for many years to come, I would never receive, for reasons beyond my control, a college degree!

The Transfer

LaCava Construction underwent some restructuring in the mid-60's; I was transferred from Cromwell to Montville, Connecticut to manage a site that was "in the ground" (site work complete and foundations in). My only knowledge of little Montville was from an occasional drive-through on the way home from Ocean Beach, but I settled in quickly. The first phase was comprised of only ten houses in various stages of construction; in no time at all things were under control. It was enjoyable to have lunch on the banks of the Thames River whenever I could grab a lunch "hour." It was a tranquil and pleasant spot, and occasionally the Yale crew team would row by during a practice. But my time in Montville was short lived, as two other tracts were experiencing brisk sales and technical and managerial skills were needed there.

So East Hartford became my next base of operation, until the early spring of 1968. Notice of my next transfer, to Bloomfield, came about quite suddenly one day, when brother Joe drove into the development and waved me over to his car. He said, "Get in—I have to brief you on something; let's go where it's quiet." At the far end of the site he stopped his vehicle under a big oak tree and brought forth a thick, rolled-up set of blueprints from the back seat. He enthusiastically suggested we get out of the car because "it will be easier." Opening the prints, he laid them on the hot trunk of his car, smiled, and said, "You know we've been working on this deal with Rocky Pasero—well, it's signed, and we're ready to start!"

Joe went on to tell me the office thought this should be my job. Then he joshed, "We need someone there with your skills, experience, and personality." We laughed as he rolled up the plans very quickly and offered to drive me back to the trailer. I motioned him on, preferring to walk.

As I started to walk the few hundred feet back to my car, hundreds of starlings swarmed in circles overhead, making a cacophony of weird sounds I had never before heard from birds. It startled me. Then they winged off hurriedly so close to one another I could scarcely see through to what was a beautiful sky. After they flew out of sight I was momentarily struck by a premonition that the transfer to Bloomfield would be very significant for my future. The feeling wasn't exceptionally monumental, like a bolt of lightning struck me, nor did I dwell on it for any length of time. Yet this curious happening was linked to another portent that would revisit me as I stood in front of a grave with a bowed head and tears in my eyes, holding the hands of two young children.

Initially, I was not happy about the transfer to Bloomfield. Traffic was a significant problem—in order to avoid the backups getting to work in the morning from Wethersfield, it was imperative to depart by six A.M. Nearby Kaman Aircraft was starting a shift change, and the highway leading to the roads for the LaCava site was a constant, proverbial parking lot. Any alternative route or routes were slow and tedious, with lots of stop and go, belying the trigonometric maxim that the shortest distance between two points is a straight line. Moreover, the return was equally exasperating—I had to either work until six or leave at three-thirty P.M. An accident in either direction—I-91 was plagued with them—-made for late arrivals and late returns. In addition, I was not familiar with Bloomfield, the codes, the inspectors, or the people. Initially, I had mixed emotions about being there, but soon that uncertainty would change, fixed by a beautiful young maiden only seen in fairy tales!

This site was divided into two large sections separated by a right-away easement of power lines and some wetlands. Although the acreage was basically without trees, it was a prime area and extremely marketable. Within the first eight months sales were beyond what had been projected. At that time the LaCava Construction Company had done very little building in Bloomfield, but its name and excellent reputation were well known throughout Hartford County. So to some extent the response was not surprising.

In a month's time I had organized and surrounded myself with an able staff of loyal and conscientious people. If the pace got too hectic (in construction, hectic was normal) the main office would augment my operation with extra men and crews from jobs that were less busy. Fortunately, this was only a seldom occurrence. But "supers" relished the help from regular crews any time it was offered. And if help wasn't available from other job sites, I would have to do some hiring.

The topography of this subdivision was relatively level in the first section, but in the second section the grade exceeded six to eight percent. The texture of soil was varied—dense and heavy with some clay interspersed, or gritty, with drainage qualities. One day as I returned to my trailer from lunch I noticed a yellow school bus parked in the development. In addition, there was a group of young people, and an older man with a black and white beard, in the open space with barrels and shovels. It appeared they were gingerly digging something up and placing it in the barrels. I slowly walked over to where the older man was conversing with six or so youngsters. About twenty-five feet from them was another group of students, I assumed, bent over and totally engrossed in something—I had no clue what. As I approached, the gentleman scratched his beard, smiled and said, "Oh, you must be Lou, I'm Professor ***** from the University of Connecticut."

"What are you doing here?" I asked politely. But before I gave him a chance to answer the first question, I whacked him with another. "Do you have any idea you're in an easement, a right-away that borders some wetlands?"

He realized I was very serious by the tone of my voice and the look on my face. LaCava Construction was extremely conscientious about preserving the wetland environment—not only because of statutes, but more importantly because we were well trained by the patriarch of the LaCava clan. George Sr. always stressed conservation, whether it be preserving trees, slopes, or meadows, and he would not tolerate operators of heavy equipment that were sloppy or careless—they would not last long on a LaCava job.

"The school called your office and they said we could take a couple of pails of white clay for our sculpture class as long as it was okay with the local and state EPA; and that was cleared." Then he added, "This is great stuff!! You just can't find this type of clay in the state to teach with." I had to admit my ignorance and asked him if he used this clay for sculpture—was it really the best he could find?

"It's just one of many methods we incorporate in curriculum. What is your job?"

"My job? I'm project manager and resident construction engineer. I still have to verify this with my office before you remove anything from the site, so please, if you'll just hold on a few minutes until I return."

When I got to my office there were people waiting to see me with structural questions and other problems. Ten minutes elapsed, then a state social worker walked in asking for help in locating a client. I told her I had never heard of the street she named, so she used the phone to glean further information from her office, and I waited, as I had a half dozen calls to make. All this time the professor was waiting outside my office. I was doing everything possible to confirm his story, but time was money, and my first responsibility was to keep the job moving.

As I was finally about to call the main office, a neighbor came in needing to talk to me. I asked her if it could wait and she said it would only take a minute. She then matter-of-factly and very somberly said word had been received that the husband of a lady who had bought the model on the end had been killed in Vietnam. Now the day was really a nightmare! I expressed my sorrow and personal feelings about the war, as well as offered support and prayers. After talking to her for a few minutes, I returned to finally make the call to the main office, receiving reassurance that it was permissible for the professor and his group to remove the clay. I then took a piece of plain white paper and wrote Please Do Not Disturb Until Three-thirty (one hour). I made my calls, planned the next day's schedule, and said to myself, "I need a couple of weeks off!"

Hawaii, Here I Come!

I had two more weeks of vacation left, and this was the perfect time to put it to good use. I was tired from a full life of work and the hubbub of other interests, which included skating up to four times a week, singing, and writing. Plus, I had a personal life—dating, attending the opera, symphony, and dinner on occasion.

At this time, there was one girl I was fond of. We had good times together and enjoyed each other's company. She was bright, cultured, and was trilingual; conversation topics ranged from the Vietnam War to the Masters to Beethoven's Fifth Symphony. After only a few months we were suddenly aware that neither of us could wait to see the other again; we would spend long periods on the phone keeping up on every detail of what had transpired since our last time together. This was getting serious, but it was an infrequent practice to allow myself to reflect on the possibility of marriage, for I was not anxious to settle down—there was too much going on in my life. Maybe it was a little selfish on my part to be unwilling to give up my interests.

We agreed not to date others, but despite our close bond and deep mutual respect, something about her always bothered me. Every time I picked her up she was either alone in her apartment or there would be a middle-aged couple she introduced as her aunt and uncle. That wasn't so strange, although I would frequently see a little baby I surmised was about three or four months old, which she volunteered was the child of her aunt and uncle. Being completely trustworthy, and as I look at it today, naive, it never entered my mind that there was another story.

We had been looking forward to a full night out, with dinner at the famous Carbone's Ristorante in Hartford, and an opera featuring the great James McCracken in *Othello*. I knew the story and main arias well, for Mario Lanza had sung them in the movie *Serenade*, and I had thoroughly digested the contents of the libretto. Regrettably, this would be the first and last time I would ever see *Othello* performed.

The anticipation of Saturday night was with me all week and I was delighted to see my lady looking quite attractive in a black cocktail dress with a plain set of pearls around her neck to accent the gleam in her eyes. As I picked her up the evening was filled with a brush of autumnal delight. The leaves were in their mutational cycle, which would surrender to nature's sacrifice for the promise of rebirth in a young and flowering spring. The air was light after a first frost had cleansed the residual effects of a rainless, sweltering summer. I was rested after a brief but refreshing nap in the early afternoon and my heart was happy with anticipation.

The performance was thrilling, and as we started to leave the orchestra area I took her hand and said, "I can't wait to read tomorrow's *Courant* and see what the critics have to say about tonight's performance. I thought it was a great rendition." Turning to her, smiling, I awaited her response; but I noted preoccupation in her eyes. "Is there anything wrong; are you feeling okay?" I asked. She told me she was fine. As we were jostled around by the enthused audience, I put my mouth close to her ear, as the level of noise made normal conversation impossible. "What did you think of the opera?"

"It—it was so good!" Then she snickered, "Some parts gave me goose bumps."

I asked if she'd like to go to Casa Loma for a cup of coffee and a sandwich. As we moved out into the open air, where we could finally hear ourselves talk, she quietly replied, "Lou, I'm not hungry. Please, do you mind if we go some place where it's quiet and we can be alone? I have to tell you something very important."

After finding a quiet, out-of-the-way spot, I stopped the car and turned to her; she was weeping. I took her hands and beseeched her to tell me what could make her so sad after such a beautiful evening. Tears streamed down her face, and I assured her time has remedial and enduring qualities.

"Please look at me, is there . . ."

She interrupted me. "Lou, I'm very fond of you."

61

I responded with a sigh of relief—"That's something to cry about?"

Her trembling hands squeezed mine as she wept and said that what she was about to confess would make me think ill of her; she was sure I would never call her again.

"I can't think of one possible thing that could make me have ill feeling toward you. I respect and like you too much. Why would I ever . . ." And I was going to continue to say "ever feel differently," when she blurted out "That baby you saw is mine!" She stopped crying immediately after that and went on to tell specific details, indicating it was not totally her fault. I stopped her, saying it was not important, that it was the past and can only be viewed as a beginning and learning experience. I told her when she got down on herself and battered by guilt to just read the lives of some of the great saints, like Francis of Assisi and Augustine. They made many mistakes. The important thing is that we learn from them, and I then continued by telling her it didn't change my feelings toward her one iota. We talked about other things until I felt she was completely relaxed and totally in control; then we left for her home.

During the drive back she sat close but remained silent. When we arrived it was late and I had to park a distance away from her apartment building. I shut off the lights and ignition, then turned and said succinctly, "Promise me one thing? Please don't dwell on the last hour of this evening; think of the beautiful and positive aspects of it." We got out and walked arm in arm to her apartment. When we said good night there were tears in her eyes. A woman's intuition had told her that our wonderful relationship had ended. She was right.

I reflected for the next few days about what had transpired on Saturday night and my overall relationship with her. I liked this girl beyond friendship. I knew she was a fine person, well bred, educated, cultured, and pretty, and I convinced myself that she was a wholesome girl that just made a mistake. Although there was still a stigma attached to illegitimacy, that didn't bother me; the truth of the matter was that I was too immature to handle a baby.

Despite my doubts about growing to accept the situation, I

liked her too much and decided to call her again for lunch the following Saturday. After three attempts with no answer, on the fourth call I was informed that she was out of the country. The next day when I reached over to put something in my glove compartment I noticed my graduation ring, which I had given her to wear as a sign of my affection, on the front seat—her sign of finality.

The girl who followed her in my life was totally the opposite. We had absolutely nothing in common, and I told her of my observation so that I would not mislead her about my feelings. She assured me I would change to cherish her company. Instead of operas, museums, symphonies, and poetry, it now was movies, bars, bowling, fast food joints—not that there was anything wrong with them, only I felt that a continual diet of these were a waste of valuable time. One night on the way home from bowling the car radio was interrupted by a special bulletin that said Martin Luther King had been assassinated. This didn't help my already depressed state of mind. My immediate reaction was that this horrendous act was a great loss to the country. I reflected that the world seemed to be veiled in a curtain of despair and chaos, and without value.

I dated this girl on a regular basis for six weeks prior to my vacation trip to Hawaii. Each date was the same dull experience. Although we had some fun, there were many times that I was preoccupied and often felt guilty. She made every effort to consume me in every way. For example, to please me she would read the current news, "bone-up" on the subjects she felt I was interested in, and on the next date would start a conversation on politics, sports, music, or poetry, trying hard to impress me. Invariably, the subjects she chose were above her head, causing inane remarks, devoid of fact and meaning, and I would cringe with embarrassment and pity for her. That's when I felt small and guilty for dating her. There was nothing wrong with her—it was me.

I take pride in the fact that I was always polite and respectful in her presence, and in reality I learned and grew in a new dimension from this relationship. I always believed that every person was unique, and by being cognizant of individuality, one could learn many things about life. With her it was no different. Her information wasn't monumental, but information that one could never find in history books; the favorite foods of her ancestry, and the clothes they wore, little pertinent details in geography—the inadvertent rerouting of a natural stream in her grandparents' village from the damaging bombing of the war. There were times when she could be very interesting; however, those times were few and far between, primarily because she wasted too much effort trying to please and impress me.

I knew this arrangement was wearing thin—it was time for me to move on when she started to flavor her conversation with risqué phrases, on the topics of sex and passion. She often asked if I was a virgin. She told me she wanted to be intimate with me, and when I replied that her chances were slim to none, she took it personally. In vain, I tried to explain that she didn't have to approach a relationship with compromise to interest a man; as a matter of fact, the converse was true, and ninety-nine percent of the time you would lose him. I told her she was a very attractive girl with much to offer—something I sincerely believed. She said she thought that I was patronizing her and continued with her try at seduction. Three days before leaving for Hawaii, I told her I would not be seeing her again.

I slept about two hours on the plane to San Francisco. Having been out late the previous night and tired from an extremely busy month on the site, it was now my time for relaxation, with no phone, problems, or deadlines. I planned a three-day side trip to the City on the Bay because I wanted to see the famous drummer Buddy Rich, who had a long-standing engagement at one of the famous San Francisco clubs situated close to the Top of the Mark Hotel. I liked good drummers and had the opportunity to see Gene Krupa and Cozy Cole in Chicago in the early 60's when I was attending some seminars in the busy Windy City. It was ironic that drummers and percussion would enter my life in an important way in the future.

The lady sitting next to me on the plane was extremely nervous and told me during lunch that this was her maiden flight; she was very talkative and apologized, saying it relieved some of her stress. Although it prevented me from additional rest, I lis-

64

tened and used the remainder of the flight to assuage some of her apprehension by explaining the particular noises coming from the aircraft that were heightening her flying fears. Upon landing, she took my hand and held it for dear life. The plane touched down and bounced up, then settled forward at a greater rate of speed than I had ever experienced before. I conjectured it had something to do with the low ceiling and heavy rain. I had told her to expect a sensation when the plane started rolling after landing, for the pilot would reverse the thrust to slow the plane's ground speed down to a manageable rate. When the pilot put it into reverse thrust, I nodded and smiled, indicating that was to be expected. The flight was now over. Her sigh of relief was easy to hear! I helped her to the luggage area, where her son awaited her arrival, and I wished her good luck on her San Francisco stay. Then I was on my way . . .

I grabbed a cab to the Hilton Hotel, settled in for a brief nap, made plans to get a haircut, shave, and trim of my Robert Taylor mustache in anticipation of dinner and Buddy Rich. I once grew a mustache in a period of weakness that was very slim and added distinction to my face, as most mustaches do. But this one was thick and black. People liked it, so it stayed with me for a few years. During my tête-à-tête with the San Francisco barber I told him I was just in town for a few days, specifically to see Buddy Rich. He suggested taking a nightclub tour, as it went to the Buddy Rich show plus four other night spots. I was never one to be kept in the confines of a tour group, but he was convincing enough, stressing other clients had liked the positive aspect of meeting people in the group. So upon my return to the hotel I stopped in the lobby to register for the tour, only to find it was full. I was assured they were trying to get another group together, and if they got six, it was a go. One hour later the concierge called to say a group would be leaving at six P.M., so payment was needed immediately. It was a few minutes past six by the time I was finally dressed and down in the lobby; he hurried through the paperwork and told me to rush and meet the guide and others anxiously waiting on the corner.

So I flew out the entrance, almost knocking someone down, ran down to the intersection where the group had congregated, and stepped off the curb to cross to the parked van, and my foot landed right in a huge, slimy pile of dog excrement! The guide let out an, "Oh! No!" and the four others in the party (three girls and an older man) and I broke into hysterics. I told the guide to let me know where we were going for dinner and I would take a cab and meet them there.

The man in the group said, "There's a shoe shine parlor across the street! Go quickly—they'll clean them. We can wait a few minutes." The guide was annoyed, indicating we were supposed to be at our first club at seven, but he said that if it was all right with the girls they would wait for me. The girls looked at each other, and one answered with a huge grin on her face, "That's okay with us—he's cute. And he looks like fun!" The guide relaxed, and as I was about to leave he yelled, "Shake a leg, my friend, and next time be careful where you walk!"

I retorted, "I just don't want to get anything on my new Kuppenheimer threads!!!" Everyone laughed again—the night had gotten off to a hilarious start, albeit at my expense.

Once across the street, I jumped up on one of the empty thrones and put my dung-covered right foot up on the shoe anvil; when the attendant looked down, his smile melted to a frown. "Hey, man, where'n the hell ya' been? This is going to be a job!"

I could only reply, "What can I say, buddy? Some days are like this!" He continued to bitch until he was done, but he made my shoes sparkle. He still had a frown on his face when I jumped off the throne; I stuck my hand into my pocket, pulled out a $50 bill, and flashed it so he could see it before pressing it into the palm of his hand. His face lit up and pearly white teeth expressed a grateful smile. Shaking my hand, he happily sang out, "Man, come back again with your shoes anytime!"

What started out as a calamity turned into a very exciting evening with a wonderful visit to that famous city of song. I met some very beautiful people, saw Buddy Rich and other great talents, sang, visited Muir Woods and the tall trees, Sausalito, Fisherman's Wharf, and then when my time was finished, sang "I Left My Heart in San Francisco"—and you know, I really did!

On route to Hawaii there was a two-hour layover in Los Angeles. It was dark upon landing; I went down to the coffee shop, bought some reading materials, ordered a soda and a Reuben, and found a quiet corner to settle in. After eating I dozed, and when I awoke I did a double take. Two hours had elapsed!!! I grabbed my carry-on and hurried down to the boarding gate, only to find my plane was delayed an hour due to mechanical trouble.

The flight over to Hawaii was one gigantic party, with singing, drinks, storytelling, and even a little dancing in the aisles. One stewardess had hunkered down in the empty seat next to me when we hit some turbulence; prompted by the book I was reading, we were soon involved in a long discussion. She had watched Bishop Fulton J. Sheen faithfully when he was on television in the 50's, and inspiration from his lectures had allowed her to persevere through a very difficult period in her life—she and millions of others, I thought.

We exchanged names and a few tidbits about ourselves, and when I told her that I came from a family of seventeen, and that I had nine brothers, she was enthralled. She then offered that she had been a stewardess for five years, on a "fluke." Desperately afraid of flying, she took a white-knuckle seminar, where she met other girls who had experienced the same apprehensions and were now flight attendants; she followed their path and had not regretted it for one minute. Our conversation moved on to personal things. For example, she asked me, "Do you drink, do you smoke, do you attend a church?" I thought this was weird. When I answered no, no, and yes to her questions, she smiled and said, "I like that!" But so as not to give the impression she was forward or overly interested in me, she qualified herself by adding, "Gee, you don't have ANY vices!" Well, I don't know . . .

In Honolulu our plane was met by a cute, hospitable Hawaiian model in a grass skirt, who, as was the custom, greeted us with "aloha," a lei around the neck, and a peck on the cheek. In the background there were several girls dancing to "The Hawaiian Love Song," the music provided by a small, colorfully dressed island band. Before entering the terminal I was offered an exotic island drink, compliments of the Chamber of Commerce, in honor of a birthday celebration for a popular historic island political figure. While unusual for such an early morning hour, this was common practice for flights later in the day, for no special occasion.

The trip to the hotel saddened me when I observed that commercialization had overrun this once beautiful paradise; I immediately considered flying northwest to the island of Maui after being assured it was relatively undefiled by large buildings and tourism. My conception of Hawaii had been that of a place to unwind in communion with nature and God's brilliant gifts, so I pictured the tranquility of clear blue water, and breathtaking, resplendent mountains immersed in golden sunsets that hover on the horizon in sheer majesty, then imperceptibly float away into the vast emptiness and cavernous universe!

The initial days of this trip were spent in museums and libraries, and on a trip to Pearl Harbor. Walking on this memorial, the *Arizona*, caused me to experience serious reflection on the brave men who valiantly gave their lives so that future generations could live in democracy, with freedom, and with the continuation of inalienable rights. It occurred to me as the guide spewed out facts, figures, and descriptions of the horrendous and catastrophic attack, that this was perpetrated by a country indoctrinated by narrow-minded leaders, whose main objective was power and who was serving the warped views of an emperor and his military. I also realized that human nature basically takes liberty and independence for granted; and the sole reason that history is recorded is not so much for posterity, but rather for continuous review by our leaders, lest the same mistakes be repeated. Filtered through my brain in meditation and prayer were thoughts of brothers who served the country in war at Normandy, the Pacific, Germany, Iwo Jima, and Korea.

When I stepped down to board the launch for our trip back to the mainland, a young lady behind me tripped and fell forward, sending me airborne—sort of in a position of the skater's flying camel. I went sprawling onto several chairs that were not secured to the floor of the boat. An elderly gentleman and a young boy prevented the rather obese girl from crashing down on me, probably averting severe injury. After assuring everyone nearby that I was fine, I took a seat in the rear of the vessel next to the lady who had tripped. She was still embarrassed, apologetic, and weepy. I told her we should always find humor in situations, especially if no injury was incurred, for it lifts the spirit and replenishes the soul. This made her laugh, as I segued into some old Italian proverbs: the face should only be frozen in death, and a smile is like a love aria from a Verdi opera. She finally relaxed. When we were leaving the vessel I said facetiously, "Be careful you don't trip," which brought about a new round of apologies. I stopped her and said, "Just think—if you didn't trip, we never would have met!" We parted as friends.

The following day it was time to get some of that brilliant Hawaiian sun. I wasn't one to sit on the beach, but I loved to watch the surfers, so I got into my bathing trunks and went down to watch the athletes as they piled in from California for the weekend. I had purchased a new state-of-the art Land Pack Polaroid camera for the trip. After snapping a picture, the film would slide out of the camera, and then you would wait about thirty seconds as the image developed before your eyes. A little felt chemically-treated squeegee was then rubbed across the photo to inhibit the film from oxidation and fading.

I went down and found myself a spot on the beach to relax and enjoy the sight of surfers as they came shooting in—riding the big wave. The number of surfers—male and female alike—was amazing, as was the obvious physical stamina and dexterity needed to maneuver their boards. I thought I'd have some fun with my Polaroid—the plan was to snap a picture of the first girl who rode in. Waves came in series, so I positioned myself to photograph the very last one. I waited patiently as boy after boy appeared, then finally a young, fully endowed blonde zoomed in, (wouldn't you know) riding an unusually big wave. She skillfully spread-eagled her board and rode it to shore, then dragged it about fifty feet, left it, and proceeded to walk up to a flat area of the sand, out of breath. As she walked in my direction with the bright sun illuminating her gorgeous, bikini-clad body, she was completely oblivious to my camera and me. I was the first of the legitimate *paparazzi,* although my intentions were really quite honorable!

I quickly removed the film from the camera, waited for the picture to develop, and coated it with the preservative. Since I had not used the camera very much, I was thrilled to find she had come out perfectly centered; the color was perfect, and her features and beauty really stood out. I blew on the picture to help the solution dry then slipped it into a case I carried in my zippered beach jacket pocket. As she walked up close by me, I said, "Hi, how've you been? I haven't seen you in a while." Now that's audacity!

She looked at me and did a double take, trying to place me in her memory while shyly answering, "Hi."

"That was a great recovery coming in. You've really been working hard on that board!"

Curiosity was getting the best of her, and she finally mustered enough sense to ask if she knew me. As it happened, a friend had called her name out as she walked up from the water, so I said, "Sandy, I can't believe it! Are you okay?"

"It's just . . . I've been surfing for a while and had a lot of sun. I'm sorry—how are you?" she apologized.

We continued to talk for a few minutes, but I knew she still was not convinced that we had met before, so I stuck my hand into my jacket and pulled out the case containing her picture. She and gathering girlfriends gasped. "Oh my God," she screamed. "Where did you get that?" She took the picture from my hand to examine it closer. But I couldn't continue the ruse, and told her how I knew her name, about the camera and my ease in not being detected snapping a picture. She was a good sport and took it in stride. And although it provided a delightful way to ask for a dinner date, I never used the camera surreptitiously again.

The next day after breakfast I bought a paper and went down to the dock area about a mile away from my hotel. Never having been there, it proved to be an enlightening experience. Naiveté had led me to envision this big island as a land of affluence, and so far I had seen nothing to disprove this notion. Commercialization was a disappointment; poverty was a heartbreak. So far I had toured areas of upper-class neighborhoods, expensive residential housing, Mercedes and Fiats, and docks that were lined with huge boat after boat—mostly impressive catamarans owned by the very wealthy. But this spot at the docks was different, and I was shocked to see such poverty. Kids of all ages—dirty, hungry, and begging. Some bore rashes and body sores, and save for a very few, all were underweight. I immediately had a new perspective of this "paradise" island.

From studying the history of the Hawaiian Islands, I knew there was great poverty at one time, but I never expected to witness this sad spectacle in so-called modern age—and amidst such tremendous wealth! My studies had enlightened me about the great Saint Damon "the leper priest," and how he dedicated his life to working with pestilence and the hungry, dying, and impoverished in this land. Damon labored incessantly to establish a city on a small island for the discarded and ostracized, using every ounce of his persuasive energy to engage the local government's help to provide for these poor disenfranchised souls. I was so moved by the sacrifices he had endured—eventually even the ultimate sacrifice—"no greater love doth a man haveth than to lay down his life for his friend"—that I later wrote a poem about this great saint who was one of my favorites.

Meandering closer to where most of these kids were begging, I noted many of them excitedly diving off the pier into the water, especially after someone would walk by and gesture with their hands. At the pier, one heavier boy, accompanied by several very thin children, came forward and stuttered, "Mis-mis-ster, have you got some fffood—mon—nney fffor the wa-a-ater?" I always carried some type of granola bar—it was a new health fad at the time, so I pulled a few out of my front pocket and threw them into the air, admonishing them to share. The words were scarcely out of my mouth as the big, taller, healthier kid with jet-black hair grabbed all three and started to move away from the pack. I yelled that he was supposed to share with the others, whereupon he turned around with a guiltless look on his face, already devouring the bars. Then I realized why he was so much bigger than the others!

One little kid, drooling and with sores on his belly, who looked about nine or ten years old, asked again if I had money for the water. People passing by were throwing coins into the channel, which the kids would dive for. This way, an old gentleman who frequented the docks told me, it was less intrusive; it gave them the opportunity to work for money! And, he added, it also helped diminish the guilty feeling that sometimes gnawed at the hearts of the rich.

My last few days in Hawaii were spent mostly with these kids, who saw me as a friend. Each day I would bring whatever was practical for them to share and appeased others by throwing money into the water. It was obvious that the kids experienced a great euphoria from the diving ritual. Each time one would emerge with a quarter or half-dollar they would beam with exhilaration. The old man was right—it did diminish the gnawing at the heart—at least momentarily.

On my last day, it was hard to tell the kids that I wouldn't be seeing them again. I don't know the reason it was so important for me to announce my departure, as I'm sure they got used to people coming and going from their lives. Their lack of concern for my departure was not surprising, until one cute, bony kid, with downcast eyes and teeth missing in front, shyly looked up at me and asked in poor English if I was going back home to get more money. I shook my head as I took out a handful of quarters and threw them into the channel; they all hurried away and dove into the water, save for little kid with the big question. I looked at his eyes and saw a reflection of Jesus; smiling sadly at him, I walked away. Then I took out my Land Pack camera, and with a backdrop of an absolutely indescribable sunset, took a few pictures as the kids emerged from the water—a paradox of unspeakable deprivation woven into God's ineffable beauty. Then I bid aloha to Hawaii.

The flight back to the mainland was hysterical. First, the plane was oversold; many people were dismayed and/or belligerent. Arguments ensued and our departure was delayed. I considered relinquishing my seat to someone who needed to get back soon, but upon learning there were too many to accommodate, I knew it couldn't make a difference so returned to my seat to enjoy the fun!

Second, at this time in aviation history, when there was a per bag weight limit of forty pounds, many people circumvented the rule by hauling everything onto the plane that wouldn't fit in their luggage. The overhead compartments were bulging, so

72

much so that the flight crew had trouble closing the bin doors, a necessity before taking off. What couldn't fit overhead was shoved under seats, which proved to be interesting once the plane ascended to 30,000 feet. Smooth boxes and other items would leave their place, sliding through the seats and into aisles every time the plane would bank and change altitude, and especially upon landing. It was a mess—and I swear the lady next to me was transporting fish back to the mainland, for the stench was obvious—until a steward announced that each passenger was responsible for securing his or her own packages. That didn't help! It was the loudest and the smokiest flight I had ever taken; the flight attendants were busy and hassled. Planes, always a restful and relaxing place for me—away from the daily grind of phones and work stress—proved the exception to the rule on this flight; I neither slept nor relaxed!

In Los Angeles a phone call to the office gave me the good news that snow was in the forecast for late morning. It was supposed to be quite heavy throughout the day and night, accompanied by strong winds; perhaps I might consider a layover for a day, as my flight was due into Bradley near midnight. The flight into a bitter cold Chicago landed at nine-thirty, where runways were in good condition and flights were departing and arriving without any trouble. During the wait, while passengers departed and new ones for the Hartford flight boarded, I left the plane and called home to verify the weather in Hartford. When informed it had only been snowing about three hours and Bradley Field was still open, I decided to continue through. I ran back to the gate, and was the last passenger to board, to the chagrin of a stewardess. Minutes later we took off. Satisfied with my decision, for this was a fast flight back to the Insurance City, courtesy of the jet stream, I was in for a huge surprise!

The scheduled arrival time at Bradley Airport was eleven-thirty P.M.; we, in fact, landed at twelve-forty-five A.M., almost an hour and a half late, in blizzard conditions, on a runway of nearly four inches of packed snow, with a half load of tired, weary passengers. Our plane was the last allowed to land, as they could no longer keep the runways cleared. The airport would not open again for many hours.

From the flight's inception, the plane had been constantly buffeted by turbulence. No drinks or snacks were distributed for fear of injury; the stewardesses were very somber, a complete contrast to their usual smiling and pleasant demeanors. The lady sitting next to me, a schoolteacher returning from a meeting, was clearly very distraught, and I had to keep reassuring her that planes were made to stand up in all types of weather. As I tried to comfort her and believe what I was telling her myself, the girl across the aisle overheard me, and she too started to ask me questions like "why doesn't the pilot talk to us?" and "it seems like the plane is going so slow and making a lot of noise." I noticed the desperate fear in her eyes; she was hoping for words of confidence that everything would be alright. It occurred to me that it would have been fitting for me to wear a white collar considering the counsel I was providing—but who was counseling me?

People seemed to relax a bit when the pilot's voice crackled over the din, din, din of the engines, telling us that we would be landing at Bradley in thirty minutes. It seemed an opportune time for me to change the subject to get "my flock's" minds off the turbulence, so I began telling them that I was a figure skater and was into pair skating now, blah, blah, blah. This didn't help. The lady across the aisle asked if a flight like this didn't frighten me. My answer was intended to be humorous: "I'm more afraid of dropping my partner from over my head onto the ice." She forced a smile, and it broke the spell.

Once we landed and retrieved baggage there were no taxis available. But I was told that the limousine taking the plane's crew to their hotel in Hartford could drop me off. Conversation in the limousine was interesting, as the flight engineer asked where I was coming from; my answer brought smiles to their tired faces, with the pilot saying, "I've had better days!" A day that started very early in an eighty-degree paradise had ended in a winter wonderland—and reality!

The Fateful Breakfast

The early and severe winter, with numerous snow, sleet, and damaging wind storms, plus extremely bitter cold temperatures, fizzled quickly in the middle of February, when we actually experienced a week of fifty-degree clime; and with the help of the sun, most of the snow quickly melted. By the time March had arrived, production had increased, sales were continuing at a brisk pace and most schedules were on line. A competent and loyal staff gave me liberty to delegate many of the non-engineering aspects of my responsibilities. I was thus afforded more time to expedite pertinent aspects of my job that took place in the office: preparing schedules, ordering materials, computing house grades, and devising topographic schematic layouts for critical landscapes with intricate cross slopes. It also provided me, on occasion, an opportunity to go out to get a milkshake, have lunch, or finally pacify a salesman who had been badgering me to accompany him to a nearby golf driving range.

A residential construction supervisor's job, in the development mode (a sub-divided parcel of land primarily used for houses) is a rewarding but very difficult profession. First, you must have the background and a plethora of knowledge in many fields: management and salesmanship, as well as construction engineering (comprised of a civil and structure working comprehension). You must be able to converse intelligently with clients and staff and deal persuasively with vendors. Moreover, you must be able to take pressure and react coherently in emergencies. Equally as important, you must have common sense. If a person possesses all the aforementioned talents and degrees without gumption, it is not the profession for him or her to be in.

Long hours were the norm for me. I would be on site most days between six and six thirty A.M. and leave at five-thirty P.M.; more often than not I had homework—plans to figure, calls to make, meetings and seminars to attend. Occasionally I would have to meet with customers who were unable to see me at the site during the day to answer specific questions and review production progress. Beyond all this, I had my skating, singing, poetry, and an occasional date.

My primary function on arrival in the morning was to review the day's production schedule, make the many calls to vendors, meet with foremen, staff, and customers and check in with the main office for messages. Around eight A.M. the initial tasks were complete, and it was time for breakfast; and before I would leave the restaurant on one particular bright and sunny mid-March day, tenderly caressed by soft, cool breezes, my life would be changed forever!

Breakfast at home while working in Bloomfield was a rarity. The wee hours of the morning were not conducive to appetite; it was much easier for a single man to eat out. A.C Petersen's was a good restaurant in the center of Bloomfield that I frequented daily. Three or four of us "regulars" enjoyed morning camaraderie, solving a few of the world's problems each day as we ate. I had become quite friendly with many of the waitresses, including the manager, and I had to admit this was pleasant—-an invigorating respite during each stressful day.

The physical layout of the restaurant was elongated; the front faced north, with the entrance at the center. If you walked straight into the restaurant, you would come to the cashier and takeout area. Left and right were stools at the counter that wrapped three quarters of the way around the sides, giving the appearance of a horseshoe. The back was fixed with booths running perpendicular to the length of the building. It was a very practical layout, with a good flow easily accommodating many people.

Our small group always sat to the right at the top of the shoe; we habitually took the same seats. I usually sat on the last stool. I liked this seat, for it provided a bit more room, where I could swivel my chair to talk to someone behind without disturbing the person next to me. It also gave me an unobstructed view of people entering and exiting. This was essential—for what reason I don't know.

76

Breakfast was usually a spirited time, with someone telling a joke or teasing one of the girls—all in clean, friendly fun. One day while telling Betty (one of the waitresses) a joke about the golfer who stopped playing to tip his hat as his wife's funeral procession was passing by, I couldn't finish the punch line; my mouth froze shut and my heart skipped a proverbial beat. I did a double take toward the entrance of the restaurant, now graced by a young girl. She was arrayed all in white—and showed sheer elegance and beauty with such bright eyes—she was truly a vision of pure loveliness! I swallowed hard, staring at her long, dark and exquisite hair, immediately aware of her quiet demeanor, thinking there was a painting—a Mona Lisa, something from Rembrandt, Da Vinci, ah!, something to espy, and I said to myself, that's my wife! And I repeated and repeated—"That's my wife!"

Now I have to admit this was unique, because although I was in my early 30's I had never given much thought to marriage! I was much too active, very much involved in life. I'll admit in lonely periods I thought it might be nice to have someone intimate, someone to cuddle up with and share your deepest secrets, ambitions, and desires—someone you really loved and wanted to protect—to give your total being to for all eternity. But these were just brief interludes and what I believed were normal fantasies that every young man experienced. So it was unusual to even subconsciously say to myself, "Behold! There's my wife!" It was not only presumptuous, but also very much out of character. I didn't want marriage, least of all at this time in my life.

Betty, puzzled that I had stopped in the middle of the punch line and noticing the distant, preoccupied look on my face, said, "Lou, are you alright?"

I called her closer so no one could hear what I was about to ask, then discretely whispered, "Betty, who is that girl?"

"Lou, look at me and listen carefully; her name is Kathleen Walsh, she's engaged to be married, her brother John is a policeman in West Hartford. And she has a big German shepherd! Is there anything else you want to know?" Just then the cook called Betty's name, indicating her order was ready for serving. She gave me the "I'm sorry" look—for her woman's intuition foretold I was smitten—and left.

On subsequent days this beauty would enter the restaurant at the same time and order to go, but would never sit down to wait. She would stand in front, very properly poised, straight, never slouched, shoulder bag hanging smartly down the left side, always looking as beautiful as ever. This continued for several days, and as time progressed I was more convinced that someday she would be my wife—how utterly presumptuous.

After she left one morning, I asked Betty during a lull if she would tell Kathleen that I was asking about her. She agreed, but intimated to me that it would be futile, that the likelihood of getting acquainted with her on a scale of one to ten, with ten the greatest chance, was less than zero. But I never got discouraged. Something told me that time would bring us together—and soon!

Unbeknownst to me, Kathleen occasionally returned to Petersen's in the afternoon. So I was completely surprised the next morning when Betty informed me that she had relayed my message with the uninterested reply, "Who is he?" I was still not discouraged, rather more convinced than ever she would look over, or even talk to me within a few days. And I was so right!

The following morning when she came in and ordered her coffee and English muffin, she appeared very serious, never giving a hint she was at all curious about the guy who was asking about her. There were very few people in the store at that time, while I was on stage telling a joke about when Saint Peter ordered the men in two lines—one for men who have been henpecked by their wives and one for those that were not. All the men filed into the henpecked line, save for one skinny little guy who, when Saint Peter asked why he was standing in the non-henpecked line, replied, "Because my wife told me to get over here and keep my big mouth shut!" My voice apparently resounded loudly throughout the restaurant, and when I finished the punch line, Kathleen looked over in my direction. Our eyes met for a brief second, and she smiled! It could have been only a nanosecond, still words could never describe the feeling that engulfed my being at that moment!

I was a prolific reader of nonfiction at one time in my life and used to read everything I could get my hands on. I would frequent library after library, museums, art galleries, and old bookstores. One day while browsing in a tiny bookstore in Hartford, I happened on a very old book written by the late Bishop Fulton J. Sheen, when he was a young Monsignor, entitled *God and Intelligence.* The book caused me to be more introspective and rely more on the tremendous positive power of absolutes. For me to think and live by this creed was essential, as opposed to the dangerous trap of living as one thinks, accepting every errant thought that comes to mind.

I also had bought a best-seller by Norman Vincent Peale called *The Power of Positive Thinking.* This book outlined the benefit of optimism and applying positive thinking to one's life. I remember reading that energy from this state of mind always worked favorably, especially when used in a righteous and moral manner. Living one's life by this holy creed resulted in good things happening, even though one might not be aware or conscious of it. Well, even though I practiced this philosophy, it never dawned on me that Kathleen's first smile was a transformation from energy of my latent positive thinking!

The following morning she didn't come in, then when Tuesday, Wednesday, and Thursday passed without seeing her I admittedly had some doubts. When I asked Betty if she had seen her during the day, her reply was negative. Dejected, I went back to my office, took out a phone book and looked up her phone number and address, weighing the advantages of calling her. My reasoning was based on the possibility she had changed her job to another town, dampening my resolve to pursue a relationship and throwing a glitch onto my radar screen of dreams. I deduced, using the Saint Thomas Aquinas method of reasoning (logically take the advantages and disadvantages of an issue and apply each to reason) that it would be a mistake at that time to call her house. More convincing, however—her number was unlisted!

Early Friday afternoon I was hungry and decided to go for a cheeseburger and shake to go, but when I got to the restaurant I saw a gentleman from our "group" just finishing lunch, so I sat down to talk. These were not our usual seats, so I was facing the back of the restaurant, with my left side next to the takeout and register area. After putting in my order I was chatting with the manager when Betty came over, looking quite earnest. Trying not to be obvious, she cleared my friend's dishes and bent over, whispering, "Lou, look who just walked in." I slowly turned, and there she was! And she was just as stunning as the first time I had laid eyes on her. She put in her order as I continued to answer the manager's questions about the LaCava development. My morning buddy got up to leave and said good luck in Italian; I knew what he was referring to! Betty brought my order, and feeling a bit uneasy checking out at this moment, I gave Betty a "sawbuck" to cash me out. She started to wipe what was already a clean counter in front of me just so we could talk; it felt as if we were planning something ominous.

"I didn't notice any ring on her finger, Lou!" she offered. Asking her what she thought, she admitted to not knowing but said that Kathy appeared very serious. I left without looking in her direction, but by now I had lost my appetite. Deep in the crevices of my brain was a warm feeling that my "secret love" and I would soon meet! It wasn't a cocky or conceited notion, for no one could feel as humble at that moment as I did. There was little doubt those words spoken the first day would come true. For there, on a balmy spring day, I became convinced that fate had arranged for our encounter.

The following morning I was extremely anxious to go for breakfast, even before my "start-up" chores were finished. Leaving my foreman in charge, I was on my way. Breakfast was finished, but I asked Betty to bring me a black coffee—which I rarely drank—then slowly nursed it, just to waste time. I just knew she would come in! Her arrival was later than usual, and after placing an order she sat down, something she had never done before. As I was trying to evaluate this new development, one of the girls came over excitedly directing us to look out the window at a snow squall. Someone said that the weatherman had forecast partly cloudy with a chance of snow flurries, when I said in an unintentionally loud voice, "I can remember shoveling five inches of partly cloudy out of my driveway one other time it was forecast in March." I never expected the reaction I got from what really was an old saying, yet everyone in earshot howled.

Surprised, I turned to convey something to Betty, who was repeating what I had said to someone else, when Kathleen's eyes met mine. She had a huge, warm grin on her face, and I smiled back!

The next day she sat down again, but this time one stool closer in my direction. Carrying on with my usual storytelling, I didn't make much of it but looked her way frequently. Some glances were for a second, some connected and lasted longer. A certain ambiance had been established, an energy that only "lovers" recognize. All previous doubts had vanished. And on each of the next four days she would sit on a stool closer, while I had moved on the other side of our little group, which put me five stools closer, slowly closing the gap! Most of the morning regulars caught on to what was happening—a love story unfolding before their very eyes, perhaps something they might only see on television or a soap opera.

This locomotion game brought us to a point where we could easily hear each other without shouting, so once we got to the four-stool mark (about six feet) we stopped moving and remained this way for one more week. It was now the end of March. Then one day, I moved to the stool next to where she had last stopped, hoping that at last we would be next to each other. To my disappointment, she sat two stools away; but at least I had my first opportunity to talk to her one on one. I said nothing monumental that would give her the impression I was "crazy" about her—just small talk about what a nice day it was. She answered in kind.

On subsequent days the conversation's substance enlarged to, "Hi, you're a little late today" in hopes I could induce her to offer a little information about herself—where she worked, time she started, anything that could get us more acquainted and feel more at ease in a young, budding relationship. I was anxious to be totally me but cautious not to be overly inquisitive or zealous, for I learned many years ago that when you try to impress someone you're doomed for failure from the start. So I "tiptoed" into conversation gingerly, careful not to be opinionated or discuss anything political or religious. I also avoided revealing my interests.

"My boss was late today, and I couldn't leave" was her reply to my comment about her late arrival.

"Oh, where do you work?"

"I work at a beauty salon." Upon further inquiry, she said she was a hair stylist there and also had her own clientele, including Mrs. Auerbach and Mrs. Firestone. I was impressed! She went on to tell me she had attended hairdressing school, plus she was required to have so many hours of medical training—mostly pertaining to the skin and hair—before being certified and licensed. The course had become more difficult in recent years and many people dropped out before completion. Then she took her bag of bagels and coffee and said, "I have to go now, Lou." This was the first time she spoke my name and it sounded so good! My eyes followed her out as I wished her a nice day. This was our first real conversation (comprised of whole sentences!); it had lasted all of three minutes, but I learned many things about this girl, now totally encouraged and pleased with her voice, modesty, intelligence, and poise. We were on a roll!

Monday and Tuesday of the following week I attended a seminar in Middletown with one of my brothers regarding the economy and building. I wasn't anxious to go, but it was part of the job. Returning Wednesday to breakfast, Betty happily said that Kathy had asked for me. I was thrilled, but she didn't come in that day, which left me feeling anxious. I learned that Wednesday was her day off, which gave me more information for my next strategy in this game of love. Thursday she came in at the same time and sat on the same stool; this time I placed myself so that we would be side by side, as long as she took her usual seat. When she arrived, it was as if I was seeing her for the first time. Such warmth encompassed me I felt awestruck! This had to be like Heaven!

She said "hi" and I really wanted to take her hand; but, putting aside temptation, I responded, "Hi, Kathleen, how are you? I missed you."

"I didn't see you for a few days. Were you sick?"

I told her that I had been at a seminar, then had to be on the job yesterday. "Bu-bu-but," I stuttered, mesmerized by her eyes and beautiful long eyelashes, "but I'm back."

She came back fast, which surprised me. "Do you have some problems with your but—buts?" Then she let out a high-pitched, contagious laugh, causing everyone around her to laugh also. I blushed, yet kind of liked the attention. The conversation continued and she asked more questions about me, but I gave her brief, non-descriptive answers and quickly refocused the discussion back in her direction, asking if she was a traveler.

"I went to Ireland last summer with my brother, sister, and father."

"Did you have a good time?" I asked, peering into her eyes. I had this urge again to lean over and peck her on the cheek, but the temptation vanished instantly.

Observing that I was intently fixed on her eyes, she exclaimed, "Is there something on my face?" And then she gave out another of her wonderful laughs; it was infectious, and now this beautiful girl and her quick Irish wit truly intrigued me. The people all around us had joined the frivolity, knowing this was the beginning of a love story—the love story of which I had written more than ten years ago!

The next day I casually disclosed a little information about my work. There was nothing about her face or body language that made me believe she was impressed with what was said; however, for the first time I felt she was scrutinizing me. Every time I would say something I thought was quite profound, her eyes would look into mine, then move up to look at my black hair, then return to my eyes again. I thought, "She's not even listening to what I'm saying," but I wasn't discouraged, as I surmised she was either sizing up my looks or was as smitten as I was with her.

Deciding to test her on what I had been saying, which I knew came with some risks, I said, "Kathleen, you weren't listening to anything I said." She quickly answered that I was a construction engineer, who was a supervisor at a site LaCava is developing on Wintonbury Avenue. I was surprised when she responded so quickly, and in addition I was astonished that she knew the name of the company, as it was something I hadn't mentioned. And despite having learned my last name from Betty, she gave no hint that she connected me to the actual business. Apparently she wasn't impressed. In fact, she had dated a lawyer and a doctor and was engaged to a policeman, so my position was of no great importance to her.

Our conversation got back to general things—she liked to dance and was going dancing this weekend. I didn't ask her with whom, although it offered an opening to ask for a date without appearing too sudden or forward. While she volunteered a litany of interests, I interrupted, saying that I knew she worked and was very busy, but what if a guy wanted to ask her out for lunch?

She looked at me, smiled, and whispered, "I don't work on Wednesday." Wow!

On the next Wednesday I picked her up at her West Hartford apartment. For our first date, I had arranged for lunch at the Casa Loma Restaurant in Hartford. My older brothers were good friends with the owner and I had gotten to know him quite well myself. When making the reservation, I said this lunch was with a special friend and asked if he would kindly save me a table in the dining room, which was separate from the noisy bar. After greeting us at the door personally, he seated us and motioned for a waiter to open the bottle of champagne that was already in an ice bucket near the table. While the waiter was reaching across to fill Kathleen's glass after I had sampled it, Carl (the owner) leaned over and assured that the waiter would "take care of" us.

Lunch at our secluded little table would have suited royalty. The food was perfectly prepared and delivered at a very slow pace. We talked about many things, including our families. Her parents were both born in Ireland—her father was from Waterford, her mother was from Mayo. Her Irish roots were important to her, and she told me more about her trip to the "old sod" and how they had fortuitously found an uncle whom her father hadn't seen in twenty years—in a pub—a moving and exhilarating surprise for all of them!

Next we moved on to my family—I told her my age and that I came from a family of fourteen children—ten boys and four girls; my father came from Italy, while my mother, though Italian, was born here. We were a family of seventeen while growing up, as my grandmother on my father's side had also come from Italy. She smiled while asking me to name all my brothers and sisters quickly, which I did without a problem, in order, from the oldest down, to boot. Wondering out loud, she said, "How did your mother do it—cook, clean, wash all the clothes, and remember all your names besides?"

After we each declined dessert, to my dismay Kathleen took out a cigarette. After talking a while longer, we left; it had been a slow, quiet, and enjoyable meal. When we got back into the car I proposed a ride to Old Saybrook, telling her my family had a house in Indiantown; I thought it would be nice to show her how pretty it was in early spring. She readily accepted. During the ride down, I told her some of the interesting history of the area; the channel there was historically important, as it had been a haven for our P.T. boats during the Second World War.

Once at Indiantown, I parked the car in the driveway and we walked down to the beach. It was a balmy, sometimes chilly, spring day. Following the main road that was parallel to Long Island Sound, we walked by the Indiantown clubhouse, and bearing left over a bridge we came to the point, which was due south as the crows fly. If you followed it to the end, passing several big beachfront houses, you would be at the water's edge. Turning west one could walk all the way to Westbrook on the sand, a distance of about six miles. We agreed we were up to the challenge.

As we slowly started walking, the breeze turned into a brisk wind. I took her hand, and as we walked there were times the wind was so strong we had difficulty hearing each other over it. After twenty minutes or so we came across some houses that had retaining walls in front as protection from high tides. Near the base of the bulwark were some big 10x10 timbers, hardened with creosote, sitting about two feet away from the structure. I put my arm around Kathy and turned her inward toward that direction, and there we sat huddled together, alone in a deserted seashore paradise, away from the howling wind that reminded one of spring's fickle nature.

As she cuddled close, I said, "How many men have told you that you have beautiful eyes?" She looked at me but didn't answer. So I repeated the question, asking if perhaps she didn't want to tell me. She looked so shy and vulnerable as she turned and said in a very soft voice, as if she didn't want me to hear, "Lou, no one ever said . . ."

I fought with every fiber of my being to resist the urge to kiss her. The wind rustled her hair back, revealing high cheekbones and bright eyes, her face a reflection of loveliness. I was then truly convinced that before the year came to a close Kathleen would be my wife. I knew that I would be her provider, protector and lover within the holy covenant of marriage forever, until death severed the holy bond!

We sat for what seemed like hours, just cuddled together, taken in by a tranquility and magic that created a mood of enchantment in the beauty and breadth of the experience. Our conversation would jump from subject to subject, and when I was talking she would suddenly interrupt me saying, "I was thinking the same thing!" Then when she was talking, I would interrupt her excitedly. "Kathy! I was just thinking of that!" We would fall into gales of laughter, sometimes bumping heads, and I would draw her closer. When it had been very quiet for a while I sang to her—love ballads, soft moving arias from operas, and popular tunes—song after song.

The name of one song was "The Old Master Painter", which I was inspired to sing because I vicariously saw her beauty on canvas. It went something like this:

The old Master Painter from the faraway hills,
painted the devil and daffodils,
painted the clouds in the deep blue skies,
painted the stars in my darling's eyes,
captured the mural with a thousand guitars . . .

When I finished she said in an apologetic voice, as if it was a crime to have a dream, "Lou, I always wanted to learn how to paint." She squeezed my hand tightly, and I pulled her up, for the timbers we were sitting on were cold and damp.

I said, "Kathy, there's no reason under this blue sky why you can't learn how to paint; you just have to take some lessons." She lamented that she didn't know if she had any talent, which made me a bit angry. I interposed, "Listen, everyone has some kind of talent that comes from God, and God wants it used, for He does not make junk. Some have more than others in respective areas, but you know something?" She shook her head from side to side, indicating she had no idea what I was going to tell her. "Do you think some of the great painters like Van Gogh and Picasso knew they had talent before they tried it? Of course not! And the degree of talent is not important; only discovering what individual gift you have, then working hard to perfect it is what matters. You'll get the most satisfaction by sharing what you have with others in your own environment. That is the fundamental reason for living." Then I added, "One never aims or strives for recognition or fame; you just try the very best in life with everything you have been given, and if success is meant to be, fine. And if you develop your talent as best you can, you become energized by the accomplishment and great in yourself, thereby surpassing those with more talent who never did much, oftentimes because they were lazy. Don't ever talk of doubts regarding a dream—this country was built on dreams—and they come true if you wish, pray, and work hard enough." I hesitated for a moment before descending from my philosophical soapbox, and added, "There's a dream unfolding right now, as we speak."

At first she didn't understand what I implied; then her eyebrows raised, her forehead wrinkled, and a big grin crossed her face. She cuddled close and said, "I like the way you talk!" Putting my arm around her again, we started our walk back.

By the time we returned to the car it was a little after four and the sun was hidden behind dark clouds; it was windy, cold, and of all things, lightly snowing. I took the contrasting weather for a great omen regarding our relationship. A day that had been basically unplanned turned out to be remarkably memorable. Love was in the air, at least the air that I was breathing!

The traffic was heavy driving back, so when we got to her apartment it was just before six. We sat in the car for another thirty minutes, reminiscing about our interesting and pleasant day. Asking permission to call her later that evening after a meeting, I was overwhelmed by her positive response. Hand-in-hand, we walked to her building, and when we got to the entrance stairway, I kissed her left hand in an old fashioned gesture of respect; she smiled, turned, and walked inside.

I called her at eleven that night and we talked for over an hour; during the conversation she expressed surprise that I didn't kiss her. When asked if she had wanted me to, she replied in the affirmative but admitted she was happy I hadn't, saying I was so different than most guys. She then shared that when I had kissed her hand then turned quickly and walked toward the car, it was so manly it sent shivers down her spine. I asked her for the pleasure of her company for dinner on Saturday night, which she readily accepted. There was heavy equipment scheduled on site, so I would not be seeing her for breakfast the next few days, but I assured her I was anxiously anticipating Saturday night. She confessed she wasn't sure what could top today's lunch! My optimism for this marriage prophecy was never greater; still, there would be a few serious pitfalls in the future.

The Saturday night dinner at Carbone's, famous for its Italian food, was a sheer delight. Afterward, we went to the Park Plaza Hotel Terrace Room in New Haven for dancing. The Terrace Room was on the top floor, overlooking the city, and on a clear night stars would "hang out" like magic; the place captured a certain ambiance, not only for its location, but also its decor. A small combo that specialized in soft romantic music, conducive to my *modus operandi,* played. We would return there many times in the future, thereby becoming a benchmark in our budding romance and "Love Story."

The month of April was a whirlwind of romantic dates, activities, and intrigue. I always had a thing about the significance in the giving of a single rose, so I brought her a rose every day in this pre-marriage romance. Five days of the week we were together, and on the other days she would drive over to my office on her lunch hour to bring me a sandwich and milkshake. There in the budding spring we would find a nice secluded spot on site and lunch together. The thirty minutes went by too quickly—as soon as we opened our bags it was time to return to my office. Gene, one of my foremen, was so impressed with Kathleen that one day he said to me with a smile, "Lou, you have great taste."

It was lunch, dinner, bowling (her sister was a nationally

recognized ten-pin bowler, and from time to time we would go to watch her, often bowling a game or two ourselves). Or there were hikes, day trips to New York City—Lincoln Center, the opera, museums, Broadway shows, the symphony, nightclubs, baseball games, skating, etc. Life was good!

One skating date in West Hartford was very amusing when I forgot to take off my rubber blade guards, so as I stepped onto the ice my feet went up in the air and I came down on my back, albeit uninjured. Kathy could not stop laughing, causing everyone around her to become hysterical. There I was in the process of showing off—I was going to impress her with spins and jumps, the whole ball of wax. She had never seen me skate before and only knew what little I had told her about my skating, so this was to be a surprise performance, and it certainly was! She would tell this story many times in the future, and each time she never failed to laugh that special way.

I showered her with gifts—a television, an air conditioner, a watch, clothes, flowers, candy, etc. I wrote poems about her and with my guitar as background would recite specially crafted lines, followed by quiet singing. At first she looked at me in such surprise, but then she became used to it, admitting she could expect just about anything from me.

This pace continued through the first week in May. We both seemed content and happy, but one night as I drove to pick her up I got a nagging premonition that something was not the same. And when I rang her bell she opened the door, still in her white work uniform. I said, "Kat, did you have to work late?" She didn't answer me at first, so I said, "Don't you feel like going to the movies?" Now I really knew things were not the same—by the look on her face. The beautiful bright eyes I was accustomed to seeing were tired, downcast, and weepy. Her usual greeting was gone—she was distant, preoccupied and sad.

As I walked closer, she turned slightly so she wouldn't have to look at me, and tearfully said, "Lou, I think we're getting too serious . . . too fast. I've been engaged before and I . . . I want to be sure that I'm doing the right thing by dating you so often."

My heart sank! I was flabbergasted and devastated. Everything was a perfect match; our personalities complemented each other. I was thrilled by her modesty, shyness, her looks, and total femininity; she had told me my values and character and my chivalry were like a refreshing, cool breeze. The girls at the restaurant told me they observed a changed lady since we started dating, and I admitted that I was a totally content man. This was the last thing I expected—the most remote possibility that we would separate. We had so often talked about our unusual chance meeting and how it had transcended all time and space.

She was crying softly when she finished. I always was optimistic and gregarious, never at a loss of words. But this was different—the exception to the rule. I couldn't say anything at first; a few minutes passed, which seemed liked an eternity, then I finally asked if she was unsure of me, or of herself, or both of us. She abruptly stopped weeping and interrupted me, saying, "Oh, no, Lou, it's just that things have happened so fast for me. I don't know . . . I like you so much . . ." She stopped, put her head down, and began to weep once again.

A minute or so passed in silence, then I said, "Kathleen, I'll leave now, but before I go please look at me and say you want me to leave and not see you again." She turned her back and lowered her head, sobbing. I went to her side, placing my hand on her shoulder briefly as a calming effect; then I turned, walked to the door, and quietly left.

The ride home was pure misery. I was in a stupor; my mind would go blank for a period, then I would relive our past month together, then become sullen. Sometimes I would smile as a humorous incident or special moment in these last many days came to mind. I would feel comforted. I thought about one date to New York City; I wanted to take her to Lincoln Center to attend one of my favorite operas, *La Bohème* (The Bohemians) by Giacomo Puccini. It's a tragic story interspersed with humor and comedy about a poor poet, philosopher, painter, and musician, living together in a small garret on the outskirts of Paris, trying to find fame. I selected this one as I thought she would thoroughly enjoy it. I had the time schedule for matinees, and called prior to leaving to be sure that tickets were available; I was assured there would be no problem. We gave ourselves plenty of time but made the mistake of stopping for a quick lunch, at which we proposed a toast to our lasting friendship. This proved to be disastrous. I had ordered a small bottle of Cinzano Asti Spumante, a popular wine, nice for a drinker, but for a non-drinker like myself there could be repercussions. One small glass sent me reeling, slightly tipsy.

For a person who is outgoing and talkative sober, this became a day to remember; between spurts of Kathleen's outbursts of uncontrollable laughter at seeing the state I was in, and our inability to hail a cab to take us to Lincoln Center, things became pretty grim. When we got to Lincoln Center I asked a "host" assisting patrons if we could still get in; he answered yes but told us to hurry along before the bell rang or we would not be seated. But in my talkative state I wanted to continue the conversation with this gentleman, asking what he thought of *La Bohème*; he would answer, "Great, great," then try to shoo us toward the ticket window. This continued for about ten minutes; he had knowledge of some of the greatest tenors and divas, and I would compare with him some of the "greats" that I was fortunate to have seen. All this time he kept saying it was getting late, to get going, while Kathleen was in stitches, trying with no luck to get me moving. In my "irrational" inquisitive state, talking with this very articulate and interesting man would result in the ultimate sacrifice of missing *La Bohème*. Sometime later I saw this "host's" picture in the paper and thought I recognized him as the Director of the Metropolitan Opera Company, Rudolf Bing!

Missing the opportunity to be a guest with Giacomo Puccini's finest, nevertheless, did not prevent us from having a good time in the Big Apple. So, decked out in my black mohair, tailor-made opera suit, and Kathleen in her thick, velvety mauve cocktail dress, we went to the Metropolitan Museum of Fine Arts, where there were some works of the finest artists on display, including something by William de Kooning—*The Standing Man*. We spent time examining the merits of each painting and its artist. Kathleen was particularly impressed with the delicate and fine hues of one painting, cognizant of detail from her new painting lessons. As she moved within arm's length of the piece, explaining something by pointing her index finger but not making contact with it, one of the security guards rushed over, reprimanding and cautioning her not to touch the paintings. She was momentarily embarrassed, then smiled and continued her assessment.

We left when the museum was about to close for the day. Having worked up a good appetite, I suggested a few places for dinner and off we went. Next to our table was a gentleman sitting alone, who on occasion would glance over and smile at our animated antics. During dinner I invited him to join us, and what ensued was an in-depth discussion of some of the great ancient philosophers of our time, during which he proceeded to run roughshod over me, although I contributed two of my favorites, Saint Thomas Aquinas and Saint Augustine. They were among many of the early fathers, the likes of St. Polycarp of Smyrna, in young years a disciple of St. John the Apostle, and St. Ignatius of Antioch—bishop of Antioch for over forty years, installed by the great Apostles Peter and Paul. Then there was St. John Chrysostom, the great scholar and rhetorician, father of the Church and patriarch of Constantinople. Other favorites were St. Basil the Great, St. Ambrose of Milan, and the beloved St. Jerome. I was well read, knew their philosophies, and often could recite passages at will from Augustine.

When he started to get into Thomas Aquinas, The Summa Theologica, he would drift over my head, until he came to faith—the cause of faith, where I briefly held my own, then started to double-talk. I read Kathy's mind, who thought it was strange discussing philosophy and the great fathers of the church in a New York City gourmet; but she enjoyed every moment of it, occasionally adding one of her famous laughs. We had in our midst our own saint, Kathleen, who listened patiently throughout this deep discussion. When he presented articulate and profound statements of angels and grace, I could tell she was impressed with my response from the look on her face. He was a brilliant man, and we thoroughly enjoyed his company and the learning experience that went with it.

Stepping out of the restaurant, we strolled arm-in-arm to the car. I was tempted to take Kathleen into some quiet, romantic nightclub and ask her to marry me, reviewing a few of the great love stories—Romeo and Juliet, Abelard and Heloise. But I suddenly was silent; Kathleen became quite concerned as I told her it was a headache, attributable to the wine we had with dinner. She said it was probably from talking too much and followed that with a notorious cackle. But very quickly she let me know she was only teasing by a squeeze to my hand and a hug. On the trip back she massaged the back of my neck, helping to ease this rare headache. It was a long but beautiful day; we were so happy and content.

Ten days passed during which I discontinued my morning breakfast at A.C. Petersen's, sending my foreman for whatever I needed. Once Betty curiously asked him if he was working in the area, and he volunteered that he was employed by LaCava Construction. Betty asked him to convey a message that she [Kathy] was asking for me. When he asked if that was all, she said she didn't know anything more but "he'll know what it means."

Even before I heard of her asking for me, I had planned to wait three weeks from the night I had left her crying before attempting a reunion. There was never any doubt that I would call her again; though the fear that our relationship was history crept into my mind frequently, I still always felt some day we would be married.

I called that same night, starting at six P.M., and continued every half-hour until she answered at ten-thirty. We talked briefly, and she gave no indication in any way that she missed me. She said she had been going dancing with friends, in addition to continuing her painting; she was also anxious to return to school for interior decoration. I made it known I had not dated but was just skating more hours and writing with greater intensity. When I asked if it would be alright to call her again tomorrow night, she said she was going dancing with her girlfriends, but that I could try her Friday night after work, around nine. I hung up the phone with renewed hope that fate had drawn a line in the sand.

I couldn't reach her at nine, but kept on until she answered at ten-fifteen. Asking her immediately if she would like to get something to eat, she enthusiastically consented. We went to the Casa Loma, the scene of our first date, which was busy even at this later hour. Brother Ozzie and his wife Lil were there, so I introduced Kathleen to them; we chatted briefly, then continued on to our table.

After some "small talk" we started to reminisce about our past month's relationship, serious at times, smiling at others. Then she surprised me with these words: "Lou, your face looks so good! And the more you talk the better you look!" What did this mean? The prophecy from the first day I saw her in A.C. Petersen's, nearly six weeks prior, flashed back. I would invite her to dinner at my house on Sunday to meet my mom and dad. Italian tradition said that when a son brought a girl over for dinner, particularly on Sunday, it was a celebration; it meant commitment, it meant love, it meant a pre-engagement for marriage. Now we just stared at each other, cognizant that the words she had just uttered would be the catalyst to change both our lives forever.

That night we were the last patrons to leave the restaurant, and while walking out the owner said, "Gracia, bona saluta," meaning thank you and good luck in Italian. Walking to the car arm-in-arm, the moon was so bright we reveled in its magic. On the ride home she snuggled up close to me, while in my head I planned the day I intended to propose to her. And this night I left her door a content man, as she thanked me for a wonderful evening and I brushed a kiss on her forehead.

The Proposal

I never doubted my love at first sight for Kathleen. Likewise, one night in June she confessed there was something about me that would not leave her. I wanted this proposal to be unique—something special and completely mine. Great men in history had made unusual proposals of marriage—some were generic, others stuffy, and a few romantically phony, but there was one by G.K. Chesterton that was unforgettable—the most tender, poetic, sentimental, picturesque, and sincere proposal of marriage I have ever read:

> There are four lamps of thanksgiving always before me.
> First, that my creation came out of the same earth from such a woman as you.
> Second, that I have not, with all my faults, gone after strange women.
> Third, that I have tried to love everything alive in dim preparation for loving you.
> Fourth, here ends my previous existence. Take it—it led me to you!

My first thought was to do something similar. But snapping back to reality, I knew our proposal had to be me and spontaneous. I would neither choose a date, nor rehearse lines, but only be prepared with the ring on my person every time we dated, lest that perfect night be lost in regrets.

Two weeks had passed; we had seen each other every night, with no talk of marriage, not even remotely close. Our dates were always unplanned, "spur of the moment" times. We basked in each other's stories, sharing details of our previous existence—joys, sadness, loneliness, and mistakes we made along the way. The more we dated the more we talked, and the more the bond between us grew. While out dancing one night she said to me, "Lou, I'm the luckiest girl alive for two reasons: first, I met you, and second, I never get sick. I don't even get colds!" These lines would become legend in my mind, prophetic in time, ironic in scope, and would end in a spiral bouquet of prayers for her throughout the land.

We would discuss at length the circumstances of our meeting, our courtship—how beautiful it had been despite mistakes that were made. And it was reassuring that we liked each other's families. She had immediately liked my brother Nick after meeting him during a visit to the hospital. Nick was a Marine veteran of World War II, involved in the Pacific Island combats. War torn, having contracted malaria, ending with diabetes, he was now very sick. When Nick joined the Marines at seventeen he was a big, muscular Adonis, the picture of health. When he was brought back to the States, he was forty pounds lighter and bore little resemblance to his former athletic prowess, ebullience, and energy. He was in the same contingent and had flown with famous Hollywood stars; Kathy was intrigued with the stories of bravery as I related how Nick had saved the life of one of the giants in the industry, a story of heroism that never came from him.

The day had come for me to meet the Walsh family. Kathy was nervous. She rationalized about her mother's cooking, repeating, "Lou, you'll like my mother's cooking. She's a good cook. I know you'll like her cooking. She's having turkey, but there will be a lot of side dishes. I think she's a very good cook."

This went on and on, until I put my hand over her mouth and asked, "Kathy, you're not concerned with me liking your mother's cooking. What's the real problem?" She put her head down, placed her little finger of her right hand to the corner of her lips, in an intense period of concentration—a pre-occupied gesture I was getting used to when she was bothered by something.

After a few minutes she said, "Alright, you can read me like a book."

I followed, "Is that a compliment or are you patronizing me? Nevermind—just tell me, or I won't go."

She quickly retorted, playing coy, "You mean you'd stand me up?" She let out that laugh that was now so familiar as she tried to put her arms around me. I gently pushed her away and begged her to please tell me. Hesitating momentarily, she said apologetically, "Lou, it's two things," whereupon I joshed, "Kat, it's always two things!"

She then got serious: "Listen, you know I've been engaged before, and my mother may not seem too enthusiastic about you; I don't want you to be hurt."

I answered, "She'll love me. Is that all you're worried about?"

"No, wait, Lou. It's my brothers and brother-in-law. They're always up for a joke, and I know it will be at your expense!"

"Kathleen, I know your brother-in-law. Don't worry; I can handle myself. Now calm down and smile—let's add today to our memory bank."

It was just like she said it would be. The food was excellent, I took the brunt of the jokes good-naturedly, and I also took an immediate liking to her parents. The Irish brogue had been somewhat softened after many years in America, but I was not surprised they retained their fine sense of Irish humor. Afterward, as Kathy and I took a ride, she was relaxed and proud of me—the way I came through the "test" with grace and self-assurance.

Several days later, when she informed her mother that we were very serious, she reminded Kathleen advisedly of past engagements and her tendency to tire of a person. Kathy answered that I was different—"he's all man." When her father heard the conversation from another room he interjected, "What's the matter with Lou?" The remarks by her mother didn't concern me, for I felt in my heart they both liked me; and apparently I had passed the "test" with flying colors, as her brothers had also given their approval.

We were ecstatic for the next few days—our families were to our respective liking and we were feeling good about each other. An air of anticipation surrounded us—here was a thirty-four-year-old who had measured instance and distance before even thinking of settling down into marriage; and here was a twenty-four-year-old, twice betrothed and unsure what direction her future would take. Now these two individuals were passionately in love. A phenomenon!

Everything was going well, except I had not asked Kathleen to marry me; neither the time nor the mood had been right. And I had to be away for three days in Washington on business. I called from my hotel and she asked if I'd mind if she went dancing with her girlfriend; her friend wanted to see someone there and didn't want to go alone. Of course I wasn't thrilled with the idea but told her to go ahead; she said she had known I would understand. But when she got home, she called me in Washington to say it didn't seem right to be there. She confessed that she had been asked to dance several times but politely refused, saying she was "taken"—meaning me!

On my first night back, we went dancing at the Park Plaza. It was a beautiful, clear night, with the sky full of stars and a waxing moon. Was there a message for me? I knew very little of astrological signs, the alignment of stars and the moon, their relationship to each other, or how it affected our biorhythms and general energy or our lives' directions. Incidentally, I was ignorant of it, and didn't care what sign I was born under, deeming it foolish superstition; but I didn't chide others if that was their belief, or for that matter, their god.

We were pleasantly surprised to meet a couple of Kathy's friends. Having heard from her about the romantic atmosphere and friendly people who frequented the Park Plaza, they had decided to give it a try themselves. They joined us at our table, and the night was filled with laughter, as well as a spirited discussion of the Bible, of all things, and about the Scripture reading "wives submit to your husbands" and its meaning. When I offered, with tongue in cheek, that man has dominion over woman, I was quickly countered from both directions. Kathy immediately reminded me to find the true meaning by following the second part. Her girlfriend said, "Doesn't it say something about, 'husbands love your wives'? And if you love your wife, do you lord dominion over them?!" Her boyfriend looked over at me with a contorted grin on his face, saying that I was getting us all into trouble. Actually, the true translation was "wives relate to your husbands." As there was no Greek word to express "relate," the next best thing was to take the closest word—"submit" or something like that. Despite the animated "discussion," we had a wonderful evening, and on the way home, unbeknownst to me yet, I would ask Kathleen to marry me.

For the drive home I took a different route, one I used to take years ago when I was skating at the old New Haven Arena on Orange Street. It was a shortcut up the mountain, circumventing traffic and dropping me north on Whitney Avenue, a short distance to the highway. On the ascent I took a dark winding road that would lead us to the "lookout," the highest point in the area, which provided a fabulous view facing south, with a peripheral view east and west. On a very clear night millions of stars would just hang bright in the backdrop, giving the illusion you could reach out and touch one.

Concerned we were getting lost, Kathy edged closer and asked if I knew where we were. I knew exactly, without a doubt, but answered, "I hope so." Arriving at the top, I found a parking place apart from the other cars already there. Taking my hand, Kathy exclaimed what a beautiful, picturesque spot this was. I looked at her face and decided she had never looked lovelier—her eyes were so bright they gave competition to the moon and the stars. Haltingly, as I knew it sounded corny, I declared, "All the stars are jealous of me!" Her beauty, the setting, and the mood had just made my statement so apropos. She smiled shyly and squeezed my hand. And now I would take center stage.

Releasing her hand, I took out my wallet, unsnapped the change pouch—she had no inclination what I was up to—and removed a beautiful diamond ring. Lifting her left hand, I declared, "Kathleen, you came into my life, and now I ask you to become my wife." And twenty years later the author would write and record a song about her for a CD, part of the lyrics being . . . "now where have you gone, Lady Kathleen?"

I slipped the ring on her finger and she started to cry. Then she put her arms around me and typically asked, "When?" I playfully questioned whether I should be asking her father for her hand in marriage, but she didn't answer and just kept looking down at the ring. We sat close to each other with some bantering—about the moon, the stars, our families. We talked about

99

the Italian tradition of personal visits to announce an engagement. She had met most, if not all, of my family by then, but it was customary, out of respect, to honor each with our presence. First there would be a general announcement so everyone would know simultaneously; then we would visit both parents, thereafter from the most senior down the line.

Every now and then Kathy would pick up her hand and hold it close to the windshield, tying to get the moon's reflection on her ring. This amused me, and I finally asked, "Kat, do you want me to turn on the light?" She answered hurriedly in the negative, then put her hand to my face, kissed me, and said this was just as nice as the very first time I had walked her to her door. The talk then turned to children, when she asked how many I would want. When I said "five," she excitedly chided, "Hey that's my number!" After more playful banter about the future we now looked to as man and wife, it was time to descend from that magical place which had been the beginning of our star-crossed journey to matrimony. On the ride down the mountain I put my arm around her and sang as she pillowed her head to my chest in joy and the serenity of her dreams. My own dreams of serenity would be locked inside of me for twenty years before I could finish them: *Lady Kathleen*, and *Love Prints:*

——*You came into my life, and soon became my wife.*
Now where have you gone, Lady Kathleen . . .

How can I go on with a new role, darling,
With your Love Prints so deep in my soul . . .

The Marriage

Word spread quickly that Lou and Kathy were engaged to be married. The next few weeks were a time for celebration, calls of congratulations, and gestures of good will. When I went into the restaurant for breakfast, those in our little group, as well as virtual strangers, were thrilled by the outcome of the pursuit they had witnessed daily.

There was no greater happiness extended to us than that from my father. I remember a time I had gone shopping for a birthstone ring, specifically looking for a certain design, not unlike anyone else who is shopping for personal jewelry. This ring had to have diamond chips imbedded at the points of a star sapphire. Well, the search continued for several months, and finally I found a ring—not exactly what I wanted, but pretty close. Despite the fact I seldom wore jewelry, I was pleased, for it was discriminatingly unique and fit my "pinkie" and personality perfectly. Proudly wearing it home—it just had to be shown off—I walked into the house and held it up to my father; he, in his own inimitable style, told me instead to "buy a ring and give it to a nice girl." It was always a "nice" girl, opposed to any other kind!

My dad already had an inclination of my intentions toward Kathleen by the way we carried on the first time she had come for dinner to meet my parents. Lovers have a distinguishable aura, an unintended amorous communicative skill—a twinkle—that's telegraphed clearly to others in their presence. Reading this message of love in our eyes, my father looked over at brother Ozzie and winked, revealing his approval and happiness; I was thirty-four, and he thought a man should be settled down by then. Although I was already involved in many other things, perhaps to him they were insignificant when compared to marriage. Myriad interests had divided my life, leaving no time for thoughts of matrimony, and I had never given a hint about

101

committing to domestic responsibilities in the near future. So when Kathy and I shared our marriage plans with my mom and dad—they were the first that we visited after I gave Kathy the ring—they were overjoyed. Knowing we would get some philosophical questions from my dad, I forewarned Kathy:

"Louie, do you love Kathleen?" I nodded affirmatively. "Kathleen, do you love Louie?" She also nodded. "Well then, your mother and I wish you both the best, and we will do everything we can to help." My father had a contented look on his face, a marked contrast to that day I showed him my birthstone ring, with his sage words of advice!

This prenuptial ritual had taken place with all of the seven siblings who had wed before me. Surely my father did not expect negative answers to his questions, but this was a way of conveying his wisdom to each of his offspring regarding the serious nature of marriage. He wanted us to realize this was a holy bond and that every day is not a honeymoon—that it was a give and take, with periods of exhilaration, as well as suffering, tears, and sometimes, tragedy. It may seem old-fashioned in the modern culture, but back then separation was a stigma, divorce unthinkable. This was the way he expressed his concern.

In the Italian household the father was at the head; he set the tone for direction and discipline and was strict when it came to expecting growth of strong values and solid character in his offspring. He and my mother were the role models, and there was no leeway or compromise when it came to right or wrong, truth or principle. The adults, as well as the children, listened intently with respect when they offered advice and shared wisdom. Their blessing was essential to all.

Kathy and I celebrated our engagement with dinner at Carbone's, and during the evening we talked about a wedding date; we both agreed it should be soon. The month, day, time, size, and location had to be decided. Once the place for the ceremony was set, we could work from there. This was easy. Saint Mark's Church, a relatively small Roman Catholic church in West Hartford, quaint with bright white decor, would be the place where we would offer ourselves to each other until death do us part.

Although we both liked the fall, particularly October, I felt she was abdicating her desire for June to satisfy me. So we tentatively looked to the end of June, knowing it would be very difficult to have arrangements made so that invitations could be printed and out in three weeks! We continued with the list. When it came to the size of the wedding we were in agreement that it would be very small—just her family and mine. During that process we laughed because when my family was added to the mix, that immediately brought a guest list to well over one hundred. The whole initial planning process took less than one hour; Monday we would commence with details.

Our plans almost immediately turned to a time in late September or early October. We agreed to think about it for a few days before our final decision, but fate would quickly make the choice for us. Plans had progressed with dispatch and we were both very relaxed, enjoying the flower of love being nurtured between us. Kathy had selected her attendant, as well as the gown color and design. We had given the church an approximate date and were going to schedule the wedding just as soon as we learned about availability of the dinner reception site.

The only uncertainty was a lack of response every time I asked Kathy if she had selected her wedding gown. She would either say "not yet" or "I'm going to do it soon." Other times she was vague; this was starting to bother me. Finally, when I confronted her with my concern, she admitted she had run short in her checking account after buying some new clothes and consequently had barely enough to even pay her apartment rent, much less buy a wedding dress. This was the first time she would experience the other side of the romantic Italian. "Kathleen (as our relationship matured she knew to expect a serious discussion when I addressed her thus), you let all this time elapse because you didn't have money in your account to pay for it?"

If something was bothering her, she usually looked away before she would answer me; this time she looked directly at me, and in an apologetic tone said, "Lou, I'm so sorry. I was too embarrassed to say anything!"

I motioned for her to sit on my lap. "Would my response have been any different if you had told me this a week ago?" She shook

103

her head, and I followed with, "Then my dearest Kathleen, next time will you promise you'll talk when something is bugging you? Do I look like a big mean bear?" She swung her arms around my neck, forcing her cheekbone tight on mine. I gently pushed her up, playfully whacked her bottom, went over to the counter and pulled a check out my wallet. Making it out for $500 for the deposit on her gown, I handed it to her and said, "Here. Put it in the bank tomorrow." Before walking out the door, I kissed her, but she yelled for me to wait.

"What is it? You startled me."

"I love you very much!"

"And I love you, Kathleen!" As I closed the door behind me, I skipped down the stairs muttering, "Women!"

Only a few days later, I was talking outside my trailer office in Bloomfield with a carpenter foreman about an alternative for constructing a certain roof when the phone rang. It was my brother Joe calling from the main office. I knew something was amiss. "Lou, we just got word that Nick died." It had occurred only a short time before, he said; I told him I would put someone in charge and be right in. I hung up the phone, terribly saddened. Nick was a great guy; he had taught me the rudiments of the building business, and we had worked closely for a number of years. Although he was older, we had an excellent rapport; he was never selfish when it came to taking his time to impart his knowledge to me.

I wanted to leave immediately but had to tie up many loose ends of the day. Appointments had to be canceled and/or rescheduled. Worksheets, vendor deliveries, the next day's schedules had to be worked on; and once my head was cleared I called Kathy at work. Her boss answered the phone and asked if she could call me back. When I assured him it was very important or I wouldn't have called her at work, he reluctantly told me to hold on. Having long ago told Kathy I would never call her at work unless there was an emergency, she quickly picked up the phone. Her greeting was shallow and very soft, with the last syllable fading to a whisper, as if she was preparing herself to hear something unpleasant. I immediately and sadly told her Nick had died. She lamented that he was so young, so good; although she had only met him once, during a lengthy hospital visit, her voice reflected her own sorrow and sympathy. It had not taken her long to observe what a fine and great man Nick was. Hearing thoughts and sorrow expressed so like my own, I knew that in Kathy I had a special person to share my life with.

People from of all walks of life—doctors, lawyers, engineers, tradesmen, military men—lined up for hours to pay their respects at Nick's funeral. The family stood by his widow, Helen, alongside the casket, shaking hands continuously with those filing through. Mom and Dad, who had endured many hardships in the struggles of raising fourteen children, were seated in front, and for the first time I noticed the lines of age running through my father's face from his many years of toil and suffering. My saintly mother, blessed with grace, was a gentle force of dignity and decorum. This loss and sadness they experienced was graciously accepted, and they persevered in faith. It was the devotion, love, and sacrifice for their huge family, however, that kept them youthful and energetic—young in mind, fulfilled in spirit: *Love makes those young whom age doth chill. And whom he finds young, keeps young still.* (William Cartwright to Chloe, 1651)

Now and then, when a break in the line allowed her a glimpse at the casket, my mother would lovingly gaze at Nick, her eyes filled with tears of memories—memories of her third born, the baby, the adolescent, the young handsome man, the athlete, the tradesman, the engineer, the Marine, the husband, the brother, the loving son. And now at forty-six he had gone home. Too young, too soon, too . . .

At the military service the guns were fired in Nick's honor. On this balmy eleventh of June 1969, the noise startled, then saddened us, and feelings lingered; taps slowly and sharply resounded off distant hills, beckoning and telling that another soldier's life was not lost in vain. "Oh Death, where is thy sting? Oh grave, where is thy victory?" (I Corinthians 15:54–55) Many wept; few were dry-eyed. "So proudly we hail . . . by the dawn's early light . . ." "The things which are seen are temporal; but the things which are not seen are eternal." (II Corinthians 3:12, 4:18) "We walk by faith, not by sight." (II Corinthians 5:7) Kathy squeezed my hand, people threw petals from roses on the casket, and through the weeping and clearing of throats the priest intoned the prayer of the dead: "The Lord is my Shepherd, I shall not want. He maketh me to lie down in green pastures . . . restoreth my soul. . . . Yea, though I walk through the valley of the shadow of death I will fear no . . ." (Psalm 23)

The priest finished, and people hugged one another and lingered until the funeral director asked everyone to please return to the cars. My brother Frank and my sister Ann walked with Mom and Dad to the limousine. The black-clad driver stood somberly as they approached, and he helped them in, then prepared for the cortege to leave a scene that would be repeated many times before they themselves would go back "home."

During the next several days Kathy and I discussed postponement of our wedding for six or eight months out of respect and mourning. After weighing heavily all the alternatives and receiving input from several family members, we decided to push the date back to November 22, 1969. This would be nearly five months from Nick's death, and both Kathy and I felt that Nick would have condoned our decision to not wait any longer.

The day of the wedding was sunny but brisk. Although she was nervous, Kathleen looked absolutely stunning, arrayed in a pure white gown with a long, flowing train. Her hair, moderate in length, was arranged back off her face, exposing the lower part of her ears adorned with small pearl earrings. Her radiant face was windowed by a fine, waist length white veil that perfectly showcased her striking beauty. Walking down the aisle on the arm of her father, with the organ resounding in an overture of wedding music, she was a picture of joy and loveliness. I looked up at her, and my heart was warm in the contentment of flame while smitten in the words of Kipling:

Cross that rules the Southern Sky!
Stars that sweep, and turn, and fly (The Lover's Litany, st. 2
    Rudyard Kipling)
Hear the Lover's Litany: Love like ours can never die!

This was her day. My thoughts digressed to the first day my eyes fell upon this shy young angel, when instantaneously I repeated to myself, "There's my wife—there's my wife—there's my wife . . . !" I remembered the night she told me she was the luckiest girl in the world for having met me, but as I viewed this beautiful picture of grace and virtue slowly walking to meet me for the rest of our lives, I knew in my heart that the converse was the real truth!

The day's festivities progressed smoothly. The dinner and reception were splendid, complemented by the music of the famed Pete DeLisa. I had asked a musician friend to inquire if Pete could play at the dinner, and he graciously obliged. Pete owned a nightclub in Hartford that was "the" place to be, attracting people from all over the state. DeLisa's not only had a special ambiance, but Pete himself was a gifted entertainer—he played the accordion and had a great voice. Kathy was pleased and honored that he would play at our wedding reception, and so was I.

The party ended at four o'clock, giving us an hour and a half to get to the airport for a flight to Kennedy International, where we would stay overnight. The apartment we had rented in Rocky Hill, a distance halfway between our work areas, was already prepared for our return after the honeymoon. Now on our wedding day, at the opened apartment door I swooped down with one motion, lifting Kathy up in my arms, and carried my bride across the threshold—a tradition ancient in the scope of modern time. I really didn't know what the significance was, but I had long planned to do it to start our honeymoon. Kathy started to giggle as I set her down gently, then kissed her tenderly on the lips and told her to shower and get dressed, recognizing that time was becoming our adversary.

The Honeymoon

I had planned an interesting two-part honeymoon. Part one would take us to Puerto Rico, that beautiful island about 1,000 miles from Florida that set the line between the Atlantic Ocean and the Caribbean Sea, and then on to Aruba, where we would stay for sixteen days. Part two would later take us to Chicago and Las Vegas for seven days. I told her some details of part one, but little of part two, as it was going to be a surprise and the thrill of her life.

In Puerto Rico we relaxed, swam, and overate. The water was exhilarating, the food was great, and the people were very accommodating; both of us would put on a few pounds! Aruba was a different story. At the time, Aruba was a young tourist and honeymooners' destination. We were booked into the new Aruba American Hotel for eleven days.

The bellhop carried the bags into our room—it was enormous!!! Our friend from the travel agency told me it was a large suite, but this was ridiculous! We were apprised of the different features in the suite, including two separate and extremely large bathrooms. On the opposite side of the suite was a small kitchenette with a refrigerator; an entertainment center featured a radio and even a television with limited channels. There was a king-size bed, private from the raised corner dining area complete with a heavy ornate round mahogany table and four chairs. This sat before a huge sliding glass door leading out to a small balcony. Above the mahogany table was there was an object that mirrored a large liberty bell, suspended from a high studio ceiling with a boatsman knotted rope that hung about three feet from the center of the table. When the bellhop drew back the floor-to-ceiling heavy lined drapes that depicted the island's history, I looked at Kathy's expression of disbelief. We both gasped—magnificent!

When informed that we were the first guests to use this suite, we found it quite believable. I was very happy and thankful for those exquisite accommodations—my agency friend had totally outdone herself. This was a joyous time for Kathy, a subject for many hours of fond recollection and nostalgia over the next few years. The days were spent swimming, dancing, gambling, and relaxing. We ordered room service on occasion, and on those days we would sleep in and lounge in our fabulous suite until early in the afternoon.

One day I leased a motorbike to take a trip around the island. This was a comical part of our journey. I hadn't ridden a motor scooter for some time, so I decided to go to the large parking lot to get used to the tricky throttle/clutch coordinates. For the first few laps I went alone until I felt comfortable. This bike was different from one I remembered operating before because you would have to let the clutch almost all the way out before gears would engage, yet the last inch you had to continue releasing. If you stopped and then let it out again, the machine would jerk forward with a thrust. I told Kathy to jump on and hold on to my waist, sure I had it mastered. I took my foot off the brake and gradually released the clutch, but instead of continuing I inadvertently stopped then quickly tried to rectify my error by letting it all the way out at once. Well, both of our heads shot back and the bike shot forward. One of her infectious laughs filled the air, and the men landscaping in the parking area went into hysterics. I stopped, stood up to regroup, and then tried again, but this time, to the disappointment of the natives expecting another spectacle, we rode off smoothly into the quiet still of the beautiful morning for a day of adventure.

The last day we went into Oranjestad, the capitol of Aruba. It was very crowded and hot, yet most of the time we were oblivious to discomfort, having a great time shopping, talking, singing together, bumping into people, and eating ice cream. A little boy walking toward us dropped his cone and started to cry. Why he was alone was a mystery, but Kathy gave him hers, as yet untouched, cautioning him to be careful. Smiling, he skipped away, and as we watched we could see he now had it under control! Aruba filled every honeymooner's needs while filling our own

Rolodex of memories. Kathleen confessed that she had never been so happy; several years later I would find myself in this same capital sitting on a bench with her young son, just people-watching. The author noticed a young couple, possibly newlyweds, laughing and carrying on, the image of my son's mother briefly reflecting in my mind. This island was truly a lover's paradise, but soon our time there would be over with a flight back to San Juan the next day. Our suite, the water, the sand, the food, the sun, the motor scooter(!), the love, would all fade slowly to a memory—a sweet, joyous, indescribable memory!

Upon our return to Connecticut we settled into a routine. Kathy was still working in Bloomfield and had her "moonlighting" jobs throughout the county; I was now working in Middletown at Wesleyan Hills. This was a new concept in design, with the main objective to preserve land in the ambiance of "mini-neighborhoods," featuring single residential homes of modest means, condominiums, and apartments, as well as some very expensive houses. In addition, it afforded many amenities, such as a huge clubhouse, swimming pools, tennis courts, its own school, and a plethora of other areas—bicycle trails, fishing ponds, etc. It was a city-within-a-city extraordinare, the vanguard, quintessential in housing; there were only two other developments like it in the country—Reston, Virginia and Columbia, Maryland. This project was underwritten by Wesleyan University, and LaCava was the principal builder. I would spend the next six months there as a technical coordinator, an experience I will never forget.

It was a bright, brisk day in February when I decided to tell Kathy about the second part of our honeymoon. She had just come up from the basement laundry area. I held the door for her, took the basket of clothes, and set it down, then picked her up and carried her to the couch and put her onto my lap. When she protested that she wasn't finished and had to return to the basement, I said, "That can wait—I have something very important to tell you." She looked at my face that was very serious and grew obviously concerned. I stopped to prolong her curiosity but couldn't let it extend too long, for now she was a little annoyed and worried. I fumbled with words, and then she caught on that it was one of my surprises. Clasping my face tight between her hands, she implored, "Come on, Lou!"

"I can't talk if you don't let up on that vise grip! Okay, tomorrow we leave on part two of our honeymoon!"

Rising, and completely incredulous to what she had just heard, she gestured, "Lou, please—I'm not finished with the wash. I don't have time to fool around!"

Again I picked her up and replaced her on my lap, bellowing loud and clear, "Honey, look at me and read my lips! (That's where President Bush coined that phase—only it didn't get me into trouble!) Tomorrow we are leaving for part two of our honeymoon. Have you ever known me to lie?"

She came back fast, "No, but you fool and tease a lot—are you really serious?" When she saw me shake my head in a certain manner, she realized that I was, then with emotion in her voice, proffered, "Lou, how can I leave tomorrow?" She proceeded to rattle off a litany of excuses, like I have to work, I don't have clothes prepared, we're not packed, I have washing to do.

While she desperately tried to convince me, I stopped her simply by kissing her, then said, "Listen, everything is prearranged with your job, with your clothes, everything. Just be ready to leave for the airport tomorrow night at six."

"Lou, can you, ah, tell...me at least where we're going?"

"Las Vegas!"

Our flight from Chicago to Vegas was anything but smooth. But I was with my Kathleen and she was with me, both of us excited in anticipation of our visit to the city that never sleeps. I had been to Las Vegas before but Kathy hadn't and didn't have the smallest clue that I had secretly planned the continuation of our honeymoon into grandiosity!

Our arrival was very late, leaving some doubt about whether the secret could be pulled off. Kathy loved Elvis Presley's music and always dreamed of seeing him in person. She figured her chances were remote after missing his appearance in Hartford. Now he was in a semi-retirement mode, and there were rumors adrift that he was involved in drugs, his voice was gone, and he had lost all desire to perform in public again. So when I heard that he was going to make a comeback, starting in

Hawaii, and from there to Las Vegas, I rescheduled our trip to coincide with his appearance.

I slipped the cab driver twenty bucks and asked him to get
us to the hotel on the double, and not by any circuitous route. He
smiled and said, "Thanks very much, sir. I'll get you there on the
double; the other thing is not my style." As we entered the lobby
to register, it was laden with stars. Next to us was Merv Griffin
of television fame, and as we registered we saw Joey Bishop and
Dean Martin. Kathleen said Ed Sullivan was getting out of a limousine in front. This was, in a sense, Presley's big comeback, and
many of the stars were there for support. He had never fared well
in Las Vegas before, so all the fanfare, while unusual, was welcomed. The glitter and buzz was certainly there that night.

Once in the elevator, Kathy said to me, "Lou, did you know
that Elvis was here?"

"Yes."

"Do you have reservations?" she asked excitedly.

"No." Her face registered disappointment, questioning why I
would bring her here without reservations for the show.

Inside our room, I requested she quickly bathe, for I wanted
to make his last show. She looked at me quizzically. "I thought
you said that you didn't have a reservation."

"I don't."

"Then please tell me, sweet Lou," she said sarcastically,
"how in the name of Jesus, Mary, and Joseph will we get in?"

I answered confidently, trying to hide any lingering doubts
from my face, "My dear Kathleen, have I ever let you down?"

"No, Lou, and I'm sorry. I . . . I . . . love you." She put her
arms around me and gave a big hug; I led her to the shower and
told her to hurry. In the back of my mind was that if we got down
there after the doors were closed my goose was cooked!

We got into the elevator at twenty-five minutes before midnight, and I was praying the doors were not yet closed. As we
walked toward the venue where Elvis was to perform, we saw a
sign that read—Sold Out. The front of the room was sheer bed-
lam. People who had tickets were already admitted, but others
were milling around outside the entrance in hope of a miracle so
they could get in to see their beloved Elvis. I took Kathy's hand

and excused myself, pushing through the mob. She nervously bent close to me and said, "Lou, it's hopeless!" I advised her to just hang on. As we approached the door there were three bouncers, a doorman, and a maitre d'. I told Kathy to stay on my left side in front of me and not to move from that position. She was confused, but I begged her to just do as I said. When I asked her later if she thought I was going to barge in past the security she just laughed.

We got to the front, ready to cross the threshold, when the maitre d' put his arms out to stop me, and in a loud voice warned "Hey! You can't get in there, it's all sol . . ." I was waiting for this line I had heard so many times before that I could have predicted the exact syntax. My right hand was in my pants pocket, my left arm was wrapped around my wife, and before he could finish what he was saying I flashed a $100 bill, which was a lot of money back then. He stopped what he was saying, asked my name, and if Kathy was my wife; when I said "LaCava . . . yes," he yelled to an usher, "Moses? Come here, please; this is the honorable Mr. and Mrs. . . . LaCada (he pronounced the name wrong, but who cared?), and they are special guests this evening; please get two chairs and meet me center stage!" His voice rose to crescendo, causing everyone in close proximity to peer in our direction.

We followed him through a maze of aisles and tables, by busy waitresses, waiters, and security people. As we proceeded, people looked up, whispering to each other, thinking we were people of importance, just unrecognizable. Kathy was so beautiful that many heads turned to get another look at her. And that night we were dressed to the hilt—me in my tailor-made duds, she in a dressy, sleek, off-the-shoulder cocktail ensemble that she rarely wore.

Halfway down to the front we had to stop because a waitress was blocking the aisle. Standing there through the commotion—the din-din of anticipation, I heard a lady in back of us referring to Kathy as someone, she was sure, who played in the soap operas. We got down to center stage where there were two long tables seating ten on each side, set perpendicular to the stage. He introduced us to the group as the honorable Mr. and

Mrs. LaCada and asked them all to stand up, and Moses with an usher moved the tables back, inserting the two chairs, which would turn out to be a handshake away from the great Elvis Presley!

Elvis was only a shadow of what he used to be—big and heavy with a gut hanging out. He was so far out of uniform that he could be on kitchen patrol for a month; in addition, he was sick with a cold or the flu. His voice was off pitch, and his rhythms were so atrocious his band had a difficult time following him—at least this was my impression. The songs that he did well were the ones where he accompanied himself. But the place showered him wildly with adulation and support, and my Kathleen was no different. When he sang, I looked over at her. Her head was fixed in his position, and he looked down at her intently as if he was singing just to her. She was in seventh heaven, with an expression of joy, of fulfillment—she had finally seen her idol! A few years later, in my loneliness and despair, I would see this image every waking hour; it would never leave; it would never leave!

The irony and the rest of the story went like this: they were filming several scenes from Elvis's appearances in Las Vegas to be used for television in the future. It was never shown until after he died, and as I was watching it with her daughter one day, there before our eyes was a glancing shot of her mother, only a handshake away from the great Elvis! I never saw that film again.

First Born

Kathy gave me a son named Louis Michael LaCava on December 18, 1970. He was a handsome guy, born with a lot of hair and sideburns. I smiled after seeing him, for I, too, had sideburns at one time in my life. She wanted to name him Michael, but out of respect for me she named him Louis, though he would not be a junior. Kathy was so happy. This was the first of the five we planned, but fate would revise the blueprint, only to stain it with heartaches, sadness, and tears.

After Louie's birth, we lost a second baby, but Kathy was once again with a child shortly thereafter. Around six and a half months into her pregnancy she was experiencing headaches. They were persistent and devastating; I took her to the doctor—a good, old-fashioned doctor from the old school, who delivered Louie and many babies in the LaCava clan—who found her blood pressure slightly elevated and subsequently diagnosed toxemia—pre-eclampsia of pregnancy. He wanted to admit her to the hospital to facilitate management of her hypertension and albuminuria. Her case was uncommon, but a doctor at the hospital told me that some women who get pregnant soon after miscarrying experience mild cases of toxemia and hypertension and that it was seldom, but occasionally, related to the miscarriage.

During her brief stay a young internist thought he recognized lupus erythematosis, a systemic immunological condition in which your body literally forgets who you are, but the anomaly is usually managed well and the patient can lead a normal life. He forwarded a diagnosis to that effect. Dr. Marino, the obstetrician, brought in a Dr. Vecchiolla, a seasoned internist on the staff, to help manage her case, if indeed lupus was the cause of Kathy's problems. Dr. Vecchiolla informed me that he wanted to bring in a lupus specialist from the UConn Medical Center to

confirm the diagnosis; in the meantime they put her on prednisone; her headaches subsided, and she was discharged.

Shortly thereafter, in early August, I brought her in for delivery; her blood pressure shot up to precarious levels, which was
of great concern to the doctors. They hooked her to an IV and
magnesium sulfate was administered; she was also placed on
Serpasil. The pressure slowly receded and contractions increased slowly, but it was a long difficult delivery for Kathy and
the good doctor Marino. A consultation eight hours after delivery, between Dr. Vecchiolla and Dr. J. Amato, confirmed they
were satisfied that "this patient is doing well." But exactly
twelve hours after delivery, Kathy had a seizure.

I had stayed with Kathleen for several hours after I brought
her to the hospital for delivery but left around noon to check on
little Louie, intending to return immediately. After having a
sandwich I fell asleep on the couch, to be awakened three hours
later by a call from the hospital; it was the good Dr. Marino, who
happily gave me the news of the delivery, although something
was different in his voice. "Lou, Kathleen gave birth to a beautiful girl. I want you to come up here."

"Doctor, is she alright?"

"Yes, but I want to talk to you." I told him I would be right
there and immediately I jumped in the car, anxious to see my
wife and new baby girl. Upon arriving at the hospital, having run
most of the red lights on the way, I met the good doctor in the
hallway, drenched with perspiration and visibly tired.

Recognizing me, Dr. Marino said, "Come, we'll go down to
Kathy." She was still hooked to the IV's, and I could tell by the
quiet breathing that she was heavily sedated. As I walked to the
bed to hold her hand the two nurses who had just finished checking the IV and monitoring her blood pressure were leaving. I
looked at Kathy's face, and even through all the difficulties, she
was still a vision of loveliness. Once the nurses had left, Dr. Marino told me she would be fine, and that he just wanted to keep
her here a few more days than usual to reassure himself. The
doctor was extremely tired, and I suspected there were some
anxious moments before our baby was born. I asked him how
long; he told me that in four or five days he would be able to re-

lease her. Mentally relieved, I was now anxious to see my baby girl. I thanked the doctor and ran down to the nursery area.

I arrived at the nursery to find three nurses inside the monitoring area "drooling over" Nancy Anne LaCava, my little girl. One of them said through the glass, "Isn't she beautiful?" I certainly agreed, for she was the image of her mother. After a long stay, I returned to Kathy's room and found her still sleeping. Her face was so peaceful, and taking her warm hand in mine I bent over and kissed her forehead, whispering "My sweet angel." Little could either of us imagine that those dedicated nurses and aides would be our baby's mothers for many days!

The Diagnosis

Three days after Kathy gave birth to Nancy Anne, I was visiting at lunchtime when she said the staff doctor wanted to talk to me about a rash she had on her hands. Kathy looked terrific, and it was apparent Dr. Marino was satisfied with the progress in her recovery, for he was anticipating her release in two days. She wanted to go home sooner; of course it was my desire also to get her home where she belonged, but I emphatically cautioned her Dr. Marino told her Thursday, and Thursday it would be.

I went to the desk to inquire what the doctor wanted me for, when the nurse tersely answered he was making his rounds and I would have to wait; she then read a message off of Kathy's chart that it was important for this doctor to talk to me. Informing her that I really needed to return to work, as I had lost so much time lately, she paged him; the doctor appeared immediately. He took me into a small office that was vacant and bid me to sit down.

"Mr. LaCava, we noticed some spots on your wife's hands and were concerned." His face was pallid, his words seriously flavored; he impressed me as being learned. I asked him what having these spots meant, and he informed me that it is one of the symptoms of lupus erythematosis.

"That's a big name, doctor. I've never heard of—what is it? But the only . . . the first time when she was pregnant they bandied it around, also," I responded, quizzically.

"Mr. LaCava, it's an immunological disorder, where one's systems can't distinguish one's own organs." I had so many questions—it's systemic? What does that mean? I sense it could be in a person's whole system. Is it serious? I needed it explained in layman's terms.

The doctor stated, "The systems go haywire, and it can be serious if we don't control it." Asking how, he informed me they

118

usually control it with steroids and other drugs. "Your wife is fine now, aside from the headaches, but—"

I interrupted him, "What headaches? She hasn't complained of headaches, the only thing she said to me is that she wants to go home."

The doctor replied, "Mr. LaCava, she is still getting headaches, and we want to put her on a higher dosage of cortisone to get her platelet count up, for it's too low, even though we gave her blood. In addition, they may want to do a kidney biopsy."

I answered respectfully but told him of my fears of cortisone, as a doctor friend had once told me that volumes had been written about contraindications and interactions and the dangers inherent in these drugs. It was now being used so indiscriminately. "Isn't the jury still out on its efficacy? Why is it you find it necessary to administer it now? She looks good, her blood pressure is down . . . several times she's asked to go home—she feels fine, and," I repeated, "she wants to go home. And now you're telling me they may want to do a kidney biopsy?"

The doctor countered, "Her blood pressure is still high for her age. I don't know who your doctor friend is, but Mr. LaCava, if your wife has what we think, it could be worse not to put her on higher dosages of prednisone. We just want to see if it clears up her hands. We called in Dr. *** to evaluate."

I shot back, "Who is he?"

"She. She wrote the book on lupus. She—she's the expert around here in that field." I asked what Kathy's doctor had to say about all this, and he replied, "Dr. Vecchiolla is an internist; he's not a specialist in this field . . . but he is receptive."

A little dismayed at what I heard and the conversation that had transpired, I concluded, "I know we have to have specialists in our advanced fields of medical science and technology, yet one can't help but get the feeling there are too many of them screwing things up. Doctor, I am against giving her exorbitant levels of these drugs if it's not necessary. And I have a twenty-year class reunion that both Kathy and I are anxious to attend." I walked toward the door and courteously thanked the doctor.

When I returned late in the day to see Kathy and Nancy Anne, I overheard the nurse outside Kathy's door ask the intern to verify the orders—the amount of increase in the levels of prednisone. I excused myself and asked to whom they were referring—"Your wife," the doctor immediately replied.

It was not my intention to be difficult. Nonetheless, as I had expressed some trepidation about these high-powered steroids and their deleterious effect on the body's systems if they are not necessary, specifically the kidneys, the liver, and the general hormonal balance, I posed a question about permanent damage from indiscriminate use. It wasn't meant to be disrespectful, only an expression of concern any good husband would have. I didn't really expect an answer but asked if Dr. Vecchiolla had approved this change. He responded that they were just following orders from her doctor and the specialist. Trying to inject comfort and reassurance regarding their mode of treatment, he briefed me that her platelet count was too low for the biopsy. I asked incredulously, "What biopsy?"

"Didn't her doctor consult with you about the kidney biopsy they deem necessary?"

"Dr. Vecchiolla never said anything to me about a biopsy. I only want to get her home, and Dr. Marino mentioned that he thought she could leave—I see now it's out of his hands."

I went into the room and said to Kathy, "Kathleen, you never told me about the added cortisone."

She looked away at the nurse that was approaching her bed, for she knew when I called her Kathleen something was bothering me. And then she turned to me and said, "Lou, did you see Nancy Anne—she has already grown!"

The nurse left the room and I asked in a very soft voice, "Kathleen, how are you really feeling, and please don't fudge the answer. I want to know if everything is alright." Then adding another statement before giving her the opportunity to reply, I said, "If you're holding something back, then I'll worry, and I can't function like that at work and home taking care of little Louie."

"Lou, I'm feeling good—really great."

"The resident informed me you were having headaches."

"Honest, Lou, I'm good. Today a Doctor *** came to see me. She said she was here to look at my hand rash and check me out.

She looked at my chest and neck to see if I had a rash there; she also asked me if I had a headache, because my blood pressure was a little high."

I cut in, "This is the doctor the resident mentioned—something about a specialist."

Remembering something else, Kathy said in almost a whisper, "Lou, she said that before I leave they want to do a kidney biopsy, but they can't do this operation until they get my platelet count up."

My eyes narrowed, and the skin furrowed on my forehead. "Operation! Platelets! Kathleen, don't let them do anything to you. I'm going down to the phone to try to reach Dr. Vecchiolla."

I was informed by Dr. Vecchiolla's secretary that it was his long weekend; he would not be back until Tuesday, and she proceeded to give me the name of the doctor who was covering for him. When I called him, he was completely vague, noncommittal, and gave me a *laissez faire* response regarding Dr. *** (the specialist). He didn't have a clue who Kathy LaCava was, nor, I got the impression, did he care. I asked God to forgive my uncharitable feelings, but this man was in a field over his head.

I called Dr. Marino and asked him if he would release Kathy from the hospital. I just wanted to get her home as soon as possible. Dr. Marino responded that as far as he was concerned he had already told the staff she could go. They briefed him on what they perceived Kathy's condition and diagnosis to be from Dr. ***'s report, and the only person who could supersede them was her own internist—Dr. Vecchiolla. Dr. Marino was very sympathetic; the intimation through his words indicated to me that the place for Kathy now was home with her children and me.

We were already approaching the end of the second week when it occurred to me to ask myself, as I hung up the phone, are rules and regulations an oxymoron when it comes to common sense? I was totally frustrated!

On Sunday, I received a call from Dr. ***, who said to me, "Mr. LaCava, I've been told you are concerned with the procedure we have to do on Kathy. I'd like you to come to my house so I can explain some things. . . . I think this is important." Apparently she had talked to the person that covered for Dr.

Vecchiolla, but I wasn't sure of that; it may have been an intern or resident.

I answered, "Doctor, I think it's normal to have concerns when I'm told that my wife has something I've never heard of, and more importantly, I don't have any inclination who you are who has diagnosed it." I then calmly and very respectfully completed my thought, "But I am willing to meet with you. Please give me your address and I'll come right away."

She lived a distance, yet even with heavier than usual Sunday traffic I arrived in less than thirty minutes. She answered the door, we cordially shook hands, and she led me to a small study. After I sat down she started right in with, "Mr. LaCava, your wife is a very sick girl!" I thought to myself not a girl, doctor, my wife is a woman and a lady in the true sense of the word. "She has lupus, and we should start treatment immediately."

I nervously said, "What do you mean she's a very sick girl? She doesn't look sick to me. Several times she's told me that she feels great. . . . Dr. Marino had released her, and . . ."

She interrupted me, sensing I was going to get adamant, for I spoke in rapid staccato progressions. "Mr. LaCava, your wife's kidneys are deteriorating, and this thing is spreading rapidly through her system . . . it may next attack her brain. It's systemic."

She continued talking, saying many things about Kathy's condition. I was starting to get annoyed, for I thought it very strange that they hadn't taken any tests to determine if she did, in fact, have lupus, and yet she was telling me all this. While she was talking I looked straight into her eyes and was frightened at what seemed a sadistic possession with her own specialty. I wanted to leave as quickly as I possibly could!

"Mr. LaCava, it is imperative that we do a kidney biopsy before she leaves the hospital."

I cut in, my voice vibrating to a steady pitch. "Dr. ***, if my wife's kidneys are deteriorating, why is it so important to have this biopsy?"

She countered, "So we know what degree of treatment to progress with. And the treatment in itself is detrimental—she'll lose all her hair, may lose weight as she will lose her appetite, fatigue will set in—. First we have to get her platelet count up before we cut her, which means raising her cortisone to extreme levels."

I asked her a naive question in layman's English. "Doctor, putting her on high dosages of cortisone, then surgery— isn't that a recipe for infection and complications?"

Succinctly, she said in a forceful voice, "We have . . . we don't have an alternative, do we?"

"Yes, Doctor, I do! Good day."

I left her house, confused and disturbed. I was determined to get my wife home. I tried to digest everything she had said by writing it down, word for word, but it played incredibly weirdly in my mind. I remembered her eyes and how frightening they seemed. I could accept sickness for my wife or me—for why not her or me, God's will be done—but this was odd. And then I asked myself a question: Why would a doctor ask a patient's husband to her house to tell him these things that had no basis in science, and that were completely irrelevant to her present condition? Although, Dr. *** played a significant role in the treatment and contributing to my wife's history, I would never see her again.

When I went to see Kathy late in the day to find out how she was doing, I was aghast that they had already raised the cortisone to tremendous levels.

Then I said, "Kathy, you know . . . I cautioned you not to let them give you any more drugs, especially cortisone. . . ."

She took my hand, pleading, "Lou, let's get this over with. They'll see that there's nothing wrong with my kidneys—they're not deteriorating—I'll be home in a short time." She would be right on one count!

I asked, "Kathy, who gave you information about your kidneys deteriorating, and why did you allow them to do this?"

Before she could answer a young nurse came bouncing in. "Mrs. LaCava, did you void?" Kathy answered yes, and she left.

"Lou, the doctors talked me into it; Dr. Vecchiolla persuaded me last week that she was the expert in the field, so what could I say?" I released my hand from hers in dismay, and while jerking it back I knocked over her pitcher of ice water with such force that it sailed splashing to my side and across the room; the stainless steel pitcher flew down to the tile with a thud. She let out one of her famous cackle laughs, so loud and so contagious that three nurses going off duty came into her room, and we all had a good, hearty, therapeutic chuckle. While an aide was cleaning up we walked over to see Nancy Anne, then I took her down to the coffee shop for a snack and some magazines. This would be the last, brief shining moment in Camelot, before all hell would break loose, and the devil himself would show his horrific face.

The Operation

After his long weekend, I called Dr. Vecchiolla to express my concerns. He had already been briefed on my demeanor. The word was out—and I had an inclination where it had come from—that I was uncooperative. Because I was alarmed about what I perceived as inconsistencies in my wife's case, I was labeled "uncooperative." I would later learn it was just a code word used when there is a screw-up, to get attention away from the patient—they label the kin in an uncomplimentary way. How often it happened, and did I want to believe it, were questions that would never be answered in my naiveté. The people working on her floor and those taking care of Kathy didn't think I was uncooperative, which would be corroborated down the line.

Four days into the high cortisone treatment obvious detrimental effects started to be seen on Kathy's body; she had put on weight, her face was bloated and moon-shaped, she was jittery and talked fast with a stutter. She was already "wired"! She told me she was keeping a precise diary of what was transpiring (it would help later) and a list of all the people that were administering to her. When I asked about her effort and the purpose of it, she explained in great detail that she wanted to thank each one personally by letter as soon as she got to go home. This was certainly vintage Kathleen, but I was deeply concerned about the havoc the high dosage of steroids was now taking and would take on her body in the future. This diary, in addition to mine, and over a thousand pages of documents, charts, x-rays, transcripts, doctors' daily records from the St. Francis Hospital in Hartford and the New England Deaconess Hospital (The Lahey Clinic), as well as hundreds, maybe thousands, of conversations with nurses, interns, and residents assigned to her case, plus doctors in Canada and other parts of the country, were destined to be the catalyst to form the basis of this story.

125

Deeply concerned when I saw her condition, I cornered Dr. Vecchiolla in the hall and told him this was insane, though not precisely in those terms. He reassured me that everything was going on schedule, that her platelet count had risen some and with any luck Dr. Fox could do the operation the following week. The only change in her condition that seemed to concern him was diminished urine output. This is common with high dosages of cortisone, and he tried to reassure me, saying they would start her on more diuretics if needed!

The next morning I left work at eight-thirty and went to the hospital. Kathy's door was closed when I got there, and I assumed she was having breakfast. A door left slightly ajar by an exiting aide allowed me to see that seven or eight doctors stood around her bed. I closed the door and went down to see Nancy Anne. A nurse was holding her when I appeared, and as I had now become a fixture there, she immediately walked close to the glass. Observing the progress Nancy had made since her birth made me proud. I could see the fine characteristics of her mother's fair beauty and smiled when the nurse took her tiny arm in animated gesture of a wave. It was satisfying to see how healthy she looked; I so appreciated the loving care and attention the nurses were extending to our baby. The whole equation had an added caveat: considering the difficulty Kathy had with headaches during pregnancy and then the subsequent "lupus" diagnosis, the doctors were concerned with the baby's health. Nancy had no abnormal vital signs—breathing, pulse, eliminating processes were working fine. There was nothing to indicate any need for the doctors' concern; she only required the normal monitoring any newborn would receive. At the end of the first week she was doing great, but they insisted on calling in her pediatrician, the venerable Dr. Golino.

Dr. Golino was truly from the old school; he could see things in a patient instantaneously. Considered a "doctor's doctor," he was highly respected, kind, gentle, compassionate, reassuring, and competent. When he was with you, he was with you, not preoccupied with his investments or lodge meeting or the golf course or who was waiting in the next cubicle. The day he came into the hospital to examine Nancy Anne I happened to be there. He went into the nursery by himself, while three other doctors waited outside for him, anxious to get his expert opinion. When he had concluded the exam, which took only a minute, he noticed me and swiftly came in my direction. I assumed he would first talk to the waiting doctors, but to my surprise he came over and shook my hand, saying, "Congratulations, what a beautiful girl you have." I quickly asked if he had found her to be healthy, and, smiling, he said she was as healthy as any baby he'd ever seen. He said he was going to tell the doctors to leave her alone and just let the nurses attend to her. He finished with, "Don't worry—she's great!"

Happy with the good doctor's findings, I returned to Kathy's room. The door was open and the first resident who had mentioned the possibility that Kathy had lupus was there with the surgeon who would perform a biopsy. After they indicated that they would possibly be putting her on a mild diuretic for fluid retention, one possible side effect of the high cortisone dosage, I questioned when the biopsy would be done. Dr. Fox, a fine doctor with an easy-going manner and empathetic personality, told me if the platelet count was right they would do it at the end of the week.

Once outside the room, I asked Dr. Fox about the chances of infection due to the high dosage of cortisone. He indicated there was, indeed, a high risk of infection, then added that he didn't like to do this type of procedure under these conditions, or when a patient is on high doses of any drugs, but because of Dr. ***'s diagnosis regarding her kidneys he had no other recourse.

By the end of the third week Kathy's platelet count was high enough and safe to perform the operation without fear of excessive bleeding. On Friday I caught up with Dr. Vecchiolla making his rounds, and he informed me the surgery was scheduled sometime during that day. I again expressed my displeasure at the change in her condition since they had started her on the high amount of cortisone. When I was with her, I was aware of unusual agitation, and her normally clear, impeccable skin now looked dry and pasty; furthermore, when she talked she would stutter. Not one of these conditions was characteristic of

Kathleen; all were classic side effects of cortisone. This was not the girl I had married.

A nurse came in with a glass of an orangy-red liquid, telling Kathy to drink it. When I inquired about this new mixture, she told me it was potassium, often necessary to counter the powerful diuretic drug Lasix, which causes the kidneys to put out tremendous amounts of fluids. Unfortunately, the diuretic also took with it everything in its way, including very important electrolyte minerals. I just shook my head in disbelief at the paradox and upside down world that we all were a part of!

While Kathy was drinking the "beverage," a nurse came into the room with two orderlies pushing a gurney and politely asked if I would step outside. They were about to prepare Kathy for the biopsy procedure. I said goodbye to Kathy and went down the hall to a small waiting room that had glass on three sides facing north, west, and east. On the north side three little kids were playing marbles up against a building, reminding me of my own childhood. Removing a 3" x 5" yellow index card from my jacket, which I always carried in case the urge to write hit me, I expressed my frame of mind:

sweet little innocent ones
how thouest play in joyous shout
neither a care a distant mood
doth free your loving world about
days will grow thee added year
time turns strife to rain
a world in discord misery
laden deep within ye' pain!

I was saddened at a thought of little Louie, whom I hadn't seen in a week. My good sister-in-law Mary and brother Tony were caring for him, and I missed him dearly.

It was after three P.M. when I called my secretary to tell her where I was. She said my basket was filled with messages and inquired if I would be back to the office today. Sullenly, I told her that I wanted to be there when Kathy came down from the OR. I then directed her to alert my painting foreman, when he made

128

his required check-in, to take over for me until I got back late the next morning. Meanwhile, Dr. Fox was operating on my beloved bride.

Three hours seemed like a light year. I nervously paced the hallway, up and down the stairs, floor to floor, and even took a walk around the hospital trying to work off apprehension and nervous energy. Sometimes even strong faith is not enough to nullify these. Passing by a room on the floor beneath Kathy's, I heard a woman's cry. I poked my head in the open door and asked if everything was all right. Yelling that her medicine was wearing off, she asked if I could press the button for the nurse and then stay until the nurse arrived.

Every now and then I would run across a nurse I knew—and in three weeks I befriended many. Kathy's case was becoming well known throughout the hospital, but if someone had told me that in a few months it would be known across the land, and in Canada, I would have asked them what they were drinking or, today, smoking. These nurses would stop and chat; on the day of the biopsy I went to the coffee shop with one and we had a long conversation over coffee and a cup of yogurt. She told me what a fine and beautiful girl Kathy was and how much she liked her. She loved Kathy's engaging manner and how she continually talked about me. The subject of Kathy's diagnosis came up, and the only thing she said was that they [doctors] try, but sometimes in their haste they harm. She had three kids home to support, and I could tell she was choosing her words very carefully so as not to jeopardize her job.

Just as we were returning to the floor, an orderly and a nurse were pushing Kathy's gurney off the elevator. Asking my nurse friend about the bottles that were hung around Kathy, she informed me it was just "SOP" (standard operating procedure—a phrase I grew to detest!).

"But I thought this was just a minor operation!"

"Mr. LaCava, she'll be alright." Then she whispered, "I have to go; God bless."

I followed the gurney down the corridor and around the corner to the end of the hall where Kathy's room was located. Two nurses were waiting for her. I stood outside the door as the four of them gently picked up the sheet with Kathy and placed her on the clean bed. One switched the IV bottles to a holding rack overhead while the others adjusted and covered her. I had positioned myself to get a better look at her when the orderly and nurse started walking out. The nurse looked over at me and asked, "Are you Louie, or Lou?" Surprised, I nodded. "She kept calling your name—go in and see her. She'll be waking up soon." Subdued, I asked if she had been in the operating room. When she indicated she had, I asked if everything had gone okay—if she was okay. "Fine," she replied, "she'll be fine."

I didn't leave Kathy's room for several hours, until she was fully awake. During that time the nurses frequently came to check her IV and blood pressure. I stood close to the bed often in an effort to communicate, but she would just mumble my name and something about the big apple. I wondered if she was mentally transferring back to the date we had in New York, when we attempted to attend the opera at Lincoln Center. I bent down to kiss her cheek and became concerned by a protrusion of the main artery in her neck. It was easily identifiable and pulsating at a rapid pace. When I kissed her, one eye opened. Seeing me, she smiled anemically, then quickly fell back to sleep. I said in a soft, but audible voice, "Sweet princess, I will take you home soon." I swallowed hard, patted her arm, and walked slowly toward the door, turned, waved, and promised, "I'll see you tonight."

Kathy was still dozing on and off when I got back in the early evening. Dr. Fox came in with a nurse shortly after my arrival. I inquired if everything was normal, and he reassured me she was doing fine but that they wanted to monitor her for a while. Asking him when he would know the outcome of the biopsy, he said that Dr. *** would talk to me or Dr. Vecchiolla the following day. Needing more information than that, I respectfully continued, "Dr. Fox, you did the biopsy, can't you give me more information so that at least I can sleep tonight?"

"Mr. LaCava, I'm just the surgeon. I don't analyze—there are smarter people in the field who do that." Then he finished with, "I think you can get some sleep." He was very comforting; I could not speak more highly of him for his professionalism, compassion, and strict code of medical ethics.

Soon after they left, Kathy awoke. She looked over at me and said, "What are you doing here instead of home with my little boy?" Then she smiled feebly with, "Come here and kiss me, you big hunk of love—and did you see Nancy Anne today?"

Infection, Complications, and Chaos

The following morning I was anxious to return to the hospital to see my wife. Despite reassurance by nurses throughout the night that Kathy was resting comfortably, I had to see for myself. The last conversation we had was about taking Nancy Anne from the hospital to stay with sister-in-law Dolly. It had been two weeks since her birth, and despite the wonderful care she was receiving in the hospital, we both thought it better for her to be in a home.

Upon entering the room, I saw that Kathy was sleeping as a nurse was working on some charts. She identified herself as the night nurse and quietly informed me that Kathy's blood pressure was high and she was experiencing some nausea, although she had slept soundly most of the time. I asked about the incision and was told the nurse on the next shift would change the dressing in a few hours with Dr. Fox. Questioning the amount of sleeping Kathy was doing, the nurse said it was normal, as the procedure was one that took a lot out of the patient.

After returning from a cafeteria breakfast, I found Kathy's door shut; I patiently waited for about twenty minutes, eager to learn more about my wife's condition. Dr. Fox exited the room with three other doctors and informed me he had just checked the incision. When I asked how it looked, he cautiously answered, "It will take time." A nurse later told me they would inspect the site frequently, due to the steroid involvement. Anxious to talk to Dr. Vecchiolla when he came in for rounds, I was told he would not be there until noon. That was too long for me to wait, because of work, so I returned to Kathy's room before leaving and found her wide awake. But I didn't like the way she looked. I attempted to engage her in a conversation that would let me know what was going through her mind, but she was distant—drained and detached from the moment and her husband. I told her to have a comfortable day and that I loved her very much, then departed.

Several attempts were made the following day to find out results of the biopsy; the resident and Dr. Vecchiolla said they would not have any answers until the next day. But upon inquiry again in the morning the responses from hospital staff were vague and unnerving. This continued for three days, until a young intern told me that there were "no significant changes in her kidney structure." I was curious how he obtained this information; was he there with the parade of doctors that held class around Kathy's bed and was privy to all the data in her case, or did he peruse her records on his own for this information? In any event, I only saw him one more time and it wasn't on her floor; he had been moved to the emergency room, which seemed odd to me. I was relieved on the one hand, but terribly disturbed on the other. Were her kidneys not deteriorating, as I had previously been led to believe? Why were they so reluctant to divulge this information to me?

Kathy's incision was not healing naturally, and when I talked to Dr. Fox he said it was, indeed, infected; he had to prescribe stronger antibiotics to help things along. This increased the number of pills she was taking indiscriminately! In addition to the infection, other changes were taking place. She was becoming extremely agitated and nervous; in addition, her face and complexion, once so bright and shining, were now drawn, pasty, and round. Her blood pressure after she gave birth was high and should have been manageable; now it was out of control. They would take blood from her frequently, sometimes three or four days in a row. When I would seek answers about the need for drawing so much blood the response was always noncommittal. Her arms were so sore and irritated from the antibiotic IV and all sites of the blood draws, that she would often moan and shriek in pain, yelling my name: Louie! Louie!

On one extremely discouraging day she cried and asked me to please take her home. I tried to comfort her, saying, "Kat, as soon as they get you off all these drugs." But the drugs were ever increasing. My heart was shattered to see my beautiful wife like this.

There were drugs for infection and blood pressure, diuretics, cortisone, and more drugs added at every new evaluation or theory. And the more drug interactions, the more varied the blood analysis; the more the symptoms, the more the diagnosis would change with more detrimental effect to her organs. One day a doctor would tell me one thing, the next day I was told something entirely different; there were so many people involved with this girl's care that ordinary hospital routine and protocol was flagrantly replaced with disorder, confusion, and perplexity. They all fed on each other, with no doctor in particular taking charge or responsibility for Kathy's well-being. It was tragic beyond doubt, partially because there was nothing her husband could do—my hands were tied. Doubts were now the norm for me regarding the ability of the staff to coherently and rationally administer on her behalf. I, along with many others close to her, was now witnessing a disaster, but we had no control or power to alleviate the downward spiral of her entire being.

The veritable cocktail of drugs being administered as each new symptom popped up seemed to be a gamble, which eventually brought about catastrophic results. We would soon be robbed of hope; the drugs were suppressing the ability of her own glands to function, and this beautiful girl's body was soon wracked by seizures! I was there once; we were talking; she smiled at me strangely—and then . . . and then . . . it was so traumatic . . . so frightening! Perhaps the drugs were not totally responsible for the convulsion but how utterly strange it was that heretofore reduction of them had reduced the frequency of the seizures.

This particular day, a nurse was there at the onset of the episode. Contrary to standard precautions, she put her hands in Kathy's mouth to prevent her from swallowing her tongue while I held her body down. It was over in only a few seconds; she didn't know what had happened, and her only complaint was a headache. But this would be the first of many convulsions. I had been warned about the cortisone, and sure enough, now it ravaged her body and spirit. It was a domino effect—an unnecessarily high dosage of cortisone, which caused the holding of water, followed by the operation ending with infection, then added complications

caused by the combination of so many drugs; so many catastrophic problems; so many doctors, so many drugs; so few answers; so little ability to halt the downward spiral. And now they
had to start her on phenobarbital for the seizures.

Although cortisone had been used for years and was
God-sent in some cases, in Kathy's it had the opposite effect; my
initial fears and concerns were becoming reality. Panic set in
from ramifications of the operation; some hearts were open, and
some semblance of truth was finally disclosed to me. Her kidneys
showed no deterioration, as I was told by Dr. ***, only minor
changes that are often shown with elevated blood pressure. The
continuous blood tests that were taken to monitor the sedimentation rate gave no scientific clue that she did in fact have systemic lupus. It was a year of many seasons, but for us the wrath
of winter forever held us in its grip.

Kathy's case was now known throughout the hospital; the
question was asked—who is the beautiful young girl, so very ill?
The answer was always Kathleen LaCava; then they asked, "Did
you see her baby?" "Did she have a baby!?" "Yes." Then it would
go on—"Do you want to see her?" " Is she still here?" "Yes. She's a
dream." Visitors would come; patients down the hall would come;
nurses with spare time would come and congregate in her room.
Finally, frustrated with the circus atmosphere surrounding her,
I requested that her room be changed—but that didn't help.

The month was imperceptibly drawing to a close. Apathy set
in with doctors, confused about how to treat this young girl.
Daily meetings around her bed became less common. Although
there was no scientific basis doctors could rely on, they still did-
n't reduce the steroids measurably. Because she was on cortisone
for so long her own adrenal glands were locked dormant. It had
to be a slow and gradual process of reduction, or other major
problems would develop. A new resident told me that depending
on the quantity given for the length of time she was on it, the ra-
tio of reduction would be slow at best. Moreover, removal of the
drug too quickly could now even increase the possibility of more
seizures!

Then there came a chest X-ray showing an enlarged heart. A
new drug for that! One doctor and a nurse told me that part of the

heart changes could be cortisone-related. The new drug was digoxin, which was supposed to give the heart a stronger beat, or so I was told. This experience for me started to add new meanings for the word incompetence. One day as I waited while they worked on Kathy's infected incision, Dr. Fox wandered over—I had no qualms about his ability; in fact, I had a lot of respect for him. We talked briefly, and before he left he said sadly, "We're at a point now where we're damned if we do and damned if we don't!" I will never forget those words, said with such empathy and altruism.

A daily increase in guilt claimed my consciousness, and I started to transfer blame from the doctors to myself. It was starting to hold me hostage for not being more forceful in insisting from the beginning that I wanted her home when Dr. Marino released her. I lamented, was all this suffering necessary or in vain? One day I scribbled this out:

Suffering, oh suffering, merit not
This gift's interred in bones to rot,
Let me find in faith to pray,
God's glory shineth thru . . . the dark of day.

I returned to Kathy; she was up in a chair and Father Crawford from the Church of the Incarnation in Wethersfield was visiting her. She was very pleased and very talkative, telling him that when she left there all the names in her diary (which she held in her hand) were going to get a letter from her, thanking them for their kindness. Kathy's mother came in while Father was still there. And when I was leaving, one nurse who took excellent care of Kathy approached me and asked, "Mr. LaCava, was that Kathy's mother?" When I replied in the affirmative, she declared matter-of-factly, "Now I know where her looks come from!"

The Nursery Princess Departs

In anticipation of her departure, the nurses had dressed Nancy but didn't bundle her until sister-in-law Dolly arrived. They asked if I wanted to hold her, and I replied (in this Catholic hospital), "Is the Pope Catholic?" After many days, Nancy Anne's features were delicately pronounced, and I could clearly distinguish her mother's beauty in her. She was displaying cute little infant gestures that initiated laughter from the regular nurses who had taken care of her for so long. In the meantime, Nancy Anne was delighted by all the attention. The longer we waited, the more the crowd grew—bringing nurses, doctors, cleaning women. Nancy Anne was voted by acclamation to be the honorary hospital mascot, and many of the girls on Kathy's floor who knew Nancy was leaving this day also congregated.

When Dolly and Kathy's mother arrived and we started to walk away with the baby, the mood was celebratory on one hand, but some of the regular nurses had tears in their eyes—such sadness and joy combined. As we walked past the nurses' station, a nun I had never seen before stopped us so that she could take a look at Nancy. She turned to me after making cute (but funny) faces at the baby, and said, "Now, Daddy, you take care of that cute little girl." It seemed as if everyone knew about Kathy's case.

Nitor in Adversum
(Strive in Opposition)

During the next week Kathy had two more grand mal seizures. She looked tired and pale and was showing increased amounts of irritability, even to the extent of being discourteous to many of the hospital staff who had cared for her so ably since her admission. It was disheartening for me to witness, for they loved her so much. She started to distrust the doctors—this feeling was certainly understandable—to the point where she became selective in the pills she would take. Certain medication she refused. The bulk of the drugs in her protocol would not cause immediate harm if stopped for a few days, but the doctors were very concerned that if she stopped taking the cortisone it would leave her without the adrenaline-family hormone that is so essential for life. The length of time she was on the tremendously high dosage of cortisone means it would take months to wean her from it and to get her own system to come back to its normal state. Now that was questionable and, I wondered, was it even possible? A plan was readied to crush her steroids and mix them in her water or cranberry juice each day. The nurses tried to reason with her to no avail; everything that had transpired devastated not only her body, but in addition, sadly, was slowly affecting her spirit. This was the most surprising change, especially for this girl who had such a strong will, constitution, and faith, plus a passionate love for people.

I persuaded Kathy to understand how important it was that she adhered to the prescribed medications at this point, until they could safely wean her off all the garbage. I told her that was the only way she could get out of there, reminding her she was needed at home to help raise the two children; she had to be strong and cooperative. She told me to call Jill, the nurse, to bring her pills, but unbeknownst to us yet another drug had been added to the mix, an antidepressant. It was never revealed, nor could data be located, who was responsible for the decision to add this medication—the *coup de grace* for poor Kathleen!

The antidepressant changed her completely. Daily concern with little Louie's and Nancy Anne's welfare suddenly diminished; she seldom asked for them. This girl, who was so homesick for "Little Louie" the first time we ever left him and went on vacation, begging me to cut the vacation short, now was completely oblivious to her children's plight and showed little interest in their well-being.

The combination of the forty drugs, plus the antidepressant, was literally a raging hell within her soul that cried out for justice and mercy. She would have periods of laughter—as her old self—and periods of extreme depression. There were times when she was loquacious and times she wouldn't talk to anyone, including her husband. Then she started to get belligerent, an emotion that was so far removed from her natural persona it was like night and day. The medications were unforgiving and totally devastating; the combinations were catastrophic. They were administered randomly, (treating the symptom *du jour*) cruelly and unscientifically, inducing unnecessary punishment, suffering, and pain.

Labor Day Visit

I made every effort to keep in close contact with Dr. Vecchiolla regarding Kathy's day-to-day progress; I asked him to take complete control of her medications since there were so many doctors involved, telling him I didn't want any more experimentation. I asked if he could begin reducing the cortisone as quickly and safely as possible. This was my statement, verbatim, witnessed by doctors and nurses, one of whom was the floor supervisor, who would subsequently confide important information to me and issue some urgent advice that would change the course of treatment. But the report P#77904904—-24–95–60, which was filed by John Vecchiolla, MD that stated: He Insisted That We Discontinue Most of the Medications, was completely without merit and inconsistent with other parts of the report, where I was quoted as *not* wanting the cortisone reduced. Now you can't have it both ways. The author certainly will admit that he had concerns, not unlike any normal man would with regard to a wife with such a diagnosis and treatment. However, the truth of the matter was that there were many inconsistencies from doctor to doctor; even the reports were imbued with contradictions and inaccuracies, so much so that at times the feedback I received from staff was alarming.

My weeks consisted of a very busy work schedule—supervising the construction of a large condominium complex, tending to the house, worrying about the kids, as well as spending several hours at the hospital each day. When I returned home at night, usually between nine and ten-thirty, the author just flopped on the bed without eating, mentally and physically exhausted.

On the third day after persuading Kathy to continue with her medication, her room was empty when I arrived. I went to the lounge; she wasn't there. I stopped a new nurse in the hall and she said she didn't know who or where she was. Finally, I went to the desk to talk to the supervisor; she was on break, and the other girls wouldn't tell me anything. I had come to know most of these people very well, so I found their silence disconcerting. One finally walked back to Kathy's vacant room with me and with sadness in her eyes, told me they had taken her "downstairs." I asked who had taken her where, and for what reason? She explained, "Lou, they came to take blood this morning and she—and she got hysterical, and we couldn't control her. Several of us tried to calm her but she was a broken girl—we couldn't get near her." She stopped momentarily to compose herself and then added, "We all just left her, but the new supervisor couldn't deal with it because she was fearful it would disrupt the floor. So she called the counselor, who advised putting her 'downstairs.' "

Ingenuously, with my voice reaching crescendo, I naively asked, "What in God's name is downstairs?!"

"Sshsss—Lou, Lou, please wait a minute—that's where they put the mentally disturbed patients—she won't be there long." With anger in my voice I asked her what floor Kathy was on, and as I started to walk away she grabbed my arm and pleaded, "Lou—Lou, please wait—one more thing. At break time, Jean went down to see her and she was okay." Thanking her for the kindness she exhibited, I hurried away—to the Psychiatric Ward!

Upon my arrival, I asked the attendant to open the iron gate and bring Kathy out. She asked who I was. Perturbed, I spit out, "Her husband!" She gave me a log to sign, asked to see my driver's license, recorded the time, and left. The thrust of the moment struck me as utterly ridiculous and cruel; remembering *The Gulag Archipelago* by Solzhenitsyn, I felt queasy. After being gone for some time, the nurse returned alone and contemptuously exclaimed that Kathy didn't want to see me! Looking at the "guard nurse," I remember thinking, is that what working in a place like this does to a person? I sat there for twenty minutes, staring at the gate, hurt, and depressed . . . I'm her husband!

Jill, one of the nurses from Kathy's floor entered, sat next to me, and asked if I was all right. The author mumbled, "Sure." She sat with me for a while until I urged her to go home to her husband and kids. Rising from the bench slowly, she looked at me, put her hand on my shoulder, and tearfully said, "I know everything will turn out okay for you." Dropping her eyes to the floor, she walked away. I cried inside; how can anyone ever forget people like that? My thoughts turned back to the iron gate and reality. I was alone, shrouded in a hopeless veil of emptiness that tempted my will, my spirit, and nearly my faith.

The next day I waited for Dr. Vecchiolla until eleven A.M. When he didn't show up, I decided to go down and see if Kathy would come out to talk to me. The supervisor was on break, so I walked toward the gate and asked the nurse inside if she would be so kind to tell Kathy that her husband was here. The nurse returned, only to inform me that Kathy didn't acknowledge the request. I moved a few feet back from the gate, musing whether to go back up to see if Dr. Vecchiolla came in for his rounds, when down the hall within the confinement I saw Kathleen come out of her room, slowly walking in my direction. I was momentarily encouraged and thought maybe she would ask to come out. These hopes were short-lived, when she advised me, standing five feet from the gate, that she was "too busy this morning to talk." Even worse, and devastatingly so, as she turned to leave, the nurse handed her a chrome pitcher filled with ice water that she took with her left hand; that's when I noticed she had removed her beautiful diamond and wedding rings!

My head was full, yet the author felt that God doesn't give anyone more than they can handle; I had already accepted that I could handle anything He presented. There was no more room for hurt. The curtain of my heart was torn from top to bottom and side to side. I was in an abyss of futility and despair! Soon it would all crystallize in sheer numbness after hearing the advice of a wise and learned veteran nurse.

Depressed and shaken, I walked back up to see if her doctor had arrived for his rounds, only to find he had come and gone. After calling my office to alert my secretary that I would not be back the rest of the day, I got into my car and went to Elizabeth Park. While sitting on a bench, meditating, and looking at the last roses of summer struggle for sustenance to prolong life, a small boy, walking alongside his mother, who was pushing a baby carriage, remarked, "Mommy, why is that sad man?" (I smiled inside, tickled by the sentence structure.) She responded, "Honey, he's not sad, just resting." I departed from my meditation, forced an outer smile thinking that wisdom is gifted to the aged and the child, but is lost to those in between, who so desperately need it.

Dr. Vecchiolla took the brunt of my wrath. I unloaded on him everything that was building in me since the meeting with Dr. ***. Most of what I said was important and justified, but tardy. That which was not, bothered me. It is almost impossible for some generalizations not to come out when emotionally conveying a message, and there is always a danger of indicting innocent people, especially in her case. Unfortunately, everything and everyone was lumped together into the whole rotten mess. I had no compunctions about expressing my feelings and anger for what I perceived to be quite obvious and legitimate reasons. This had nothing to do with catharsis, but for two days after this big "discussion" the voice of my father was loud and clear in my head—the advice he gave his children so often. "Before you speak, be very careful what your mind and heart really want to say, for after the words roll off your tongue, it's too late to retrieve them. It's done; they're gone." In retrospect, there were some words that I would have eliminated, or at least rephrased, but the composite of my indignation was totally justified and woefully overdue.

Dr. Vecchiolla then started to take complete charge of Kathy's case. During the frank exchange of views he told me that although her kidneys were not deteriorating, there were some changes that they had to monitor carefully. But, he added, the seizures and her enlarged heart were of great concern to all, emphasizing this was very serious. I reminded him that neither the seizures nor the enlarged heart were there when she entered the hospital; he intimated that it was water under the bridge. There were no ill feelings between us; on the contrary, I respected him as a competent doctor, liked him, and was empathetic toward him and the stresses doctors have to endure. The only thing the author questioned was his abdication of responsibility as Kathy's primary doctor—he was depending too much on the so-called "experts" and not using his own knowledge.

143

Sadly, the "expert" had candidly explained to me at her house one gloomy Sunday that Kathy's kidneys were deteriorating. But studies would show that to be untrue. Report 24–9560 #79074802 stated: A renal biopsy was done which was not really consistent with SLE. (!) Report 24–95–60 #77904904 showed: Fluorescent Ana Studies Were Negative. The diagnosis was determined solely on the rash and low platelet count. Some of the doctors were under the impression that the rash was due to the medication. But this "expert" was so sure SHE was right!

The next three days I would visit Kathy with the same pattern; three times a day the director would announce me to her and each time she would say she was too busy to talk. I asked the nurse if any of her medication had been reduced, and she told me that the doctor had reduced the cortisone minutely, but the rest of the protocol remained the same. The only real difference was that they had changed to another antidepressant. As her husband, I beseeched the nurse to stop giving her the antidepressants; she said she couldn't without the doctor's permission. So I made it known to her doctor, in no uncertain terms, that I wanted it stopped immediately; he said he had no authority—the only person that could discontinue it, he bluntly told me, was the psychiatrist. Reminding him that he was her doctor and it was ethically his responsibility, I told him once again that I wanted those dangerous tranquilizers discontinued today. I left him no alternative; later I was to find out that this anti-depressant drug, Thorazine, had caused severe liver damage in many trial studies. The pill was discontinued the same day.

On the next visit, Kathy still wouldn't come out to talk to me, but on the following day, to my surprise, she was by the gate at my arrival. I quickly walked toward her and immediately noticed the rings were still missing from her finger. I timidly asked how she was feeling. She said, "I'm alright—a little restless, tired. I didn't sleep last night." The nurse cut in, yelling down to her that lunch was here. My spirits were rekindled, albeit only temporarily, and I left saying, "Kathleen, I'll be back tonight." This was the first time she looked directly at me in many days; the patent twinkle in her eyes was still gone, but at least she acknowledged me with an "okay, Lou."

Each day I observed favorable changes in Kathy's appearance and temperament. On the fourth day she had her rings back on; I was ecstatic. One nurse told me this behavior was a normal reaction from some high-powered drugs, and on a daily basis they were prepared to expect anything from their patients. She also intimated that the place was a "snake pit"—a potential hazard, especially for those who weren't really mentally ill and were placed there indiscriminately. This information was somewhat startling in that staff would voice this opinion—but it would not hinder the slight bit of encouragement I had received from Kathy. Discontinuation of the tranquilizers, along with the reduced cortisone, was allowing the re-emergence of the real Kathy—the girl I knew and loved so much. In a few days she was back upstairs among her friends. The moon face was slowly diminishing, and I could see some of her natural features returning. She started to talk about the children and the house, asked about my parents and said that she missed everyone, particularly the kids.

One day when we were alone Kathy declared that she would like to come home for Labor Day weekend and asked, with tears in her eyes, if I could bring the kids home while she was there. She understood they were still having problems with her blood pressure, but I agreed that if the doctors thought it was alright, I was willing to give it a try.

In his wisdom, the doctor felt a weekend would be too much, because they were reducing her cortisone at a rapid pace, and he was concerned with the ability of her body to handle the extra stress, especially with the children home. In addition, they were still "monkeying" with her blood pressure pills, but he saw nothing detrimental about a day visit.

Kathy was so excited. I had decided the baby would be too much and we would just have Louie come home. I called my kind sister-in-law Mary and informed her that Kathy would be home at nine A.M., asking if she could bring Louie over a short time after. I told Kathy's mother she was welcome, as well as Dolly and George. My fear was that too many people would potentially stress Kathy's already overtaxed system.

We prepared for her homecoming by bringing the comfortable family room couch up to the kitchen, thereby eliminating a need for her to walk down any more stairs than necessary in this house of so many levels. The nurses wished her well—four of them put her in a wheelchair, and wheeled her down to wait as I brought the car around!!! As I facetiously asked who was minding the store, they laughed and sent us on our way.

When we arrived home, I carried Kathy through the doorway from the garage, as she was extremely weak. I couldn't help but smile when greeting her mother holding the door open, for my mind returned to our wedding day when I carried my beautiful bride over the threshold into our apartment on that bright, promising day. Settling her on the sofa, I could see she was breathing heavily and again noted the artery in her neck protruding and beating rapidly. She looked around without saying anything; I knew she was familiarizing herself again with the house. She had her mother open some of the cabinets, joking that she wanted to see if I had changed the way she had things organized; I feigned exasperation, laughing, since in the order of important tasks that would have been a zero on a scale of one to ten.

Suddenly the door swung open and in bounced little Louie, all dressed in the sailor suit his mother had loved so much. Mary had prepared Louie to see Kathy, for up to this point, the only thing he had been told was that his mother was tired after having a baby and needed rest in the hospital. His little mind had no inclination, no conception after such a long time, of what to expect of his mother's condition.

Louie stopped, looked at his grandmother, his aunts, and his uncles, and then noticed his mother sitting on the sofa at the other end of the kitchen. He made a grand dash for her and tried to put his chubby little arms around her, but they fell short; and she mustered every fiber of energy she possessed at that moment, engulfing him with her own arms. Tears filled her eyes and the eyes of others who were there. But the tears abruptly changed into spontaneous laughter when the ebullient little Louie said, "Mommy, where have you been? I missed you—hey, wait a minute—why is this (couch) up here?"

It was a delightful day up to this point; Kathy was very happy to see Louie, who stayed about two hours. She was in her home, the environment she loved so much. But I was anxious to take her blood pressure when I noticed extreme fatigue and increasingly labored breathing. Reading everything I could get my hands on, I had become proficient in monitoring her blood pressure and evaluating danger signs. I knew the number of significance of the diastolic and systolic and the danger zone for imminent seizure. I had become well aware of exterior signs of peril three to five minutes before she would convulse—there would be changes in facial expression with increased difficulty in her breathing due to pulmonary edema. All this was caused by the inadequacy of her kidneys to eliminate fluids, and that was caused by the inability of the doctors to regulate her medication, brought about by the indiscriminate initial administration of cortisone. I knew the signs so precisely that some doctors were amazed when I would put in a warning signal. The doctors that ignored me were panic stricken when a seizure would follow. Obviously shaken to the core, this brought out both the ire and chagrin of the nurses.

Now Kathy's blood pressure was high. Assessing the imminent danger, I informed her mother I was going to take her back after she had some rest. I wanted her to calm down from the excitement, hoping her blood pressure would not climb any higher, but after observing her inability to rest, a decision was made to return as soon as possible.

We were less than a mile from the house. Kathy was telling me what an exceptional day it was, how good it was to see Louie and that she missed him so much, how great it felt to give him a big hug and kiss and that next time she wanted both children home. Some of the familiar telltale signs were present, so I said to her, "Kat, I'm very happy, too. Now don't talk anymore—I want you to rest. Put your head back, please, and close your eyes."

She started to respond, "Lou, I lovvv—" I knew it was close; she started to convulse, and when traffic stopped I slipped through a red light across the highway into a gas station and instructed the attendant to get me an ambulance—pronto. Luckily, one was strategically positioned nearby on this Sunday afternoon and arrived within three minutes. The attendants put

147

Kathy on a stretcher and into the ambulance, turned on the sirens (a sound that was in my nightmares for a week) and had her at the hospital in less than twelve minutes.

At the emergency room, ironically, was the intern who first revealed to me that Kathy's kidneys weren't deteriorating. He was familiar with her case, gave her a shot of adrenaline, and never left her side for the next half hour. When he was satisfied she was stabilized he took her upstairs himself. Once the nurses got her into bed, he checked her again; she was resting quietly. As he started to leave, I walked him down the hall, expressing appreciation for his competence, calmness, and compassion. He humbly thanked me for my words and ran down the stairs. Our lives would never intersect again.

The next week was back to square one. They raised Kathy's cortisone, telling me her own glands were not returning at a safe pace. They changed some blood pressure meds and added something new—another diuretic that was supposed to make the Lasix work more efficiently. There was another chest X-ray to check her enlarged heart. Then they started to take blood again—every day, every day, every day—causing her much discomfort.

All of these changes and experiments were making her condition worse. Once again the moon face was evident. Sometimes she was irritable. But I could still communicate with her, and she was very dependent on me. Often when we were alone she would reiterate how happy she was that we met and how lucky she was, saying, "You could have married any girl you wanted, but you married me." Before I was thrilled to hear her say that, but now I wasn't sure she was so lucky.

On one evening visit Kathy was sleeping. I inquired at the nurses' station why, as she was seldom sleeping this early. Jill told me she had had a bad day and said that frankly she thought the continual changes were doing more harm than good. And I thought of what Dr. Fox had so candidly expressed to me a few weeks back. . . ."At this point they're damned if they do and damned if they don't."

I said to tell Kathy, if she should awaken, that I had gone to the coffee shop for something to eat and would be back. And while waiting at the counter to be served, an older nurse who was a floor supervisor and very familiar with Kathy's case approached and said, "Mr. LaCava, when you get back upstairs could I talk with you?" I had no idea what she wanted but assumed she just wanted to give me support and tell me to keep the faith. As she was leaving, she came back to remind me.

Back on the floor, I stopped by the nurses' station; the supervisor asked me to wait in the lounge while she attended to one patient. Except for the chatter on the television, the room was quiet and empty. Turning off the TV, I picked up a magazine and sat down to read. In about twenty minutes she came in and got straight to the point. Some of the following was chronicled that same night by the author; other parts are paraphrased through memory; all will be treated as translation: "Mr. LaCava, you're aware that there have been many nurses and doctors involved with your wife's care. And there is much affection for both of you." She stopped talking when another nurse came in to ask a question. I wondered to myself why she was telling me this. If anyone knows how great the nurses and doctors have been, it has to be me, which I acknowledged many times in many forms.

Alone once again, she continued, "I've been with your wife since she first came in, and every . . ." She stopped again when two people came in and asked to put on the television. When she told them that visiting hours were over, they indicated they were waiting for a doctor. She asked them to wait near the nurses' station, ushered them out, and closed the door. She then repeated, "I've been with your wife since she first came in, and I am very familiar with her case—everything that transpired from the biopsy to the tranquilizers. Now, I'm an old time nurse of thirty-five years and believe me when I tell you this, I've seen everything—great doctors, poor doctors, and downright incompetent ones. I've seen brilliant treatment, miracles, and screw-ups. I could lose my job for what I am about to tell you, and maybe I wouldn't have been this courageous ten years ago, but this case has been bothering me for a long time. Please, Mr. LaCava, for your own peace of mind and for your wife's welfare, get her out of here and up to Boston! I worked there, and that's where some of the best doctors practice, especially the Lahey Clinic; maybe they can help her or maybe not. I can't answer that question. The only thing I'm certain of is that they don't know what the hell they're doing here with your wife!" She would not be the only one to offer that opinion.

I was numb. I knew Kathy never should have had the biopsy—but how can laymen second-guess doctors? I knew there was experimentation going on, and I even observed doctors who should have chosen another field—but a head nurse telling me this blew my mind. Testing her, I asked, "Are you telling me that there has been malpractice?" She stood up as one of her nurses came in and said, "Mr. LaCava, think over what I've said to you." When I agreed to take it under advisement, she shook my hand and walked out.

I just sat there, realizing she risked her job talking like that. Then I was overcome with a chill, realizing that perhaps my assessment was accurate from the beginning; I felt opposite passions of guilt and anger—guilt for allowing it to happen, and anger for it happening. I was leaning forward with my head in my hands, trying to arrive at some decision, when Jill came in to say Kathy was awake and asking for me.

Upon my arrival at her room, Kathy was in a chair talking to a nurse while an aide changed the bed. After we exchanged pleasantries, I said succinctly, "Kathy, tomorrow I am taking you to Boston." The two girls, after hearing that, quickly helped Kathy back in bed and hurried out. Kathy never questioned me—she only said she would do whatever I thought would help. I kissed her, she closed her eyes and fell asleep, and I left.

It was a bold decision that was made walking from the lounge to her room. I had to notify Dr. Vecchiolla, who had to call Boston to see if they had room in the Deaconess Hospital (where Lahey Clinic patients reside), schedule an ambulance, and get the necessary records to take up there. Would he be open-minded enough to release her from his care?

When I got home I called his answering service and asked them to have the doctor call me tonight, for it was important. His return call came around eleven P.M. When I shared with him what I wanted to do, he never questioned me; he was very cooperative and receptive. The author even had a momentary lapse of charity when a thought came that the doctor was happy to release her from his responsibility. Dr. Vecchiolla said the transfer could not be until the following day, for it would be difficult to get an ambulance scheduled this late for tomorrow. Gratefully, I asked him to do what he could; in addition, I wanted Jill or Jean to go with me, which he could not guarantee. But he assured me that some nurse would escort Kathy.

Accompanied by Jill, the trip to the Deaconess on Tuesday, September 19, 1972 was uneventful. The doctor had notified staff at the Deaconess of our departure time, so when we arrived there were two nurses and an orderly at the entrance. The orderly and one nurse quickly rolled Kathy in and put her on an elevator while the other nurse took the packet of records from Jill and showed me to a seat in the admitting area. She said to me, "We heard about your wife's case. I hope they can help. We have some of the best doctors in the world right here in this group." I answered that I hoped that was true, thinking it interesting she already knew about Kathy. Noting that I looked tired, she asked if I was returning to Hartford that day; I told her I was going to stay here close to Kathy, residing in the Deaconess Hotel, which was adjacent to the hospital and connected by a long underground tunnel which also housed the hospital cafeteria. I had taken an extended period of leave from work and was prepared to stay until tests were complete to determine why they could not regulate her blood pressure.

This young woman was very gregarious and sported a continuous smile on her face; she boldly inquired where and how Kathy and I had met. Not being in the mood to talk, I was short or absent on answers to her questions. She was very nice, but I had unfairly formed an early opinion about her professional manner. Before we left Boston, Kathy and I would develop a close friendship with this fine, dedicated nurse, who was truly a credit to her profession.

On the first day, the medical staff studied Kathy's case, from the headaches starting in her seventh month of pregnancy to her arrival there. Because an uncontrollable high blood pressure in such a young girl was unique, they assigned a blood pressure

151

specialist from the Lahey Clinic, whose name was Dr. Breslin. He was young, intense, and brilliant.

He introduced himself on the third day and told me before they could make any assessment they had to slowly wean Kathy off many of the drugs she was currently on. Upon my inquiry about the necessity of those drugs, he swallowed hard, then answered reluctantly with a question: "Is her body a computer to know and guide each drug to its proper use? Mr. LaCava, I'll do everything possible to get her pressure regulated to manageable norms before it has a disastrous effect on her kidneys." His voice became angry and acerbic as he said, "The amount of medications they had her on for so long hasn't helped." He then continued to ask questions regarding her hospital stay in Hartford.

Over the next four weeks they performed every type of test scientifically available, attempting to accurately evaluate Kathleen's condition and precisely diagnose the exact cause of the high blood pressure and related problems, like pulmonary edema, enlarged heart, and seizures. Dr. Breslin, working closely with Dr. Fernandez, a brilliant lupus specialist, slowly removed unnecessary medications from her regimen, reducing the cortisone to half of the initial dose.

From the middle of October to Christmas I stayed in Boston to be by my wife's side, save for six times for important work-related day trips. Normally I would return early the next morning, except for one time when I called and was informed by our nurse friend that Kathy's blood pressure was dangerously high. Then I returned that same day.

When she was sleeping or undergoing tests, I stayed either in my hotel room reading or writing, or in a church or a library or just walked the streets of Boston, observing life that was so far removed from mine. This was another world—the carefree facade of children going or returning from school, college students rushing about, minds centered on a mission, a horde of busy executives hustling hither and yon to the beat of car horns, and the discordant sounds of whistles from traffic policemen who were so frantically waving their arms. It reminded me of Arthur Fiedler directing the Boston Pops Orchestra.

One day while Kathy was undergoing a special kidney test I

was unable to see her for about five hours. Having been assured there was no danger in the procedure, I planned a long morning walk.

I walked. I walked in no special direction, with so many thoughts passing through my mind—up Boyleston Street, across Commonwealth, across Massachusetts Avenue. I finally found myself on Lansdowne Street, where I stopped and looked up to find myself by Fenway Park. I envisioned many home runs the great Ted Williams hit out onto this road and wistfully went back in memory. Tremendous nostalgic warmth feathered my entire body. The Boston Red Sox—they were my team! I remembered some of their good years, and like a falling set of dominoes set on edge, I came out of myself and into a playoff game in 1948 between the Cleveland Indians and the mighty Boston Red Sox. Oh! What a team we had! It was the greatest on paper and in conversation. There was Denny Galehouse, Bobby Doerr, Johnny Pesky, Manager Lou Boudreau, Dom DiMaggio, the great Ted Williams . . . come on . . . hit a home run . . . tie it up . . . get your hot dogs, hot dogs here . . . cold soda . . . ice cold beer here . . . strike him out, ya' bum . . . come on, take Galehouse out of there. . . .

I walked across the street, sat on a broken-down bench in front of two small, smelly, overflowing dumpsters and looked back at that baseball park—a quaint, homey, and historic classic institution. My thoughts went to Kathy, wondering how she was doing, then strangely wondering about her age at the time of the 1946 World Series—the Boston Red Sox versus the St. Louis Cardinals—was she three? No, one. And let's see how old was . . . My mind wandered back in time to the series; I could still hear Mel Allen's loud emotional cry, his voice in strong lament, "He held the ball, he held the ball! Johnny Pesky just froze—he held the ball!" And Enos Slaughter rounded third and never stopped!

I was snapped back into reality by the sound of a loud, low-flying helicopter. I raised my head, scanning from left to right over the building tops. Anxious to get back to Kathy, I started a fast-paced walk up Boyleston Street, where my eyes became fixed on a Roman Catholic Church set on the corner of Ipswich and Boyleston. Directly across the street was an ambulance in front of a building, with its siren screaming. The ambulance sped away, but my eyes remained fixed on that building; then I stopped in a coffee shop to get a soda and didn't question why. I seldom drank soda but now stood slowly sipping, mesmerized, gazing at the building as perspiration filtered through my clothes like paint through a sieve.

The mysterious feeling that swept over my entire body would not be understood for years to come, its significance locked inside for twenty years until our son took up residence there while attending college in Boston. It happened quite unexpectedly, yet the memory remains with me still. While attending his performance recital required for seniors, my car across the street from that same building was ticketed for a parking violation. I noticed the pink slip while approaching the vehicle after the recital, turned around, and removed it from under the wiper, then subconsciously looked up at the building; there with a smile, in beautiful silhouette shadowed from a dim street lamp was a vision, the image of his proud mother. And I heard her soft voice in my head saying, "Well done, son!" Oblivious to the first part of a question his sister asked, chills went down my spine, as I opened the doors for the family and we left.

Kathy's prognosis remained grim. The paradox of her test results baffled the staff. One doctor was noncommittal when I asked if the test of her kidneys had revealed anything. Symptoms she was experiencing were not compatible with the test results. The doctors were exasperated by not having more definitive answers. They never de-emphasized the seriousness of her condition, but good results from tests like the sedimentation and other blood tests were testimony to their frustrations. Even her white blood cell count, which had been extremely high in Hartford, causing worries about pneumonia, had improved. The tests not only baffled the doctors, but answers I got about lupus involvement also bewildered me to no end; specific questions posed revealed some contradiction with the original diagnosis and were subsequently recorded in several documents filed with her case. LC#87–86–44 stated: During This Hospitalization In NEDH, CNS Studies Failed To Reveal Lupus Involvement. [!]

Dr. *** in Hartford had minced no words when telling me

154

that Kathy definitely had lupus, her kidneys were deteriorating, and it was going to her brain! Totally inaccurate! Possibly negligent! But I was brought up to love, and to respect doctors; I had to be charitable and harbor no animosity.

Despite the many down and discouraging days, despite worry, suffering, and stress, neither Kathy nor I ever lost hope. We would talk for hours about the future and our family. We agreed to reach the number of children we had dreamed one romantic moonlit night at a "lookout" area by Long Island Sound. If not naturally, adoption was the answer. We became closer than ever, revealing the most insignificant things from our past. I confessed my love of parades, comic strips, and old-time funny books. She told me public speaking made her nervous, and although she was talkative she was really shy, which was not really a secret to me. Sometimes we would go to the chapel together and during service we would sit with our arms crossed, each sliding the opposite hand under the arm to a hidden clasp we maintained until the service was complete. On a few good days, I'd rationalize that if it was God's will to take her I had known a love that few will experience—my cup had runneth over!

For Thanksgiving the hospital prepared a fine turkey dinner for the staff, patients, and guests. Two of the nurses we had become friends with joined us, rather than spending it with others. We enjoyed an afternoon of good food, jokes, laughter, and sharing; Kathy was having an exceptional day. And when one of her doctors came in to check her, he observed she was fine, then sat down and joined us, also. The early 70's were still the me-me-me years—I've got to do my own thing years—and yet all around us we found compassionate people who put themselves last, not only this day but many days. However, this particular Thanksgiving was a great afternoon for which I gave special thanks to God; that day has never left me.

After dinner I presented the nurses with a heartfelt poem I had penned on the back of our dinner placemat; they read it together with teary eyes, and I later noticed it was hung on a bulletin board next to the nurses' desk. The verse sincerely expressed how I felt about the people at that facility and those who compassionately cared on a daily basis for my lovely wife. Many people read the "ode":

If asked to come some would come
If asked to help many would help
If asked to give a few would give
If asked to share several would share
If asked for an ear, most would listen
All because they were asked—that's sympathy.
You were neither summoned nor asked—
That's Love!

I'll Be Home for Christmas

The next three weeks were a combination of poor and stable days. Kathy's blood pressure was all over the place from a range of 172/90 to 230/130. I was with her one morning and noticed the familiar signs; I alerted a doctor in the hall that my wife was in a precarious state and would convulse unless she received an injection. He came in and questioned me about the signs while directing a nurse to prepare the shot. But before she returned, Kathy had had a seizure. He looked at me puzzled, shook his head, and administered the medication, still wondering what my signs were.

It became increasingly apparent to the medical personnel that my close proximity to the day-to-day trauma related to Kathy's illness had started to take a toll on my own health and personality. Once robust, athletic, and gregarious, I was now experiencing lethargy, vertigo, and introversion. In addition, I had lost thirteen pounds. Leaving Kathy's room one morning I was forced to sit down immediately, upon experiencing extreme dizziness. A nurse asked if I'd been eating on a regular basis; my negative response told her something had to be done. She left but quickly returned with a turkey sandwich, along with a lecture about the danger in neglecting my body, especially at this time. I vowed to work more on maintaining my health.

Christmas was coming, and we fervently hoped that Kathy could be home. I had discussed this with many of the nurses; their feelings wavered between optimistic and cautious. When I asked Drs. Breslin and Fernandez they said it was possible, for she had a few consistent days of stability. They both cautioned not to allow her to be overly involved in the frivolities of the holiday, for since they weaned her from most of the cortisone her body would not handle continual excitement. The ability of her own glands to produce the adrenaline hormone was far from

157

back to normal. They warmly agreed to contact Dr. Vecchiolla and update him on her case, and told me to make arrangements to leave the day after tomorrow, which was two days before Christmas.

I was filled with such elation—words could not describe the extent of joy in my heart. And the news had an immediate effect on Kathy. She wouldn't stop talking, telling every nurse and doctor who came into her room—"I'll be home for Christmas!" It was fun when we got home to relate the scenes—so many—of Kathy telling everyone she came in contact with—from the man who vacuumed the carpet to the lady who delivered her meals—about going home, and her schedule once she got there! I would intersperse her storytelling with Bing Crosby's rendition of "I'll Be Home for Christmas," so popular during World War II. Everyone was thrilled for her; it was the high point of her hospital stay, doing wonders for her inner spirit and well-being—how anxious she was to see the children. Tears would well up in her eyes when she mentioned it.

The last time Kathy had held Louie was when Mary and I brought him up to Boston in October. She had seen recent pictures of him and wanted to cut his long hair. What a day to remember! He had charmed the nurses and was the talk of her floor. But Kathy had not seen Nancy Anne since the day she left Saint Francis Hospital, and now she talked about her incessantly. To characterize her mood as ecstatic would be an understatement!

The morning I told her she would be home for the holiday, six doctors had come into her room for their weekly consultation. Before they could start with the questions, she made them listen to her story about seeing the kids and Christmas. It was a contagious moment parked in my memory. There were tales, laughter, and teasing from the doctors and sharp, jovial repartee from Kathy; then she would give—although very reserved—one of her famous cackle laughs. It was so good to see her like this; I made a wish in prayer that she soon would get well.

It had been five months since Kathy had stayed in her house overnight. Once home, she said it felt strange but good. I tried to make it as "Christmassy" as possible without extreme exertion on her part. We were invited to her mother's, but the visit could only be a few hours. Fearing Kathy would tire, it had been arranged to have the kids overnight with help from her mother, my sister, and my sisters-in-law. I surprised her with jewelry and some clothes. My family prepared a turkey dinner and I even opened a bottle of Asti Spumonti champagne—to recall memories of our reunion dinner a few short years prior. It was difficult to relax, for I had to monitor her blood pressure periodically as well as be cognizant of telltale signs. Kathleen was very happy, and it was a quiet, beautiful, intimate Christmas to celebrate the birth of Jesus Christ our Savior.

If the months spent in Saint Francis Hospital were exasperating and stressful, the days in Boston were hopeful, encouraging, and educational. Upon our return after Christmas I learned quite unexpectedly that Kathy's case was receiving widespread publicity throughout the medical circuit. The reason, conveyed to me by one of the doctors, was because they never had a patient so young and relatively "healthy" with blood pressure problems of this magnitude. It bothered me sometimes when I only wanted to be alone with my wife and suddenly an entourage of staff would come barging in. Likewise, a visiting Catholic priest from a local parish and the hospital chaplain were amazed by the number of doctors interrupting their brief stay.

For the most part, Kathleen handled the attention relatively well; sometimes she excelled in her relationship with these groups. I noticed her true personality taking charge with tremendous expansiveness as she communicated her feelings to these doctors while answering their questions. She was confident, with articulation that was exact and expressive; her thoughts were completed quickly, to the point that even Dale Carnegie would have been proud of her. Most of these sessions were time consuming, but light and jovial. They were certainly a training class for many medical students and interns. Kathy came out of most of them with flying colors; I was very proud of her.

We had no idea how well-known Kathy's case was until one night, as I sat in the hotel room saying my rosary, the phone rang. It was a woman from Los Angeles who introduced herself

159

as part of a prayer bank and then continued, telling me that she had heard of Kathy's case. She did not say how she knew, and I did not think to ask her source. She was calling to make me aware that prayers were being said for Kathy and me; she told me to "keep the faith," offering encouragement and urging me to pray, also. After fifteen minutes or so of conversation I told her how kind she was to call, then asked how she had gotten my number and why she had picked this time to call. She replied that the number, name, and time came to her spontaneously. I questioned her no further and we said goodbye.

Immediately after I hung up the phone, there was a knock on my door, and when I opened it a cleaning lady was standing back about five feet from the entrance. She said in a wonderful Irish brogue, "I hope—did I wake you now?" When I said she had-n't, she continued, "But you've been here so long that—that—I want you to know—I'd been prayin' for ye and ye wife now." I told her she was very kind and gracious. She stepped back a few more feet and said, "God will watch over—God is good. Keep the faith, please." She slowly turned and walked away.

I closed the door, and as I reached for my rosary beads on the chair, instead I was moved to pick up the nearby Bible, randomly opening it to Ecclesiastes: "Woe to him that is alone when he falleth, for he hath not another to help him up." I felt several emotions—pain and suffering, disappointment and loneliness from the illness of my wife and the separation from the kids. And yet so many good people surrounded us—some that didn't even know us, who cared and wanted to share our burden, to lend their ear, who wanted to feel our hurt, if it was possible! There were those who would cry for us and those who would pray for us, and those and those and those—those too numerous to count, too numerous to see, too numerous to remember—in all parts of this country and Canada.

Who were we to deserve such compassion? I mused. When it seemed that everything one read was highlighting the evil peo-ple in the world, on the contrary, we were experiencing the oppo-site. We found that people were basically good, generous, compassionate, kind, and loving. I didn't try to analyze every-thing that transpired that night as coincidence; rather I realized

160

people were giving of themselves totally for their need to help another human being. When Ralph Waldo Emerson's "make yourself necessary to someone" came to mind, I reflected that these people are making themselves "necessary" to us, and what a tremendous pick-me-up that is on down days; it was a grace which proved to be sustaining.

Though Dr. Breslin used every facet of scientific knowledge available to him, he couldn't consistently stabilize Kathy's blood pressure. Kathy, thinner than she had been, still looked bright and optimistic, despite bouts of difficulty in breathing due to pulmonary edema brought on by the unstable blood pressure. But since her sedimentation rate was very low, my curiosity drew me to ask Dr. Fernandez one day, point blank, if she did in fact have lupus. His answer so surprised me I immediately recorded it in my journal: "It depends on how she was initially treated in Hartford." My head dropped; my eyelids blinked. I had been expecting a positive affirmation of my question, and here this brilliant doctor was telling me that they were not sure! He continued, "Mr. LaCava, sometimes drugs can trigger these things . . . our main concern is the damage to her kidneys. We are having such a difficult time getting her to a safe level."

I had assumed from the "get-go" that when she first entered the hospital in Hartford Kathy did have lupus. At least most of the doctors there were telling me that lupus was her main problem. Now came this answer—we don't know—by one of the top lupus experts in the country, or world for that matter; and even more surprising was his implication that it was unlikely her problem, even if she was genetically inclined!

I hurried back to my hotel room, sat down on my bed, and tried to sort out the millions of thoughts flooding my brain! Had the astute senior nurse who urged me to "get her out of here, for they don't know what the hell they're doing," known more than she told me? If all of these things were true, or some of them, how often did it happen?; who was to take the responsibility for malpractice? Was it all the doctors? Was it some? Was it one? Was . . . Did . . . Should? I looked at my watch; two hours had passed so quickly and I was now besieged by an extraordinary sense of guilt. As I went to pour a glass of water from a pitcher left by the

161

maid, there was a knock on the door. "Telegram. Are you Mr. LaCava?" I nodded. "Please sign here," she said. After signing and retrieving a two-dollar bill (remember the two-dollar bill?) for a tip, I closed the door and slowly opened the message. It read as follows:

Dear Mr. LaCava,
This is to inform you that there is a world prayer bank offered in your wife's name. Trust in Him; continue to stand strong in His mercy.

Faith in Christ!

I never knew who sent it but suspect it was connected to the call from California. Whatever the origin, I was extremely moved.

Clandestinely Outside the Walls

The morning after Dr. Fernandez talked to me about his doubts of Kathy's lupus diagnosis, Dr. Breslin hit me with another blow. He voiced his frustration at the inability to regulate her blood pressure and admitted it was highly unlikely she would ever see her children grow up. I had slept very little the previous night and was shaky from lack of breakfast; so when he dropped this on me it was like being hit with a "sucker punch!" When I expressed faith in the Lord, he dropped his head and walked away. I went to the cafeteria like a zombie, took a cheeseburger, stuck it in a new machine called a microwave oven, and stood behind the white line required to reduce chances of absorbing radiation.

After Dr. Breslin informed me there was a remote chance Kathy would ever see her children mature to adulthood, desperation I had never before experienced engulfed me. It reminded me of an old radio program called *Mr. Anthony* that was aired back in late 40's and 50's, which presented the most desperate people and their problems in a public forum; the only difference between this program and today's television spectacles, where they dredge up the most pathetic cases and exploit the participants, was that *Mr. Anthony* participants actually received professional counseling on the air.

I sat in the cafeteria, tired and alone. I wasn't hungry but the nurses kept badgering me daily about the necessity of eating good meals with meat and vegetables, so I decided to get the dinner they were featuring that day of spinach, baked potato, and broiled chicken. I particularly remember that meal, for it was part of the scene around a springboard of an ensuing drama. Two nurse friends had come out of the line and asked if they could sit with me. As they ate "delicious" beef barley soup, I tried to stay with my "featured" meal. Our conversation varied, but ended with Kathy's condition and my desperation. I reiterated what Dr.

Breslin had said and told them that at this point I wanted to bring in the Shute Clinic from London, Ontario, Canada as consultants; I planned to make my feelings known to Dr. Breslin in the morning by asking him to contact the clinic.

The Shute Clinic was named after two brothers, Wilfred and Evan Shute. At that time they were using Vitamin E therapy with tremendous documented success on over 25,000 patients throughout the world with heart, kidney, and skin problems. Many had come from other clinics where they had been given little or no hope; many had been sent home to die.

During this conversation one of the nurses mentioned a doctor who practiced orthomolecular medicine and natural technique modality (Dr. Linus Pauling coined this term). His name was Dr. Louis Billotti, an M.D. educated at Harvard and a maverick in a sense. He had his own clinic in the Boston area and believed that the body had a remarkable ability to heal itself if left free from synthetic drugs and other harmful medicines and fortified itself with natural substances, good food, and exercise. It was said that he was having great success in this method of treatment until "conventional establishment" investigative pressures were forced upon him and his clinical license was revoked. The story was related by several people, that despite thousands of positive letters to the State affirming his competence, his clinical license was never reissued. He was ignominiously routed from standard medicine but continued practice at his home in Wakefield, Massachusetts for many years; although he was for the most part ostracized by his confreres, he helped literally thousands of people. It can now be said that he was years ahead of his time with vitamin therapy.

It so happened I had already heard of this doctor. He had helped a skating friend of mine who was arthritic from a young age; in addition, a local health store proprietor had mentioned him to me. In the future, I would see him myself for trouble with periodic bouts of asthma when I couldn't take the medications local doctors prescribed. After surprising the nurses that I also knew of Dr. Billotti, one suggested that despite her profession and not believing in miracle fixes, she felt I should give him a call to see if he could offer any insight into Kathy's problem or had anything at all to offer. At this point I was willing to listen to any advice, but pondered the severity of Kathy's condition and the improbability that the doctors would agree to call him as a consultant. Merely asking advice didn't make much sense because he had to see her to perform his own tests, and that would be impossible at this stage. As they were leaving, I thanked the nurses for their thoughtful suggestion.

While eating a dish of rice pudding for dessert, I started to mull over the rationale of calling Dr. Billotti. What could be lost? I could at least tell him the specifics of her case and ask if he thought he could help. If he had a positive response, I would inquire whether the Lahey Clinic would allow him to work with them. I knew in my heart that it was wishful thinking, but before I finished my pudding my decision was made—to call.

Upon returning to my room I immediately phoned Dr. Louis Billotti. A lengthy discussion of Kathy's case ensued, and the doctor agreed to see her. Even though his office was only a half hour away, it was important to advise him it would be almost impossible to get Kathy to his office without a nurse to help, but that I would do my best. His office hours were from nine A.M. to well past midnight, and the office was always packed with people from all parts of the country. His schedule was booked for five months, but once you got in he was very thorough; it wasn't rare for a person to wait for hours before seeing him. So before the conversation was ended, I made it clear to the doctor that Kathy was too weak to wait any length of time; he assured me that they would take her right in when we arrived, if I could get her there any day between six and seven P.M.

I hung up the phone and was anxious to tell the nurses of my decision to take Kathy to see Dr. Billotti. After actually running downstairs and through the tunnel, I arrived at the nurses' station to find the girls had left for the day, and when I asked about their hours the next day the new nurse told me she did not have that information. I went in to see Kathy. She was sleeping; her breathing was labored. I could see the artery in her neck pulsating heavily and hear the water in her lungs. I sat down and picked up a magazine, and shortly thereafter a doctor came in and took her blood pressure. He did it quickly and left; she never woke up during the process. An aide came to take her dinner tray. It was untouched. He looked at me, wondering what to do and I said to please leave her the banana. Kathy opened her eyes when she heard my voice and smiled, then said, "Lou, did you get a good meal?" She was still thinking of me, despite all her problems! When I broke the news about Dr. Billotti she just looked at me and said she'd do whatever I thought was best.

The nurse who made the suggestion was off for two days, and when she returned I gave her the news that I had called Dr. Billotti, telling her about the conversation that ensued. I admitted I wanted to take Kathy to see him but was concerned it would be difficult without the assistance of a nurse. She agreed to help me obtain some test records, get some specimens from her, and in addition, get her prepared the day we planned to go.

About four days after the conversation with Dr. Billotti, I took Kathy to his office. It was a tense journey. She was extremely weak and a little apprehensive, but handled it like a trooper. As I expected, the waiting room was jam-packed when we arrived—every chair and space was taken and people were standing. Observing Kathy's condition, several people rose to offer us their seats, and we gratefully accepted chairs closest to the office. I had called the doctor before we left to inform him we were on our way, and before we could sit down he poked his head from behind the door to say he would be right with us.

The examination and review of tests took a little over an hour. When he finished he took me in an outer room a distance from where Kathy was lying and said to me, "I don't know what they did in Hartford, but the one thing I am certain of is that she is a very sick girl." Then he went on to tell me about her condition, which was not encouraging. At the conclusion of his analysis I sullenly asked, "Dr. Billotti, is there any hope for Kathy's future?" Without hesitation he replied, "There is always hope, (and he emphasized the always) but I don't have a clinic here, and she needs careful daily attention." I cut in, asking what my alternative was, and he said, "These other substances have to be introduced one at a time and monitored by someone who has knowledge of their efficacy."

"Can I do it myself?"

"That could be dangerous," he admitted. When I asked if he would work with the Lahey Clinic as a consultant, he said it was highly unlikely they would do that, but he would always be available if he could be of assistance. He reiterated that we should not give up; there is always hope. I thanked him for his compassion, helped Kathy up, braced her carefully, and walked out.

A short time after the clandestine trip to see Dr. Billotti, I called and talked to a director at the Shute Clinic in London, Ontario, Canada. I outlined the situation and asked about their policy in hope the Shute Clinic would agree to come in as consultants. I spoke with a very gracious woman who asked me to detail Kathy's case, and when I finished she explained in very specific terms she was a nurse for many years and it was true the clinic had helped many people with vitamin E therapy, especially with heart and kidney problems. However, she phrased her words carefully so as not to impress me and cause my hopes to soar. I told her I was realistic yet had much faith. I also shared my feeling that if I didn't pursue all the options and alternatives available to this lady I certainly would be derelict in my responsibilities as a husband, and almost as importantly, as a human. She frankly addressed the fact that Kathy's doctors would have to sanction the Shute Clinic involvement with her case; a doctor would have to call the clinic and mail a report on her present condition before they could commit. She closed by saying, "In the meantime, I'll pray for your wife." This nurse didn't know us from Adam; still, she was going to pray for Kathy. . . .

The next morning I waited at the nurses' station for Dr. Breslin, who repeated his dire opinion of Kathy's future. This was the first time since Kathy was admitted that he talked at any length with me about the situation and her plight; usually it was a brief update and he would leave. When he finished I asked him if he would call in the Shute Clinic as consultants. He refused. Asking for his reason, he told me it would not do any good. I answered him, "Dr. Breslin, on the one hand you're telling me the prognosis for my wife's recovery is not promising, and on the other you won't call in another consultant. Isn't it a prerogative of the patient and loved ones to make decisions based on the facts presented to them?"

"Mr. LaCava, I've seen many patients with problems similar to your wife's. Most of the time we are able to regulate the blood pressure. With her we can't get it down consistently to safe levels; her heart is still enlarged and fluid is constantly building up in her lungs."

I cut in, "Well, isn't that all the more reason for me to request another approach, another avenue, maybe another method of treatment—to try to explore all the areas in science?"

I felt he wasn't too pleased with my insistence, and he said, "Your wife has a unique set of complex problems, and we don't know why. I doubt that vitamin E will help her blood pressure, but if you insist I will call Dr. Shute." I thanked him and we returned to Kathy's room, where we were surprised to find her sitting in a chair eating her breakfast. She looked up at the doctor, smiled, and said to him, as only she could, "Hi! You're certainly here bright and early—must have gotten up before breakfast." A rare smile cracked his face as he asked how she was feeling.

Kathy's daily medication was fixed. She was on diuretics, several types of blood pressure derivatives, and digoxin, which was an adjunct to strengthen the heart. She still was on a small amount of prednisone, as well as Phenobarbital for seizures. The daily number of pills she consumed compared to when she was in Hartford was down more than sixty-five percent. For the most part, Kathy tolerated the medication, had a good appetite, and was in a *status quo* mode, despite erratic blood pressure swings.

Sometime later Dr. Breslin briefed me on his conversation with Dr. Shute. He had been advised to put her on 1,600 International Units of D-alpha tocopheryl acetate, the one part of the vitamin E family that did work like a drug in high doses. Moreover, Dr. Shute said it had to come from a pharmacy in Michigan called Wilson and Wolfer, for their product was completely natural, (non-synthetic) and they knew the exact strength of this product. Dr. Breslin said the nurse would order it and have it sent to me in Connecticut and that Kathy could go home, for there was not much more that they could do for her in Boston. He demanded that I keep in close contact with him on a daily basis for a few weeks so that they could monitor her progress.

After the morning visit by the doctors, breakfast, clean-up, and packing, it was a tearful goodbye from nurses, aides, doctors, and staff in general. The drive home was very pleasant; Kathy was in a very positive mood. We talked about everything she had experienced in Boston, but most of all we talked about the kids. She was so anxious to see Louis Michael and Nancy Anne it monopolized her conversation until I persuaded her to try to rest. She had great plans for the kids; guidance was her objective. She wanted to offer them opportunities in sports, education, and the arts. She was so optimistic and loved them so dearly. After sleeping for a brief period she awoke talking about having more kids or adopting, asking my feelings on having kids from a different race and culture as part of our extended family. When I answered positively she smiled, saying she really didn't have to ask that question, knowing that would be my answer.

Before we reached the Connecticut line it was time to inform her I had hired a very competent full-time nurse. Sue was her name, and I was convinced Kathy would like her. I also threw into the mix at that time that a comfortable hospital bed was in the kitchen so she would not have to climb the stairs every day. In addition, I had purchased a stationary bicycle and placed it next to the bed, as Dr. Breslin wanted her to exercise a minute or two, twice daily, to help her adrenal glands start to function again on their own.

After wending our way through Wethersfield, as I turned into Pyquag Village a stressful, bizarre episode that had once occurred not far from there came to mind. Returning from work one day, immediately after passing the Highcrest School I was stopped by a policeman who informed me the area was surrounded by police officers—local and state officers, a special sharpshooter and, someone else said, the FBI. He explained that a man with a gun was holding a bank president in his house on Highcrest Road, demanding he go with him to open the bank. This man was serious. He wanted money—a lot of it. When I told the police that my wife was home alone with a small child, he had tried to comfort me, saying all the people inside Pyquag Village were notified to stay inside their houses with their doors locked. At the time there was only one way into the village, so I asked him if I could walk through some yards circumventing the line of action to get home to be with my wife and child. The sergeant said he had orders to keep everyone away, for they were not sure how many ruffians there were. Details were very sketchy, and I was concerned about the possibility of multiple perpetrators in the neighborhood.

While making a quick U-turn to go find a phone to caution Kathy to stay away from the windows, a special bulletin about the incident came across my car radio. Those who lived in Pyquag Village were concerned there were others in a getaway car, for reports had circulated about a strange vehicle parked inside; it proved to be just a rumor, but there was no way for us to know beforehand, causing much anxiety and mental anguish. After calling, I returned to find the area swarming with people, to the chagrin of the police. It was an extremely tense period until finally the man was taken into custody from the home.

Twenty minutes later the street was open for those who lived in the village to go home. It was like something you would see at the movies—excitement, action, and plenty of drama! Now, when I asked Kathy if she remembered that bizarre night of the hostage taking and the closed passage, and how I couldn't get home, she put her head on my shoulder and said, "Lou, it's so good to be home again!" I took her hand in mine and said to myself, let's hope and pray it turns out alright.

The adjustment time was brief, and Kathy settled in nicely with Sue. They liked each other immediately, and Kathy listened to and followed her instructions regarding medication, diet, and exercise to the letter. I brought Little Louie home within a week, and his mother's spirits soared. Family, friends, neighbors, priests, and nurses from St. Francis showered the household with much attention. There was an occasional visit by local doctors; at times it got hysterical. One nurse would cook extra and frequently bring special treats over for dinner. One remarkable dinner I will never forget was eggplant parmesan. Kathy had mentioned it was my favorite dish, so she surprised me one night with a huge pan full. It certainly made my day! Kathy continually remarked how lucky she was to have so many friends.

I was back at work again, and my life started to take on a semblance of normalcy. Sleep was through the night, which hadn't happened for over a year, and surprisingly I regained the thirteen pounds I had lost, plus two additional ones. The vitamin E arrived the day after we got home, but the nurse wanted to update Dr. Breslin before she started Kathy on it. She was given two (2) 800 international units of d-alpha tocopheryl acetate capsules of vitamin E at ten A.M. and through that night she got rid of 1000 cc's of fluid. The next morning, less then twenty-four hours after her first dose of vitamin E, her blood pressure was unbelievable. Sue repeated the test several times, then came down to my office, where I was finishing some calls and preparing my day. She very seriously said, "Mr. LaCava . . ."

I stopped her. "Sue, please call me Lou."

"I'm sorry. But I just wanted to tell you I don't think you'll need me much longer." I stood up and away from my chair. She continued, "I took Kathy's blood pressure, and it was incredibly low." I asked her how low. She said, "On the first reading it was 90/60, but I took it again and it was 90/50."

I exclaimed, "90/50!!!"

"Lou, I took it a third time and it was the same." I replied that I wouldn't stand Kathy up yet, until she had had some breakfast. Sue said she had kept asking for cranberry juice and had drunk two eight-ounce glasses. I conjectured that she was craving potassium because of the diuretics. Sue said she was going to wait and see what developed in the next few days before contacting the doctor.

We all were quite pleased with her blood pressure's return to normal. When the nurse notified the doctors in Boston they were surprised, but cautiously optimistic. I was hopeful that she had started on the road to full recovery but was realistic enough to understand the harm that six months of drugs had done to her kidneys. I also remembered that Dr. Shute had said in one of his books that vitamin E had a quick and immediate effect on the eradication of scar tissue and other debris in the kidney, but that E would not repair damaged or sick kidneys. We knew from these recent changes that it cleared out dead cells and debris to make a passage for her kidneys to work in eliminating fluid that had backed up in her lungs and other tissue. The question remained whether the kidneys, now cleansed of extraneous residue, would be able to heal, or were they irreparably damaged?

Extremely delighted by the turn of events with Kathy's health, I became paradoxically cautious in the days that followed. I became justifiably dismayed when made privy to a report sent to the Saint Francis Hospital in October of 1972, in care of Dr. Vecchiolla, from Dr. Fernandez at the Lahey Clinic:

. . . THAT HER KIDNEY BIOPSY WAS MORE REPRESENTATIVE OF HYPERTENSION THAN LUPUS. THAT THE STEROIDS SHOULD BE KEPT AT THE MINIMUM DOSE NECESSARY TO CONTROL EVIDENCE THERE MIGHT BE OF LUPUS ACTIVITY. I PERSONALLY FEEL THAT IN HER CASE THE LOWER THE DOSE OF STEROID THAT SHE CAN GET BY WITH THE BETTER IT WILL BE, AS FAR AS EASE IN MANAGEMENT OF HER RENAL AND HYPERTENSIVE PROBLEMS.

Here was the documented proof—something I believed from the onset, that lupus was not Kathy's problem! I read the copy of this report over several times, dismayed. In my mind's eye came the four words of the Hippocratic oath—first do no harm!

Over the next two weeks Kathy's condition improved immeasurably. Sue had her out for a walk, she was eating like the Kathy I knew—she loved good food and every imaginable spice there was. And one day she even asked for her books from the interior decorating courses she had been taking before she got sick—it was a miracle she felt so good and enthused enough to study. She was doing so well on the vitamin E therapy that other vitamins were added to her diet, but after several days minor changes became evident; we questioned if the added vitamins were causing the kidneys to overwork and whether they should be discontinued.

During the three-day period Kathy was on the added vitamins her blood pressure elevated a little but then had returned to below normal, enough that the doctors lowered her blood pressure medication. This stability continued for a brief period, and then she started to feel lethargic and fatigued, sleeping more than usual. I became concerned when her pressure rose again for no apparent reason on a few nights. This continued for a few days, but the strange thing was that it usually started to elevate at night.

One time after the nurse left for the day, Kathy asked if she could sleep in her own bed with me. I said to her warmly that I felt that she should have the benefit of the hospital bed, as her head should be elevated to help her breathing and also because the oxygen tank was too cumbersome to bring upstairs. She was good in debate, and against my better judgment I carried her upstairs to her own suite. After I carefully placed her on the bed she just sat there, looking around. It was twilight, the sun still hovered low on a brisk spring evening, inspiring her to say, "Lou, please open the drapes to the balcony doors. I want to look out to Dolly's house." I opened the drapes on the large slider; then she asked me to open the door. I argued that it was too cold to do that, but she insisted that she would be fine, she only wanted it open for a few minutes. Reluctantly, I acceded to her wishes.

She slept very little that night, as did I. In the morning I asked her how she felt, as a few telltale signs concerned me. When she was slow to respond to my question I went down to get the apparatus to check her pressure. Upon my return, she was laboring to breathe. I immediately sat her up and the labored breathing subsided, but I could hear gurgles, indicating a return of the pulmonary edema. Indeed, her blood pressure registered 210/120. Very concerned, I decided to contact the doctor, but before reaching the phone Kathy was in seizure. I called for an ambulance and we took her to St. Francis Hospital.

Upon placing a call to the Shute Clinic I was fortunate to talk with Dr. Evan Shute himself. After briefing him on Kathy's condition and setback, I asked if it would help to raise the dosage of the vitamin E. He informed me she was on the maximum dose for her diagnosis; any added strength was a waste of money and time, as it wouldn't increase efficacy of the treatment. He also repeated what I had read in his book: Vitamin E therapy clears scar tissue from the kidneys and helps the heart, but does not correct damaged or sick kidneys. He was very professional and compassionate.

I was now receiving advice from well-meaning people and friends from all walks of life. I would get calls from nurses, doctor friends, skaters, relatives, clergy, etc. Some told me of a specific clinic or special treatment; some would urge me to have Kathy eat a lot of fruit. Another would talk about acupuncture and how it helped someone they knew who had kidney disease, and someone else would educate me about homeopathy, and on and on and on. I would listen politely and thank them for caring. Each person really felt bad and wanted to help; if they took the time to call it indicated their sincerity, but I had to make decisions based on some scientific background. I was aware that medicine was not an exact science; nevertheless, there would be no more experimentation.

I did agree, however, to listen to a suggestion by a friend's doctor from a clinic in the South where they worked not only with drugs but also with a holistic approach. The doctors were M.D.s and D.O.s and introduced natural substances individually, carefully monitoring progress on a daily basis.

Supposedly it involved a long process that had proved extremely successful with many maladies, and they had an exceptional record with people who were deemed terminal, discarded by other clinics. I had read enough to be well versed about it; yet I was not naive and gullible. The drawback was that I had to fly Kathleen there, but no airline would take the responsibility—this was a policy of five carriers that I called who flew that route. The other alternative was to lease a private jet, but before I would agree to such a drastic measure I wanted a doctor from the clinic to examine her.

A week after Kathy came back home from St. Francis Hospital I flew a doctor in from the clinic. I picked him up at the airport and briefed him as much as I could on her case. During the process of conveying the essentials to him, he asked how they treated her on the first admission to the hospital—it seemed every doctor was concerned with the initial treatment. This briefing was carefully worded so as to leave out any emotional bias, while including everything that was germane; the doctor listened intently, then said he would need her charts from both hospitals.

During the examination of Kathy he checked her heart, checked her temperature three times, looked at her tongue several times, took some blood, and read her blood pressure, which was rather high. He then did a few pressure points on her, which hurt one time. After he finished, the nurse asked him what he had done. The response was he wanted to bring her pressure down and listen to her heart again. When the nurse questioned what science he was using, he tersely replied, "Take her pressure." It was normal. Sue shook her head. The doctor checked her heart and found it had a strong beat, questioning if she was on vitamin E. This bothered me, for he was given this information on the ride from the airport. He completed the examination with only one negative statement before this one—he said he didn't like what he heard in the lungs, and he asked to use the phone.

After completing his call, the doctor asked to talk to the nurse and me in private. The words that rolled off his lips must have been taken from the same script that Dr. Billotti and Dr. Fernandez had used: "She is a very sick girl. But there is always hope." He added that if we could get her to the clinic they would do everything they could to help. He stressed there were no guarantees and it would be a slow process. His sincerity may have been noble; he seemed very knowledgeable and anxious to try a new modality. But he impressed me as being arrogant and involved in his own science. I thanked him for making the trip, telling him we would discuss it with local doctors and call the clinic to schedule a room. In the back of my mind I first wanted to talk to Boston. Besides, it would take two to three weeks to secure a private jet.

Sue, Kathleen, and I had a lengthy discussion on the advantages and disadvantages of pursuing this new approach. They both were willing; confidentially, I was skeptical. There was no way that I was going to jump into something helter-skelter; for me to move her that distance required advice and positive data on the clinic's competence. This was my logical background speaking. The doctors in Boston were professional, assiduous, and compassionate; I trusted them implicitly. Now I didn't want to make a rash move!

I pondered and agonized over this decision for three days. In my heart I wanted to give Kathy every available option where there was a flicker of light on the candle of hope. Conversely, leaning to the extreme could result in discouragement and total despair. Beyond that, my head was full; all days were coming together; the situation became surreal—a nightmare that was unfathomable had taken over our lives.

Four days after the doctor examined Kathy a decision was reached to transfer her to the clinic. When I got home from work I called my brother-in-law, who had some connections at Pratt and Whitney, hoping he could secure a jet for me as soon as possible. He called back the next day to inform me that the earliest plane available was three days hence; it would cost $6,000, for they had to fly with two pilots, which was federal law. I asked him to schedule the plane and said a check for payment would be there in the morning.

The next day Sue was instructed to prepare Kathy for this trip and to pack herself a bag, as it was apparent we would spend at least several days in that city—there was no way to know how long. I talked to Kathy that night, and she was willing do anything that we thought would help. Her optimism, her hope, her enthusiasm had never left since she first entered the hospital pregnant with a headache. She certainly had been through Hell and her will to fight on never ceased to amaze me! Anything I thought would help she said she was willing to try. The words made me swallow hard; I kissed her on the forehead and went to bed.

I tossed and turned. The decision to go had been made, but there were a million thoughts rummaging through my head—doubts, questions, but no answers. I fell into a deep sleep and awoke at three A.M. heavily perspiring; a voice inside my head was telling me—Lou, don't take her to that clinic, and it repeated—Lou, you can't take her to that clinic. I jumped up out of bed and went into the bathroom; the sweat was pouring off my body, which was eerie, for I never perspired heavily. The voice continued for over an hour and when it finally ceased I fell back into a deep sleep.

I awoke at six A.M., very rested with regained lucidity and vigor. Jumping up and out of bed, I hurried down to check Kathy, who was sleeping peacefully, returned to my room and went to the dresser to brush my hair. It was there that I saw a message on the pad I kept for jotting down reminders or a poetry inspiration. I didn't recall writing it, and spooky enough, it didn't look like my handwriting. But it read, "This is so bizarre, Lou. You can't bring her to that clinic."

If it was God's will to call my wife home at an early age, no matter what was done here or wherever we took her would not help. I turned it over to Him! Sue was happy I had changed my mind, for she had some misgivings. She was a fine nurse, dedicated, loyal, and professional. She was very experienced in many areas of her profession, having even served on a medical ship. I held the deepest respect for her—she was like one of the family.

Following the decision not to go south to the clinic, our lives started to take on a whole new dimension. I lived every day thanking God for another day with Kathy, sharing and giving totally the love that was known the first time my eyes fell upon her—a brief four years past. Our relationship became fused in ways never imaginable. We were so closely grafted that thoughts became one and the same; when together we would often be thinking alike. When I was at work and put in a call to her, she would say she had just been thinking of me and the phone rang. Occasionally in the afternoon she would say to Sue, "Lou will be here soon." I very seldom came home in the afternoon—and before Sue could question if she was expecting me, the door would open and there I was.

I wanted Kathy to spend time with Nancy Anne, so I had arranged with my sister Rose, who was caring for Nancy, to bring her to the house; but it was important that Kathy was having a good day before this event. So on one Monday morning it happened; Kathy was having an exceptionally fine period of well-being—her blood pressure and breathing were normal, her spirits were excellent, and she mysteriously kept asking for Nancy Anne. Unbeknownst to her, Rosemarie was, indeed, on her way over with Nancy. It was eerily strange, for every once in a while Little Louie would go over to where his mother was sitting and say something about his sister. Kathy would look at him lovingly and say, "You're the sweetest little boy in the whole wide world." He would smile

177

and then repeat what he had said before. This time his mother would answer, "Yes, your sister is coming over now!" How she knew that I can't explain, for neither Sue nor I had forewarned her about Nancy Anne's visit. And when the bell rang and the door opened, we were all surprised when Kathy said, "Well, it's about time. What took you so long? We've been waiting for you!!" And then one of her wonderful, famous laughs filled the air.

Nancy Anne was precociously learning to walk, and when Kathy chided Rose jokingly about being the one to experience Nancy Anne taking her first step, everyone broke up hysterically. Nancy Anne was a bit shy and sadly didn't have a clue how the author was related. Now and then I would catch her taking a cautious look in my direction, as if to think this guy looks awfully familiar. When I would smile at her she would turn her head and run for her Aunt Rose and Uncle Paul. Taking care of her mother and the responsibilities of my job left me very little time to visit her in seven months, and although she seemed to know who her mother was, she felt alienated from her father. It made me extremely sad that she didn't know who I was, but how could one blame her for the lack of positive response toward a dad she had rarely seen?

Over the next few months Kathy's health was like a pendulum. It would oscillate from good days to bad, scary ones. She would have days with an abundance of energy, and other days of extreme lethargy. There were times where she would not even take a nap, and other times where she would sleep all day. Her appetite was spotty. She would crave something exotic, or conversely wouldn't eat at all. From the start she was in and out of hospitals, so often that I forgot the number of times. But all through the maelstrom she was a fighter—a soldier who never lost faith in God. Her optimism and cheer were something to behold. Even when I was having a down and depressing day, to see her like that could only lift me up. I admired, respected, and deeply loved her. And above that, I was very proud of her—she was truly my hero!

August 14, 1973—10:20 A.M.

June and July sales slacked way off, but I had missed so much time from work I was still trying to catch up. My day would start at six and end at six. My employees were very understanding if I was short at times, and they all co-operated to keep the job running smoothly when I was absent. Meanwhile, I made the effort to give as much time to my family as humanly possible. I was watching over Kathy plus attending to Little Louie's needs; in addition, I was trying to visit Nancy Anne more frequently.

Kathy went into the hospital again for what we hoped would be a short stay, although, seeing some definite changes in her health, I was realistic about how much her body could endure. I would visit her each morning before work, at lunchtime, and would stay at night for two, three, or four hours. Little Louie was back with Aunt Mary and Uncle Tony. As there was no need for Sue at this time I told her I would call when Kathy returned home.

One morning I went in and found Kathy in terrible pain after having had blood drawn. Upon inquiring what had transpired, the head nurse told me the person taking the blood was a novice. My immediate concern was why they would allow a student to draw blood from someone who is so sick and whose arms had been pierced so many times. This was just not the situation for practicing. After telling her it was beyond my comprehension how this was allowed to happen, she admitted it was a mistake and apologized while applying ice to Kathy's arm to alleviate the swelling. This was a different floor than the last time; most of the nurses, although professional, were unfamiliar with Kathy's case. A few became friendly with her, and occasionally someone from the maternity area would come by.

For some reason I can't explain, one particular day I left work at eleven A.M. instead of noon to visit her. When I arrived she was sitting up in bed; her appearance was bright and shining, and she had a happy smile on her face. Actually, she was radiant and glowing—absolutely stunning—something I had not seen for such a long time. My heart was filled with joy. As I walked over to her she said, "You're late. I've been waiting for you for a half hour." I was flabbergasted—even her voice sounded different.

I answered deliberately, "Kathy, you know I always come at noon."

"Yeah," she said, "but I've been sending you messages since I woke up. Come here and sit down—I have something to ask you."

I went over and sat on the bed; she took my hand and I teasingly apologized for being late—then she started. "Lou, I want you to promise me two things."

I responded, "Kathy, two things again?" But she was very serious.

"First, I want you to take my diary and write a note to thank everyone for taking such good care of me, and also," she said, hesitating for a few seconds, looking in my eyes, and emphasizing "for being so kind."

Ordinarily a person can take in, absorb, and process 400 words a minute when someone is talking to them, while we can only speak about 200 words per minute. There is usually a lot of time and space to think of other things in between, even as others speak. But I was wondering why she was telling me this; we had continually thanked people—nurses, doctors, orderlies, aides and staff. But then I remembered her telling Father Crawford when he visited her many months now passed that when she got well she wanted to send a personal note to all the people who took care of her. My heart sank, anticipating what was coming next.

And then she said it: "Lou, I want you to get married again." I was stunned—shocked—and devastated!!!!!

"Kathleen! What are you telling me?"

"Lou, I'm going to die."

The words rolled off her lips clearly, steadily and eloquently as I sat there in shock. I would never have expected this to come from her. Here was this pillar of strength—never with a com-

180

plaint, never a cry in anguish—this model of endurance, patience, and perseverance, my Joan of Arc, always able to tolerate pain and suffering and injustice, and now she was giving up—giving in. I couldn't believe what I was hearing. She fought the good fight and now was cashing in the leftover chips!

"Lou, I want our kids to have a mother. I want our dreams to be yours and their new mother's dreams. The five kids we planned can still be a reality, and I'm as sure as my name is Kathleen that these—these kids, and their mother will receive all the love you gave me, and more, and that's a lot of love!"

All the time she was talking her face was resplendently fixed, each word was chosen carefully, slowly, and meaningfully. She knew what she wanted to say. Her voice was clear and strong, and as lonely and empty as I felt, I marveled at her composure. During this monologue it appeared as if someone was talking through her.

I couldn't respond. She looked at me and continued. "Lou, I didn't want to hurt you. You've been through so much, but something inside inspired me to share this with you. I'm . . . I'm not quitting. Lou, won't you say something to me?"

I swallowed hard and tried to talk, but nothing came out. An aide came in to ask Kathy if she wanted the water pitcher refilled; she quickly left when Kathy answered no. Finally, and emotionally, I chastised God. "Kathleen! You're not going to die. How can this romance and our dreams end? This world, this life," I continued, my voice trailing off almost to a whisper, "won't make a bit of sense if you die." She cut in after listening intently for a moment to the last part of my sentence.

Gripping my hand tighter, she pleaded for me to look at her, but I couldn't. "Lou, why can't I die?" There was no answer I could give to that question, nor did she give me a chance.

"Kings and queens die, Popes die, great people die. Who am I to stay alive or to say I shouldn't die? If we believe in God we have to accept His will." I thought while she continued that this was the crux of the story—"WAS it His will?"

"Lou, you have done everything imaginable—you have certainly proved your love for me and upheld your vows—you've been wonderful. It's not for us to question His will. There is meaning in everything, especially what God ordains, and there will be meaning for you after I'm gone." Her words had broken me down to where I was utterly speechless. But she continued, "Lou, didn't a priest tell you one night in Boston that some day this will all make sense? Please don't say life will make no sense if I die; every time you pick up Little Louie and swing him over your head and through your legs—that's sense. Every time you pick up Nancy Anne and hug and kiss her—that's sense. Every time they talk and smile and cry—that's sense. Lou, can't you see, God has left you a legacy—is that not sense? He has left you our history. I want our kids to have a mother, Lou. Will you promise me that? And Lou, let it be recorded in our history book that everyone tried. Lou, look at me please. Lou, please don't leave."

I could neither look at her nor respond. I released my hand from hers and left. I walked out into the hall by the nurses' station and turned the corner toward the lounge. When I walked in, the television set was on and I went over to turn it off but stopped, for there was a rerun just ending from the series *Life is Worth Living* with Bishop Fulton J. Sheen, and he was reciting:

I slipped His fingers, I escaped His feet,
I ran and hid, for Him I feared to meet.
One day I passed Him, fettered on a Tree,
He turned his head, looked, and beckoned me.

Neither by speed, nor strength could He prevail.
Each hand and foot was pinioned by a nail.
He could not run and clasp me if He tried,
But with His eye, He bade me reach his side.
For pity's sake, thought I, I'll set you free.
"Nay—hold this cross," He said, "and follow Me.

"This yoke is easy, this burden light,
Not hard or grievous if you wear it tight."
So did I follow Him Who could not move,
An uncaught captive in the hands of Love.

Turning the television off, I felt terribly alone. Shame and guilt overwhelmed me for feeling sorry for myself and challenging God's Will.

Upon arriving home that evening I pulled out a book *Life Is Worth Living* of Bishop Sheen's television shows and found the lecture that poem had come from. It was entitled *Pain and Suffering!* Desperately alone with my thoughts, brokenhearted and drained, I relived in awe Kathy's bravery that I had experienced that day. I was proud of the gumption she possessed in telling me what she thought was so essential to life. I had never heard her more poetic nor so articulate. The word "sense" clung to me like the ubiquitous pricker in a blackberry patch and remained in me for years until I could garner enough strength—courage to drag the meaning out which was inspired by Kathleen's answer to my disheartening retort when she told me she was going to die:

Sense (prologue)
never flee from dreams
afraid they may come true
every heart deep inside
waits God's latent wish
for you . . .

yes, sometimes dreams get shattered
deep in suffered pain
but there can never be a rainbow
without first the touch of rain.

Sense
every time you hug your little boy—that's sense
every time you kiss your little girl—that's sense
sense is a thousand times a thousands times:
in a young one's smile
a child's first step
its garbled first word

sense is the glitter of all the stars in the heaven
shooting barbs of mysteries and intrigue

sense is the first tender spring blossom—flower in sunshine
caressed by the brilliance of a butterfly, the elusive firefly

sense is the fragrance of a rose
the stature of a lily,
and the beauty of a daffodil.

sense
is helping others
the down-trodden
the sick
feeding the poor
holding the hand of the aged
listening to a lonely soul.

sense
is good morning
please
thank you
encouragement (you did great!)

sense: sense: sense:
is sincerity
sympathy
perseverance
patience

Sense is hope
Sense is faith
Sense, above all, is Love!

Goodbye, My Sweet Princess

Ten minutes had passed when two nuns came into the lounge. I was in deep thought and meditation. One of them looked over and asked if everything was all right. I nodded affirmatively, but they could tell by my facial expression there was pain. I picked up a magazine and was thumbing through it when a tall, very thin nurse I had never seen before came in and asked if I was Lou LaCava. She walked over, put her hand on my shoulder and said, "Your wife is very upset and asked the desk to please check if you were still here. She wants you to come back to her room." As she turned to leave I looked up, and on her uniform was a name tag—Betty! I hurried back to Kathy.

On Monday, 14 August 1973, a few days after Kathy asked me to promise her I would get married again, a terrible sense of discouragement engulfed me because of her declining health. I decided to make my visits to the hospital earlier in the morning, affording me more time to spend with her when she was the happiest. Today she looked tired, drawn, and drowsy; nevertheless, she quickly recognized me when I got a few feet from the bed. Despite her listlessness and difficulty breathing, we carried on spurts of conversation, mainly about the kids. Every time she asked a question about our precious little girl her face became as radiant as the sun, and I would think to myself there's the Kathy I once knew. Her breath control failed when she attempted to say how much she loved the kids and me; in order to be sure she had expressed her emotions to her satisfaction, with great effort she would repeat herself twice. I reciprocated her feelings, saying she knew I'd loved her from the first time she walked into the restaurant. But I was preoccupied, for her breathing was very labored.

She dozed off again. Her breakfast tray, untouched, was still on the swivel table when the kitchen aide came to collect it. Seeing that Kathy was asleep, she looked at me, unsure of what to do. I motioned to take it, but gestured with my finger to my lips to do so quietly; but when the aide came over to pick it up, Kathy opened her eyes and mumbled, "Lou, please leave it." She fell back to sleep after a few minutes, and I went to the nurses' station to ask how long she had been in this state of drowsiness. They said it had been for a few days. But this was the first time I'd seen her doze on and off with such regularity. I had faithfully been visiting her three times a day and had never observed her in this state of lassitude before. The supervisor informed me that her kidneys were not doing the job of cleansing her blood thoroughly, which caused her present state. I returned to find her still sleeping, with the breakfast still untouched.

Heavy equipment on the job site forced me to return to work. As I turned to leave, Kathy stopped me, reached out and touched my hand, squeezed it tight, and just as quickly fell back to sleep. It was seven-thirty A.M. Before departing the hospital I asked the head nurse, Jean, to please tell Kathy when she awoke that I would be back about one o'clock.

I was unable to get back to the trailer office until late morning because it was extremely busy on site. I had just finished making a call to the town hall requesting an inspection and was in the process of another call when I noticed my brother Peter's car pull into the parking space outside. Peter was district manager, on the road visiting several sites a day and always in touch with the main office. His presence was rather surprising, for rarely did he visit my development. Curious, I quickly walked out to meet him. The look on his face as he got out of his car told me that something was very wrong. We met about halfway near the back of my office when he looked up at me and soberly spoke. "Lou, the office was trying to reach you." Before he had a chance to finish, something inside compelled me to ask, "Pete, did Kathy die?" He shook his head I'm sorry and mournfully said Dr. Vecchiolla was trying to reach me.

I spoke with Dr. Vecchiolla, who stoically informed me (as he must have done hundreds of times before) that Kathy had died at ten-twenty A.M. I asked him about the official cause of death—what was on the death certificate? He responded that the immediate cause was uremia! He then asked me the following: "Lou, they want to do a postmortem but need your release."

I responded in a calm, sorrowful monotone, "Dr. Vecchiolla, I'll leave that decision to you, but keep in mind that a lot has transpired in my wife's case that you are well aware of. It goes without saying, far beyond contradictions between hospitals and doctors, and I know things can be simplified on the death certificate by stamping in uremia . . . you have to do what you have to do. If they want to perform an autopsy, well and good, but if they don't find any systemic deterioration . . . a clue or involvement that this was caused by so-called lupus, Hell will have no fury compared to what I . . ."

I then reiterated, "Sir, there are a lot of good doctors that were assiduously dedicated to Kathy in her illness, and I hold great esteem and a lot of admiration for many and don't have it in my heart for Kathy's death to be the indictment of all doctors. Why don't you let me just put her in the ground?"

He laconically replied "Fine," without making an effort to challenge my thinking. I had a strong feeling that the doctor, deep inside, acknowledged big mistakes dealing with Kathy's case—erroneous, flagrant screw-ups—and held regrets about ever bringing in the "expert" doctor. This was only my gut feeling and supposition. He never offered his sorrow, a condolence, or a bit of remorse. He was cold and unfeeling. And they never did the autopsy.

I started to lament that I had never left Kathy's side for one year, yet I wasn't there to hold her hand while she died. What merit was there in being with her daily if I wasn't there at the end? Word quickly spread throughout the condominium site where I was now working that Lou's young wife had died. As I drove to one of the buildings to tell the foreman he would be in charge for an indefinite period of time, I noticed several small groups—employees and residents huddled together in deep discussion. I talked to my foreman, accepted sympathy from several workers, and left immediately for the hospital.

When I walked by the nurses' station it was so quiet you could hear the squeak from the rubber sole of my shoes on the freshly waxed floor. Nurses were congregating around the main station looking busy. An intern poked his head out of an adjacent office to ask about a patient's medication. I walked into Kathy's room, where the curtain was pulled around her bed. How often had I seen the curtain like that! But this time it was different—there would be no doctors, no nurses, no one taking blood, no one poking her, no one—no one . . . this time she would be alone. I swished the curtain aside and there she was, lying so peacefully, still a vision of loveliness. I said, "Kathleen, no more pain, no more hurt, no more suffering, no more disappointment—no more . . ." I stared at her lovely face and said, "I'm sorry, Lady Kathleen, I let you down! I let you down. . . . Not only was I not forceful enough in making the right decisions on your behalf, but I was conspicuously absent to hold your hand when you died. . . . I failed you miserably!" Heartbroken and in complete despair I leaned over, kissed her, and whispered unpoetically, "Lady Kathleen, I wasn't worthy for the likes of you!"

Standing there with glassy eyes fixed on this beautiful woman, I quickly looked back in time. Horrible guilt engulfed me, and I laid the blame on my shoulders for all her pain and all her suffering, for all the apprehension that she experienced and endured in the last year, and finally blamed myself for her death. Why! Why! Why! I took her hand and it was still warm, and I thought, wait a minute—she's not dead—maybe it's a miracle. Bodies dead don't stay warm. Why would God bring us together and tear us asunder? You blasphemed! Don't blame God. He had nothing to do with this. This is human frailty, human pride, human ego! Why blame God?! He gave us free will to do good . . . do right, and sometimes we don't perform! So many unanswered questions were now so irrelevant.

My eyes never left her face, but I could see the stages of our lives happily unfolding together; shadowed on the beige wall above her head was an image of a dove: "There's my wife, there's my wife, some day she'll be my wife. Her name is Kathleen Walsh and she's engaged and her brother's a cop, is there anything else you want to know, Lou?! What if a boy wants to ask you out to lunch . . . you work all the time; I don't work on Wednesdays! Tomorrow I want to take you to New York's Lincoln Center to see an opera. That sounds good! How many boys have told you you have beautiful eyes? I like the way you talk! Lou, did you know

Elvis was here? Lou, today I found out that we're going to have a baby!

A cold chill brailed my skin and I said, "Lord, take my beloved into your kingdom; she was good; she has suffered so," and then I said a prayer. A young nurse I didn't recognize came inside the curtain, put her arm around my waist, and held a brief silent vigil with me. When I turned my eyes away from Kathy momentarily, she nudged me gently outside the curtain and from the room, then walked away into the crowd of nurses. Curious, I later asked her name and was told she didn't work on that floor. I thought of compassion and the Good Samaritan, wondering what element possessed the heart to make a person so kind. I wanted to thank her personally, but unfortunately I would not see her again.

I went down to the lounge and sat thinking of what had transpired at this hospital in a little over one year, then left abruptly when some talkative employees came in to have their break. Walking out into the hallway and to the exit, I made my way down a side stairway onto the sidewalk and shuffled a short distance before a policeman stopped me as I started to cross over to Collins Street, where my car was parked. An ambulance with its flashing lights and wailing siren came speeding down the car-lined street, swiftly turning into the emergency entrance circle. A girl and two burly men dressed in white exited the vehicle with dispatch, opened the rear doors, and carefully rolled out a gurney while a doctor and a nurse hurried out to meet them. As they adjusted the stretcher around to make the trek toward the entrance, I caught a glimpse of the person on the gurney and did a double take. It was a very attractive young girl with dark hair, eyes closed, one arm tied flat, attached to an IV. In my despondency, through blurry eyes, it was Lady Kathleen! The policeman waved on those of us who were stopped; I stood there, mesmerized momentarily; the policeman looked at me and quietly repeated, "Sir, you can cross now." I crossed over, walked to my car, and drove away—I never looked back—heartbroken, fatigued, and emotionally drained, saying to myself, "I'll never step foot into that hospital again." I never remembered that trip back home!

The Funeral

The initial scene at D'Esopo's Funeral Home, owned by the author's cousin, transpired without small talk. The type of casket, how long the wake would be, the time of the Mass and burial were all fixed in my mind. We had decided to delay the wake for an extra day to give family, relatives, and business associates out of state the opportunity to attend—but only if I could reduce the wake from two days, morning and evening, to one day with combined hours.

Twenty-four hours after Kathy's death, calls and messages started to arrive at the office, Saint Francis Hospital, the Deaconess Hospital, our house—from friends, nurses, doctors, church groups, the Lupus Foundation, the Heart Association, the Kidney Foundation. Messages of condolence, messages of sorrow, messages of hope, messages of prayer, poems, and even a letter from an old girlfriend—such expressions continued for months!

But before the obituary was sent in for publication we decided to extend the hours, anticipating large crowds. I arrived very early in the afternoon, hoping to spend some time alone with Kathleen. When I walked into the parlor I was overjoyed at the sight—and this image is still with me today—all four walls were hidden from floor to ceiling with beautiful arrays of flowers—every type of arrangement imaginable! The combination was a gigantic fragrance of God's sweet gifts. I knew Kathy would have been pleased, for she loved flowers. Carefully examining the bouquets, I momentarily felt guilty about once having reprimanded her for cutting through poly-weed-prohibitor in a birch tree planting area on our lot to plant flowers she loved so much. I would tolerate all the weeds in the world to have her back again, I mused!

I walked slowly toward the open casket, then just stood and

looked at her. She was outfitted in a new dress—white with light green highlights, and a narrow rose colored with plain augmented sequins. Green was one of her favorite colors. Her dark thick hair was set like I had seen it many times before, to the side, back and off her shoulders. She looked so elegant, so majestic, so regal. I placed my hand on hers, now folded and graced with rosary beads. Her face was so angelic it brought a feeling of tranquility to me. The longer I gazed at her image it appeared as if she was smiling to me with a message of her own—Lou, it's alright, Lou it's alright, I'm happy now.

I knelt and prayed the rosary alone, unlike before, the way we used to say it many times together. Every bead a prayer, ten to make a decade, five to make a rosary, repeated three times to offer spiritual power. Hail Marys rolled off my lips into the quiet and stillness of the moment, uniting us for the last time. A romance that fortuitously ignited on a bright March day, four and a half years ago, was ended in the autumn with a tear. Gone was the pretty girl with the pleasant smile. Gone were the sense of humor and infectious laugh that lifted my spirits after a long stressful day at work. Gone was the generous, caring, tender wife and mother. Gone! Gone! Gone! But as she had scolded me, she left me a legacy in her children and in the memories.

Looking at my watch I was surprised to learn I had been with Kathy over thirty minutes. It was only fifteen minutes until the scheduled time, and people were already starting to file in. A state policeman friend walked to the casket and knelt for a short while, then came over to offer condolences, "Lou, she was so beautiful." No one could deny that. One hour after the start of calling hours I was informed by brother George that my cousin suggested we remove the kneeler in front of the casket to facilitate the flow of people paying their respects. Apparently the line was already out the door and down the steps, stretching about 100 feet in both directions on the sidewalk, blocking the entrance and exit to the parking lot and causing traffic to back up in the street. I agreed but also said we would not rudely rush people by who wanted to talk. Regardless, it didn't help facilitate the process, so the police in front enjoined the two lines in one direction to make the parking lot accessible.

191

It was a slow, austere and emotional display of people that filed past the bier of this twenty-eight-year-old girl. There were family members, carpenters, painters, plumbers, electricians, general contractors, lawyers, engineers, vendors, agents, laborers, landscapers, hairdressers, doctors, nurses, clergymen, and friends from AC Peterson's. This continued throughout the evening, until the line stopped when Sue came through. She put her arms around me and sobbed, her grief unlike anything I had experienced until that moment. And I thought of Scripture: "There will be the gnashing and grinding of teeth." How was this to be interpreted? What did it all mean? I put my arm around her and we went to see Kathy together. After a few minutes she touched Kathy in an affectionate gesture, and then I walked her to the back of the parlor, where she took a seat beside a lady on the hospital staff.

While I was going back to stand in front of the casket one lady in a group of five that came to represent the Lupus Foundation stepped from line to offer her sympathy. While we were talking I overheard one at the end say, "Why couldn't they have sent all this money to the Lupus Foundation instead of wasting it on flowers?" I had an answer, but the narrowness of the remark would not have brought understanding to the recipient. And beyond that, Lupus wasn't Kathy's problem. I thanked them for coming, but as I walked away another flash of Scripture came to mind regarding expensive ointment. Kathy was dead. She loved flowers. What was more fitting than offering the sweet-smelling fragrance and beauty of one of God's finest miracles . . . flowers?

Two hours after the scheduled end to calling hours, the last person expressed his sorrow and condolences. He was an old retired judge with failing eyesight who had worked for my father for many years. I was very moved that he would come, and expressed my heartfelt thanks. When everyone had left, my cousin quietly came, bidding me to stay as long as I wanted. Words could not be enough to express my feelings of gratitude for her kindness as I knelt down on the floor in front of Kathy until the kneeler was returned.

Physically exhausted and emotionally drained, my heart was damp from the flow of tears. I was fixed in a sorrowful state.

It seemed surreal—like a nightmare I was trying to awaken from. Then the scent from the flowers, the roses, carnations, lilies . . . brought me back to reality. My eyes left my wife momentarily to see that above the casket top there was a stand holding a beautiful arrangement laced with a red heart. The inscription read, "We love you, Mommy. Love, Louie and Nancy Anne." A tear rolled down my face. I kissed my wife for the last time and walked slowly out the door.

Morning/Mourning

On the morning of the funeral a limousine picked me up at home and brought me to the funeral parlor about half an hour early. D'Esopo's parking lot and the street as far as the eye could see were overflowing with cars carrying people who wanted to be part of the procession to the church and cemetery. I went in and sat in front of Kathy in a quiet, prayerful manner. The rest of the family followed. Very quickly the parlor was filled to standing room; Father Crawford from Church of the Incarnation in Wethersfield came, expressed condolences again, and said one decade of the rosary.

Immediately after he finished, Mike D'Esopo said in a clear voice, "As your name is called please pay your last respects, then return to your car in the line of procession." Soon all were called and the parlor was empty. I went up to Kathy to say my very last goodbye: "My fondest wish, Lady Kathleen, is that you will be happy beyond all worldly beauty the eye could ever experience here . . . any measure of joy a poor wretched soul like myself could ever offer you. No, I couldn't promise you that I would marry again, but I promise that I will, with all my being, love and take care of your . . . our children." My final thoughts came to me in verse:

young hearts in spring
'neath heaven's light
two in love
it seemed so right
evening shadows
glazed the stars on high
cruel bewilderment . . .
Sweet princess goodbye!

194

Cousin Eleanor came over, put her hand on my shoulder, and walked me to the waiting limousine while attendants closed the casket and wheeled it away.

I had made a decision to have Little Louie attend the funeral Mass. Despite the consternation of a few in the family, my reasoning was soundly based on the fact that Mass was the highest form of Catholic worship. We believe bread and wine is changed into the body and blood of Jesus Christ in a miraculous process called transubstantiation. It is made possible through the power of the Holy Spirit and consecrated by traditional authority given to the ordained priest, instituted down through the ages at the Last Supper by Jesus Christ Himself. And if we as Catholics believe that Jesus Christ is really there in the tabernacle, what was more fitting than to have a baptized family sharing this Holy Sacrament, regardless of the solemnity of the funeral service? Despite the logic in my sound thinking, I had misgivings at the end of the service as they wheeled the draped casket of Louie's mother down the aisle. Her young son clearly understood the significance of the moment and was immediately comforted by his aunt when the reality of the moment so grieved him.

I had met before the Mass with Father Crawford to request two pieces of music Kathy loved so much, and in the process of conversation, I asked Father to do the eulogy. Father assured me he had intended to express a few words; however, he admitted it was going to be one of his most difficult eulogies. Father was an excellent speaker. He never used notes, never went off on a tangent, and always returned to the original thought for closure in short order. It was no different with Kathy's eulogy. He opened by saying how important it was to Kathy she thank everyone who took care of her with a personal letter when she got better, and then talked specifically about some of her fine qualities. He enlarged upon the mystery of our faith and how Kathy had an abundance of it. And although we can't understand this now, especially the complexity of her illness and subsequent death, we have to go on, and the family has to continue with hope and fulfill her dreams. He ended with something that forever remained with me in time: "Sometimes God picks His most tender, brightest, His most resplendent flowers early to help beautify His heavenly gardens of Love." I never experienced Father Crawford being poetic; nonetheless, it was Father at his best.

A custom that originated from Europe was to light a candle upon a person's death and leave it burning for forty-eight hours. The significance was votive in prayer—make way—to light the way to heaven. I thought there was sentimentality attached to this tradition, yet I left all the outside and interior lights in the house switched on for only twenty-four hours. When the procession left the church, my cousin didn't forget the request I had made to take the procession by the house one more time so that Kathy could say goodbye to the home she loved so much. As we approached the front of the house, I asked the driver to stop for a minute. I put down my window and said a brief prayer. It was a very warm August day and I could see several pretty butterflies around Kathy's geraniums and impatiens planted in the raised area above the quarrystone wall to the right of the entrance. The locusts were busily working in the hemlocks, making a cacophony of sounds and being quite oblivious to a sparrow winging in and out of the maple trees. Comforted by tranquility that prevailed at that moment about her earthly abode, I gave the driver permission to go on.

The cemetery was quiet, save for a lone man in the distance cutting grass. After the family was seated, Father Crawford recited a litany of prayers for the dead. When he had finished he came over and shook hands again—a token of remorse, sympathy, and respect. I thought as he was leaving about how many thousands of times he had done this during his priestly life, and how only through his strong faith would his job be bearable. Taking a red rose from the casket, I kissed it, broke the petals away, and placed them back on the casket—an ancient gesture signifying the fragrance of love eternal. I looked down at the casket one more time and noticed five petals; the dreams of love are detached only in death—but the memories of the living never fade. She had carried a dream in her heart since my proposal, a little over four and half years; it was now laid to rest. Everyone picked off petals to place on the casket. As I turned to move outside the tent to make room for those standing to place their petals, a cowlick blew in front of my blurry eyes from a swift, warm

196

summer breeze that swept the tent area. It flapped the canvas sides and billowed the pointed top. The five rose petals I had placed on the casket butterflied momentarily around people close to the casket, finally swirling out to freedom as if to announce, unobtrusively, it is finished. I left.

The limousine driver had the door open. I requested he not leave until all the family limousines were loaded. As the procession moved slowly through winding roads lined with trees, my thoughts flashed back to Boston and a young intern's never-to-be-forgotten words: "All our mistakes end up in the cemetery." Up the hill, down the slope, around a bend, so serene, so peaceful—a heavenly scene with flags, markers, flower stanchions, bushes, trees—and Lady Kathleen.

Alone with My Children and a New Life

Traditionally after a funeral, there is a gathering of family and friends. With Kathy's funeral, it was no different. Everyone was invited to brother George and sister-in-law Dolly's home. They were the godparents to Louie and Nancy. The limousine dropped me off with Kathy's mother and father, who were mournful but accepting of God's will. The house was very crowded, with people of every age and gender, and at one point my father quietly lamented that he was an old man, and asked why the good Lord didn't take him and let her be; that is all I remember of that afternoon.

While I was appreciative that so many had done so much for this gathering, the time seemed like an eternity, and despite the huge crowd, loneliness wracked my very soul. I returned home in mid afternoon, exhausted, and fell asleep on Kathy's favorite sofa. Upon arising I took a pen and recorded my feelings. I remember in school reading something in a memo written by Samuel Webb (a patriot in the Revolutionary War and an aide to George Washington) to his brother-in-law Joseph Barrell, a Boston merchant, dated 25 November 1781, one week after Samuel's wife, Eliza, died. They had been married two years. The words precisely mirrored my feelings that day:

"I was completely happy as this world could make me; I am as miserable as man can be. My Dear Partner, all that was Dear to me in life, is no more to be seen among the walks of men. She has left us in the early bloom of life, and I verily believe is now singing hallelujahs with the just in heaven. This, my dear friend, is my only consolation in this hour of affliction. I wished her life for my own sake, I wished it for the sake of my friends—they must have loved her—but Heaven forbade it. The subject is too painful for me to dwell on. Hereafter, when the mind is less agitated, I may renew it. At present my friends must take upon themselves patience. . . ."

With ink on white-lined paper, the author wrote:

I expended every ounce of energy and spirit; each frayed fiber this weary body could offer in the comfort that you could remain with the children and me. I gave of myself unconditionally all that was humanly possible, thereof, written and pledged in our vows—not from commitment or contractual necessity, rather, in the union of Holy Sacrament and desperately out of love! Although my heart is torn—dislodged with unmitigated grief—so pained, nothing conceivable can remove your image; I will always miss you . . . the curative gift of time and faith is solely the essence of my future; henceforth, our children's growth and happiness. Rest with solace, my dear Lady Kathleen, that I will continue undaunted by obstacles of loneliness from fear, forged with the help of the Holy Spirit and proudly inspired by the courage you have exemplified. I will carry on the difficult task of existence in your absence; your memory is a beacon of hope—a symbol of valor. You will always be my "hero." . . .

My mouth was parched and in need of moisture. Slowly sipping on a glass of cold water to quench my thirst, I was pensively filled with awe by the brilliant fiery flame of the August sunset in the westerly sky. Placing the glass on the counter, I mentally recited a passage from the late Pope John XXIII, written upon finding his life would be shortened by an incurable illness: "Any time is a good time to be born, any time is a good time to live, and any time is a good day to die." If Kathy had to die young, she certainly chose a brilliant day. . . .

I returned to the kitchen table where I had been writing. In front of me was a hospital bed with a blood pressure apparatus, in the corner near the sliding glass doors was an oxygen canister. I took another piece of paper and added a footnote:

I pledge my heart, never to garner hostility, animosity, or malice toward anyone associated with my wife's initial discourse, diagnosis, treatment, and evaluation. Truth records many fine doctors, compassionate and caring, generous and dedicated throughout this country and Canada that were involved with her case, who wanted sincerely and desperately for her recovery. Unfortunately, the few that lacked professional character, ethical esteem and simple gumption resulting in irreversible harm will

199

eventually be weeded into areas of less concern. Yes, Lady Kathleen, I will uphold your wish that "everyone tried."

Before I could date and sign it I heard this tap, tap, tap on the back door. It was my neighbor from across the street, Roy Pierson. When I opened the door he looked up at me sheepishly and said, "I didn't know if you would open the door or tell me to go home and leave you alone, but I had to come over. I just couldn't stand the thought of you here by yourself in this big house."

I said, "Roy, how long have we been friends? You know me better than that. Please come in."

At first we both sat quietly, working with small talk. Then he said, "I hope you don't mind me telling you this, but to all the neighbors, you and Kathy were our 'Love Story.' " He didn't know about me having written the first "Love Story" that was rejected by the *Saturday Evening Post* and one other magazine. For over an hour we talked about many things, and before he left he offered that he was aware I had a lot of help, but if there was anything he could do, to just get on the phone. "Just being here tonight shows empathy and compassion," I responded. Throughout more than a year Kathy and I had met so many generous and sympathetic people, but people like Roy pass by only once in a lifetime.

My first priority was getting the kids home. The tremendous void in my heart and stark reality that Kathy was dead suddenly took hold. It was almost unbearable, but I had a responsibility as a parent and a promise to fulfill. The day after the funeral I called Mary, thanking her and my brother Tony for their immense kindness and sacrifice for the care and love they had provided for little Louie. I also asked if it would be possible to have him ready to be picked up in an hour. I was determined to have him home as soon as possible. She graciously obliged, offering to bring him by herself.

Once we were alone in the house, Louie took my hand and asked for some orange juice, then urged, "Dad come—Dad come!" Asking what the hurry was, he proceeded to lead me throughout the house. And every place we went, he would say, "Dad! Hear Mommy." Then he would point to a certain area, holding his hand fixed in the same direction, repeating, "Dad, there Mommy.

200

Dad, hear Mommy?" His face, tentative and bright, appeared as if someone was conversing with him. He stopped suddenly and said, "Okay Mommy!" This continued for over an hour, and not once did he release my hand—he went first to his mother's bedroom, then to her dressing area, pointing to her vanity stool. He took me to the laundry room and family room, and to the porch—where his mother used to paint—and then we were back upstairs again in her bedroom. Each time he would repeat, "Dad look, Dad hear Mommy," and urgently move to another location as if someone was prodding him to follow. Finally, he stopped abruptly and released my hand. His bright little smile changed to a sad, forlorn pout as he slowly walked down the stairs.

I was perplexed on the one hand and curious on the other. Although I believed in mutually active communication channels of a spiritual nature, including premonition, I wasn't a good enough student to be convinced of communicative skills after death. I always thought that attached to it was a measure of superstition and the occult. Stories pertaining to after-death experiences or things that transpired at a séance left me incredulous. I'd listen politely out of respect, although I never could be convinced of their authenticity. But alas, this brief experience with Little Louie brought a chill to my spine and a new dimension in maturity. I had no answers for what took place that day; was it the excitement of him being home again? Was he just telling me that he remembered the house? His mother's daily schedule? Or was he actually communicating with her? It was a mysterious, unsolved phenomenon that I was unwilling to dwell on. I never understood that hour and confess that the only satisfaction derived from the experience I kept sealed in my heart for twenty-five years, only revisiting it reluctantly in rare times of nostalgia.

One week to the day after Little Louie came back, Rosie and Paul brought Nancy home! There was Little Louie, Kathy's mother and father, godparents Dolly and George, and myself, sitting in the family room waiting excitedly for her arrival. My biggest concern was that she would be set in a "cocoon" mode, oblivious to the people around and incessantly clinging to her aunt and uncle. To my surprise she was quite congenial. Nancy Anne was precocious for a one-year-old, talking, walking, and

201

setting up a happy camaraderie with many people. The most intriguing development was that she and her brother, who had met only a few times, were drawn to one another. I was pleased, despite her notion that I was some alien rather than her father.

She would bounce around to everyone that was there but was careful to steer away from me. At one point she was so involved with jumping from person to person, smiling happily, that she forgot to avoid me. I stuck out my arms, quickly lifting her into the air, and planted a big kiss on her cheek—to her surprise and the delight of everyone there that day.

After many weeks of continual nocturnal crying, and many periods of defiance, she realized that this "guy" she was living with was nice, and she eventually settled in to accept the love that was offered in her home. But it would be a long time before she would fully understand the circumstances surrounding her birth.

My life was finally returning to a routine. To supervise the children, I hired Kathy's mother, who had worked in a nursing home for a number of years and was experienced with the care of people, in addition to bringing up her own four children. My day would begin at five in the morning; I didn't need an alarm clock, for the kids would run in, jump on the bed, and bounce and bounce until I got their message—they wanted something to eat. After tending to the kids, I would shower and get dressed, then work in my office with blueprints, estimates, and calls, with an audience of two. They would sit quietly together, Little Louie holding his bunny and sucking his thumb, and Nancy Anne, cuddled close with her head on his shoulder, clutching her pink stuffed bunny; they looked so content. At six-thirty A.M. the doorbell would ring, and they would both make a beeline for the door, singing, "Grammy, Grammy!"

The schedule became fixed; life imperceptibly slipped into a normal pattern with a joint effort. The kids, always with an abundance of energy, were happy, healthy, and satisfied. They were showered with love and attention from so many directions, and often I prayed it would not spoil them, despite the fact they got their share of spankings. I was so blessed with family and friends that came from every direction; even nurses from the lo-

202

cal hospital that took care of Kathy were frequent visitors. People would stop to spend time with the kids and do errands for me, and every evening upon my return there would be a hot dinner waiting, so that cooking was seldom necessary. I did everything in my power to be a good single parent, completely dedicating my life to the children in every possible way—they were my life. Despite Kathy's plea, I had no intention to ever marry again.

I wanted the first Christmas alone to be a grand time for the children. I mulled over whether to have a tree, but because the kids were sometimes alone while their grandmother was busy washing clothes and cleaning, I decided it would be too chancy. Fearful they would get overly enthusiastic with the lights, I chose not to take the risk. Yet Little Louie often asked when we would get a Christmas tree. The problem was solved when Rosie brought in a small silver artificial one, complete with a rotating colored wheel light, which spun brilliant hues for a wonderful Christmas odyssey. During the day I placed the light high on the shelf in the closet so they couldn't get at it, but upon my return after work, with great anticipation they would both come charging at me, "Dad! Dad! Put the lights in the tree!" Normalcy was slowly entering my life once again.

Although I dearly missed Kathy, at times experiencing profound loneliness and a terrible void, we had a wonderful Christmas. Cuddled together on the couch in the family room, Nancy Anne on my lap and Little Louie snuggled up close with a comforter draped around all of us, I told them the Christmas story of Mary, Baby Jesus in the manger and the Wise Men. We also read other Christmas stories and seasonal poems. And when I would finish to rest awhile, Little Louie would say, "More, Dad! Dad, more!" So I would start over again until I just couldn't talk anymore. Some evenings I would let them stay up longer and we would watch special Christmas programs until they fell asleep, then I would carry them up one by one and tuck them in. Many times they would both come into my bedroom to say they were scared and crawl into bed with me, but I only allowed this on special occasions, if I was convinced they were really afraid. And there was also the week of the untimely ice storm in Connecticut, when we were powerless and heatless for many days; then cuddling was a true necessity!

That first Christmas was filled with presents, Santa Claus, carols, the tree, stockings hanging from the fireplace, a LaCava family Christmas dinner, and lots of love. Inasmuch as the children were adjusted and happy, so too, the author was contentedly filled with joy and thankfulness.

My father wanted me to get married again, and advised me many times that it was essential for kids to have a mother. Some of my close friends would tactfully intimate I should get out, that it wasn't healthy for me to be in the house night after night. Often they would suggest going with them to a social, discreetly adding that there was someone they wanted me to meet; I would smile politely, indicating I was completely satisfied with my lot. Moreover, I was content using my extra time to write, which I enjoyed so very much. An old skating friend called to ask me to attend a competition and [maybe] skate afterwards. I thanked him for thinking of me and noted it was a kind gesture, although I hadn't skated in five years and had no interest in sitting through a competition.

All other efforts on my behalf by family, friends, and business associates, to get me active again in social circles, were to no avail. I was determined not to marry again, although admittedly it would have been nice to have an adult companion to confide in from time to time. But I was concerned that any arrangement could be misconstrued and had the potential to turn serious. The mores of the 60's had spilled over into the 70's; divorce had increased exponentially, domestic confrontation and violence were rampant. Since the Supreme Court had sanctioned the legal killing of a baby inside the mother's womb through Roe v. Wade on Monday, 22 January 1973, the family nucleus was deteriorating. My ultimate concern was not the financial risks of marriage going bad, but more importantly, losing my children in the process. I was determined to go it alone.

The first month after Kathy's death I received a letter from an old girlfriend who had recently divorced. Our relationship had come to an abrupt end when she left me for another guy. This was fine with me, as "all's fair in love and war," but I was disappointed then because she never said anything to indicate she was dating someone else at the same time. It left a bad taste in my mouth. Her letter was filled with romantically passionate, detailed descriptions of her love for me. In five handwritten pages she purged her soul in poetic soliloquy. Catharsis! While I was slightly amused, I was also embarrassed for her, feeling pity that she was so desperate she would attempt to ingratiate herself with a widower of thirty days. This was just a start . . . this naive boy got an education in the next seven months!

There were several girls living in the condominium complex where I worked who showed obvious interest in a relationship with me. Some were very coy and discreet; others were forward and bold. One, a widow several years my senior, was very pleasant, educated, and extremely nice to talk with. Once she moved in we had many enjoyable and interesting conversations, as she was very bright with a broad base of knowledge. Somehow she knew of my love for writing poetry, although I never remembered telling her; it was not the author's habit of talking about himself. However, I grew uncomfortable when her interest turned to making obvious, forward gestures.

In retrospect, I was aghast, for it was not my *modus operandi*; though probably innocent, it made me uncomfortable. But to say I was totally surprised would perhaps be somewhat untruthful, as she admitted her attraction later on. I must confess—not to win a badge of honor or proclaim my saintliness—that nothing ever came of it.

And a photographer who worked nearby told me several times she wanted to take some pictures of my kids, whom I frequently took to the condo site on weekends when checking on the sales staff. One day as I took their sled and pulled them up the hills and around the complex she came out and asked again if she could take some pictures. Telling her courteously that they were very shy and would probably not pose, I then facetiously added it was a free country so she could do what she pleased. As she worked, one could easily observe she was a professional, and one day she presented the outcome to me. They were exceptional, really great pictures—centered, clear in every detail and naturally focused. I thanked her and insisted on paying for them; but she refused, telling me it was an after-work hobby and she wanted to do something good. End of case? Hardly!

A week later I was in my trailer and had just finished a call when there was a knock on my door. It was the photographer, nervously asking if she could talk to me. I bade her to come in and sit down, but before I could listen to what she had to say, one of the foremen walked in to inform me that a potential client waiting in front of the model unit wanted to see me immediately. She was on lunch break from work and was short on time. I asked the foreman to show her the units, saying I would try to get there in a few minutes, and in the meantime the photographer said she would come back, but I assured her it was all right. After another phone interruption, she asked me in a halting voice if I ever entertained the thought of going out with her on a date. It would have taken a lot at this point in my adjustment period to surprise me, yet, and wrongly so, I felt this was audacious on her part. But it really wasn't. Now, she was a fine girl—attractive, intelligent, and talented; but I had absolutely no knowledge what her motive was, considering she already had a boyfriend. I was not interested in a dating relationship with her or anyone, and besides, it was against company policy. I politely responded in a way that would not encourage her in the future.

One young schoolteacher invited me, with the kids, over for dinner. I thought she was kind and without any ulterior motive, but I would soon find that she had a strategy all lined out. Yet another girl said she liked the way I talked and always went out of her way to find me. What these girls wanted from a man with two small children was difficult for me to understand. One day I asked a supervisor why I never got this adulation when I was single! The efforts these girls extended to capture my attention or pursue me were without merit. It would take a girl who had no interest in me to break my resolve.

Her name was Janet Young. She was ten years my junior, single, tall, willowy, pretty, and very intelligent. As fate is fickle, I had met her father in early spring when he came to look at a penthouse unit overlooking the pool that his daughter was interested in. He walked up to me and introduced himself. "Oh, I'm

Ronald Young. My daughter was down and said she was interested in an upper floor unit. Can I take a look?"

I replied, "Sure, I have one open in that building over there (I indicated by pointing with my right hand that was holding a lock level)—it's building number ten. Walk up the front tower, and on the top landing you'll see an entrance door that should be unlocked."

He asked if that was the one overlooking the pool area. I indicated that one was not open and I had just opened the model. But he wanted to see the one overlooking the pool, as that was the one she was interested in. I asked if he could wait until I got a message to one of my employees; he said that he could and would walk over to look at the pool. Once he saw the unit he was pleased. The unit was spacious, with two eight-foot glass sliding patio doors, one off the master bedroom and one off the living room, with an unobstructed view of the pool area. It had cathedral ceilings and a mammoth living/dining room combination. In summary, this was a lot of condominium for the dollar. As we were leaving the unit, his daughter arrived. He asked if we had met; we had not, so he made a quick introduction. He told her he liked the unit he had seen but wanted to also see one on the first floor. We sauntered across the street, where there was a ground floor flat.

Ronald Young and I talked for well over half an hour. He asked me several questions about the type of construction, heating costs, taxes, condo fees. All the time we talked, his daughter was at the other end of the room, waiting patiently; eventually when I realized her proximity, I thought of what a respectful girl she was to just step aside and let the men talk. Later I would find out she had been anxious to return to work but had had to convey a message to her dad first. Finally, when our conversation left business and turned to world events, she came in and excused herself with, "Dad, I have to get back." She then looked over at me and asked, "Mr. LaCava, can I bring my brother back later—will there be someone here so he can see it?" I told her that I had to leave early this particular day to take my boy to the doctor but said I would have a supervisor open the unit if she could tell me a time. She said she'd call to let me know, and within an hour a message said her brother was not available to inspect the

207

unit that day. Neither of us had any idea what that fateful meeting meant. She saw me only as an older man with kids; I saw in her a young, bright girl, and her father a very distinguished and intelligent man—a highly respected officer of the Hartford Insurance Group. But only a short time later, after she had settled into this state-of-the-art condominium, the office had asked her to work part-time in sales for the company, and our paths would meet again!

My first favorable observation of Janet was on a routine visit to the site one Sunday afternoon in the spring of 1974 to check on my sales staff. I scanned the schedule (sales log) and saw the name Janet Young penciled in for this particular day. I knew she was the new girl who was recently hired, and remembered several conversations we had had during the process of purchasing her condominium unit, though I was utterly unfamiliar with her ability as a sales person.

Part of the job description as project manager was to monitor the sales department, which included oversight of the models, and making sure the units were clean, the sales literature was frequently replenished, and the sales journal was properly kept. In addition, I was supposed to stop by the sales office briefly on weekends as a support visit—*esprit de corps*. That spring was rather cloudy and unseasonably cold, and I had the kids bundled up, with Nancy Anne in the back strapped into her safety seat, and Little Louie in the front seat next to me secured with the seat belt. I pulled into the parking space directly in front of the models, released Louie's belt and told Nancy Anne that Dad and Louie would be right out so she would not be frightened. I reassured her that Dad could see her all the time and pointed to a big picture window where I would be, less than twenty feet from my car. I left her there for two reasons: time lost in undoing her straps, and the hassle of two kids in the model condo. I later found this reasoning to be unsound; at the very least, I should have left Little Louie with her.

I walked into the model with Little Louie, and though Janet was sitting down with a client, she immediately stood up, excused herself, and walked from behind her desk to greet me. I thought this was real class. Inquiring about the turnout for the day, I asked if there were any prospective buyers or if there were any problems, and because this was her first weekend, reminded her to recheck all the thermostats before she locked the models. I then bid her *adieu*. The whole process had taken less than three minutes, and all the time I never took my eyes off Nancy; but upon my return to the car she was crying, and by the look on her face I knew she had been crying for some time. I felt terrible for leaving her alone; prior to this, she had had another stressful experience, and both in one day were too much for her.

The kids liked when I swung them over my head and under my legs, and they were constantly asking me to repeat it. Early Sunday morning while swinging Nancy Anne, I took her over my head using a skating lift (overhead with my hands extended). She was thrilled at first, but when we left for dinner at my mother's she started to cry and continued crying intermittently throughout the entire dinner, often holding her arm. I was concerned and decided to bring her to the hospital for X-rays. Two doctors examined her and couldn't detect anything wrong but wanted to take some pictures to be certain. While we were waiting for the technician, Nancy Anne continued to cry as a pleasant Asian doctor walked by. He stopped and asked my brother Frank, who had accompanied me, what was wrong. Learning she had been crying and holding her arm for the last three hours, he went over to her and looked at the area she was holding. Then he smoothly ran the palm of his left hand slowly three or four times over her elbow joint, clasped her bicep, and with the other hand instituted a gentle quick jerk, pulling down on the arm. There was a little click (like cracking a knuckle) and Nancy Anne brimmed with a smile from ear to ear. The doctor said the joint was dislodged from the socket. There was no need for X-rays, and we could go home.

Janet worked the next three Sundays. She was pleasant, respectable, and very able when it came to selling, and being knowledgeable about the product; moreover, she was loquacious, gregarious, and very attractive. She would greet me congenially each time I arrived to collect the day's numbers, always addressing me as "Mr. LaCava." I liked her poise and performance, and informed the office in this regard.

One day, parked in front of the trailer office waiting for the rain to let up, I noticed an unusual rainbow in the southeastern sky—a mammoth arc interrupted by bright blue space, and before the continuation of the bow was a dark, ominous sky. I thought it was weird—not only had I never witnessed anything like it, I had never seen a rainbow this early in the morning. Then, I attributed it to the angle of the rising sun, the heavy volume of showers, and the atmospheric pressure, but to this day I believe it was an omen that would change the course of my future.

I finished talks with my vendors, checked production stages, scheduled town inspection, had my daily meeting with my foremen, and called into the main office, then left for my first set of daily rounds throughout all the buildings. The time was nine twenty A.M., exactly. I would now let the day evolve systematically, save for one fateful diversion. Having been informed by a supervisor of some vandalism overnight in a building near the end of my normal route, I digressed from the usual pattern of inspections. In a voice tinged with anger, he said that someone had kicked big holes in the soundboard of one of the buildings (soundboard was used as a new technique for party walls, the inside walls that separate units). Since the Sheetrock workers were anxious to finish, he wanted me to take a look.

I went into the townhouse to assess the damage, advising what had to be replaced and patched. Upon leaving the second floor I noticed a metal lock grab was missing from a sliding glass window, and asked one of the men installing wallboard if he had seen it. He informed me it had fallen off when they removed the window to deliver the Sheetrock, but that he would reinstall it before the end of the day. A vinyl piece on the fixed glass section of the same window unit was loose, and in the process of snapping it back in place, I observed Janet Young standing by her car in front of the rubbish dumpster with a disturbed look on her face.

Arriving at street level, I realized she couldn't start her car, as an odor of petrol filled the nearby air. It appeared the automatic choke was stuck open, saturating the carburetor. I yelled to her, "Jan, what's the matter? Won't start?"

"I just stopped for a minute to throw my trash in the dumpster and it stalled. Now I can't get it started again." I told her I thought it was flooded and to let it sit for a few minutes, then it should start right up. She tried it again after a few minutes, to no avail, so I told her to let me try. We knew each other pretty well by now; I had sold her a condominium and had met with her several times regarding her interior selections, and also during my Sunday sales staff checks we had an opportunity for friendly conversations. As she left her car and walked in my direction, something happened to me. I noticed she was an exceptionally attractive woman—tall and extremely shapely, dressed in a short light brown skirt, well above the knee, with a white jersey covered partially by a tan jacket. Her brown hair was smartly combed out down to her shoulders, showcasing pretty features. I thought, with a bit of guilt, that she had a stunning figure that would catch any eye.

I had been very careful up to this point to keep my sensibilities intact; so I was surprised by this different feeling that had unexpectedly engulfed me, especially at work, and came from an employee, no less. Quickly, before she could distinguish the change in my facial expression, I jumped into her car, slammed my foot on the gas pedal, and turned the key while continuing to pump the accelerator. It started up immediately. She graciously thanked me as we dodged a cloud of black exhaust. I wanted Janet to think of me as chivalrous! However, the car and I were the farthest things from her mind—she had to get to work. Over lunch, though, my thoughts returned to that fortuitous morning episode with a car, a dumpster, and a pretty young maiden. Then I rationalized the mood as silly, ascertaining the enchantment was just a moment of weakness, and cast it off as probable indigestion.

The following day we had a late concrete pour on a new building. The forecast was heavy rain at night, and we decided to get the footing in so the men wouldn't waste time pumping water out of the hole the next day. While I was leaning on my car at an adjacent building, Janet stopped by to tell me that she had been having trouble opening her front door. I explained to her that at this time of year sometimes the heat pulls the top and the bottom out on exterior fire-rated doors, causing pressure at the lock.

211

This was before exterior metal doors had been perfected to be certified fire-rated. I told her that it just needed a minor adjustment at the striker plate and eventually the door would dry out completely so she wouldn't have this problem anymore. I offered to adjust it myself in half an hour if she was going to be there. She wanted to know how long it would take and, hearing only ten minutes, said she could wait.

While I was adjusting the door, Janet inquired about the cost of having her laundry area concealed with louvered doors. It was getting late and I knew the babysitter would be wondering where I was, so I told her I would get a price sometime during the week. That night I couldn't get her out of my mind. Inwardly, I'd rationalize her many fine attributes. She was young, very pretty, and extremely smart—I would find out later that she had graduated second in her class at college—and very pleasant and gregarious.

Three days later I called to give her the cost to close in the laundry area, and in the conversation she also inquired about a peek-a-view for her front door; I acknowledged getting one would be a smart idea, and that it was only a $25 item. It was during this exchange that I got to know her much better. She revealed to me that in 1968 her fiancee had died tragically in a house fire, and that she liked to ski and had been to Vail. She was an avid reader, once lived summers on an island in the Sound, was a water skier, and loved all kinds of boating. We had a lot in common, I thought, as she told me these things, but when she informed me that she had known my wife Kathy and attended her wake, I was astonished. Genuine fond feelings started to cultivate in my heart toward her; nevertheless, I would soon realize the feeling was far from mutual.

Sales activity started to improve in the late spring of 1974 after a severe recessional period had totally devastated the industry nationally, putting many people out of work. Although there were several unsold units, the main office wanted to start a building that had been designed with three-bedrooms units. Surveys and demographic studies indicated a strong potential demand for this type of unit and the company wanted to take advantage of an untapped market. This data, known prior to the

212

prolonged downturn, would now be used to stimulate sales and catapult the firm quickly out from the lull the industry was still experiencing.

I decided to take a long weekend away by myself to rest before the orders came to break ground and commence construction on the three-bedroom building. It had been three years of worry and stress, and I had been in a routine alone at home with the kids—which I loved—day in and day out, but now it was time for a needed change of venue. I had been to Las Vegas several times, and although I wasn't an avid gambler, I enjoyed the entertainment, the people, and the sheer ambiance of the town.

A week before my scheduled departure, I asked Janet to have lunch with me at a park in Newington, and was delighted when she accepted. I told her I would bring the lunch and to meet me at the picnic tables near the Little League baseball field at the agreed-upon time. It was twelve-thirty when I left the site, giving me plenty of time to pick up lunch and drive to the park for a one o'clock date. The sky had been filled with light, and weird cirrus clouds; when grouped together covering the sun they gave the appearance of several rows of cotton candy balls standing together upright without the sticks. During lunch, fortunately, the sun was shining brightly, which brought comfort on an otherwise cool, windy day.

And when Jan's bright, shiny, new red Mustang pulled into the park, a warm feeling feathered my body. I went to greet her by opening her door, and when she got out of the car a strong gust of wind slightly lifted her flowery spring dress. She said, "Lou, isn't it too cold to eat outside today?" I responded facetiously, "Ah c'mon, we're not weaklings—other people are out here. And listen, if it gets too cold we can sit in my station wagon—a deal?" She took the bag from my hand and answered reluctantly, "A deal—but I'll be the judge."

I chided that from the beginning of time it's been a woman's world. And what a discussion on man/woman philosophies that started! She asked me if I really believed the male was the dominant fixture in a relationship and the woman's role was secondary. Not wanting to spend the whole time on this topic I auspiciously rambled that my family was raised basically from a religious point of view, where the man is the sole provider and protector of the woman and the family, and he is supposed to love and cherish her forever, until death do part. I qualified my thinking by adding this is scriptural and has nothing to do with the restriction of the woman's rights in any capacity. She cut in and said, her voice rising with each phrase to bring out a point, "You may say all that and be sincere, but there are a lot of men I know who believe the same thing but treat their wives as if they were property instead of a partner."

"Yeah, but I'm not other men."

"I wasn't directing these remarks toward you."

"I didn't say you were—d—did you have a bad morning?"

"You started it."

"I was just answering your question." Then we both laughed, and I asked if she was cold. She said she wasn't, then asked excitedly if I played golf. I told her not often, but that I had been a figure skater years ago, had been off the ice for several years, and was anxious to get back into it. She admitted she did not play golf herself but her Dad wanted her to start, as he was a golf lover and had even played in the Pro/Am of the Greater Hartford Open a few years back. When I questioned her reluctance to play, she admitted to me that she was nervous at the thought of delaying the game for other golfers. I asked if she had been to a driving range, and she said her experience was only at miniature and three-hole golf courses. Testing her, I asked if she wanted to go to a driving range tomorrow at lunch hour, an invitation she enthusiastically accepted.

A driving range was located about ten minutes between our respective jobs, so that day when she came home to her condo for lunch we went out to hit a pail of balls. Although I wasn't an expert in the game, driving seemed natural to me; therefore, I gave Jan little suggestions on how to improve her distance with the correct body position while focusing an eye on the center of the ball. When she tried, the ball topped over. Looking at her smile, and feigning disdain, I yelled over, "It works for me!" It was a pleasant time which we repeated at lunch, and once after work when the babysitter could stay late. I enjoyed the time spent with her and hoped she was happy with me.

After our evening date at the range, I thought about asking Jan to join me on my long Las Vegas weekend, weighing the advantages and disadvantages of her company—my only compunction being that fine line between valor and discretion. It didn't bother me what people would think—the only significant thing was knowing who I was and how I conducted myself; whether people thought I was discreet was secondary—that was their little problem. When I arrived at work the next day I decided to call Jan around eight A.M., just before she left for work, and ask her to stop at my office on the way out. In front of my trailer I carefully explained to her the long weekend plan and said I was wondering if she would join me. She cautiously asked, "Lou, where are you going?"

I looked at her and casually answered, "Las Vegas."

Nervously, and in a rather loud voice, she said, "Las Vegas! Did you say Las Vegas? You've got to be kidding!"

"Oh, I'm serious. It's not my style to joke around—especially interrupting your work for something frivolous. We'd leave at six P.M. on Thursday evening and return on Sunday night. We've had fun together, and I thought it would be nice to have someone to go to shows with and maybe take a trip to Hoover Dam and Lake Mead—have you ever been?" She said yes, but that it had been quite a while ago, and only for one night.

I continued, "If you're . . ."

She interrupted me, "Lou, that's a long way!" Then, nervously, she took my hand, obviously contemplating my invitation.

I looked in her eyes and said, "If you're worried that it's not the right thing to do, I can assure you my . . . my intentions are completely honorable and respectful. Of course, we'll have separate rooms, and if it will make you feel better, different hotels. But I'm sure we'd have a good time."

"No, no, it's not that I can't trust you," she said as she squeezed my hand tighter, "it's—it's just that I don't like to fly that much and . . ." I noticed my concrete representative Hank had driven into the parking area near the trailer, so I cut her off.

"Jan, look . . . if flying's the only thing that concerns you, remember you'll be with me, and I'll explain everything . . . promise, everything about airplanes. They're safer than cars. But I have to go now. We have a big pour today. Give me a call and let me know tonight, okay?" She nodded and slowly walked away, greeting Hank as she went.

I was confident that she would accept my invitation, but after I didn't hear from her that night, I went to her condo the next day before she left for work. She didn't answer the door, and I wondered if she had overslept. I made my rounds and became concerned, for her car was still there and it was well after eleven o'clock. Returning to my office, I decided to call her, but before I could the phone rang; it was Jan. She asked whether I had rung her bell this morning. I admitted I had, reminding her that I hadn't heard from her and needed an answer about Las Vegas. She apologized, saying she was sick with the bug and had forgotten to call to let me know she had something already planned for the next weekend. Disappointed, I offered that maybe there would be another time and wished her a speedy recovery from the flu.

It was May of 1974. The economy was showing some feeble signs that we would soon pull from one of the most serious recessions since 1948, but not many had predicted it would lead us into a boom period in building during the latter part of the decade. I was busier at work than ever since starting at the condominium, my health was good, and I went skating for the first time in over six years. Despite having dull blades, I had a good workout, surprisingly so, with good spins and jumps. I even attempted to pull off a double lutz. Returning home, I informed the kids that Daddy was going to buy them some skates, with the hope there would be another skater in the house. That wish was short-lived when they drifted toward other interests.

I hadn't seen Jan since she turned me down during the first week in June—nearly two weeks before. Then one day as I was coming out of a model she came to see me on her way to work and said, "Lou, did you get my message?"

I replied, feigning chagrin, "Loud and clear!" Her message had been in reference to the model condos, which hadn't been cleaned. They were usually done on Friday afternoons, to be ready for the weekend, but the maintenance person assigned was ill and the replacement was delayed on another job; consequently, cleaning was never done. I had to leave early that day and was unaware the models hadn't been attended to, so she wrote me a cute note in which she pleaded, chastised, and cajoled as to why the units were not cleaned.

I took her note home with me and analyzed the writing, then later called to explain what I had done, jokingly adding there was some information I felt she should have. I proposed we go hit some balls out at lunch, but she said she couldn't, as she had promised a co-worker to go dress shopping, but asked for an alternative time; perhaps we could meet at the range after work. I had to be home early to relieve the babysitter so I suggested we try for the next week, some day at lunch. She agreed.

Insight collected from her handwriting at first glance impressed me as common, save for one exceptional difference: legibility—it was so intriguingly perfect. On Sunday I went to check the sales office, something required every weekend, and it was no secret she was scheduled. I asked if I could call her later at home; she said that would be fine. We discussed many things on many topics, for she was well informed and a prolific reader. She asked about the kids, whom she had gotten to know after many Sunday visits, though she impressed me as having a more than casual interest in them. At first I figured it was because everyone on the staff was congenial and playful with them, but I came to realize later that she had a more attached feeling—the others were just respectful with the boss's kids, but with Jan it was different—she was genuine and sincere.

Before our phone conversation ended on Sunday evening I asked if I could call her in the morning, as I had something important to ask; she was curious why I could not ask then, on the phone. I told her it was something that had to be asked in person, preceded first by a call. After her dramatic demand to know if it was another trip, I assured her it wasn't, but now her curiosity was piqued and she obliged, while reiterating her fear of another trip invitation.

One thing Jan didn't understand was that my day started at five o'clock A.M. So when I was making some of my early morning vendor calls, she was included on my list. While dialing her number I looked at my watch and it read five-thirty. The phone rang several times; finally, it was answered. The voice on the other end said, "Uuhh, hel—hel—hel—lo?"

"Jan, this is Lou. How are you this morning?"

"Lou? Lou?"

"Yes."

She hesitated, then repeated, "Lou? What . . . what time is it?"

"It's late. I'm getting ready to leave in about twenty minutes."

"Lou, what time is it?"

"About twenty minutes to six."

"Do you always call your friends this early?"

"Friends can call friends anytime—that's how the word is defined." I continued, "Last night you said I could call this morning, or did you forget? I have to ask you something. . . ."

"What could be so important at this ungodly hour?"

"Would you like to go out to dinner Saturday night—a double date with one other couple?"

"Sure, that sounds good, but—unn . . . unnnn . . . but it's early now, Lou. (yawn). Who's the other couple?"

"My brother George and his wife Dolly—you know George."

"I'll stop and see you on my way out today—good night!"

I had just finished with a client in the model condo when Jan drove in. She looked very pretty that day, wearing a lilac spring dress with a ruffled front. When she walked in, I welcomed her with a big grin; she tersely greeted me with, "Lou, you had better redefine the word morning!" She continued with a very stern voice, "Now the answer to your question this morning or last night is . . ." she then softly smiled, "yes—where are we going?" I told her I thought it would be the Log Cabin in Holyoke, Massachusetts. She said she'd been there and had loved the food; she thought I would, too. And then she smiled again. "Is that the word you want?" She was amused, but when she noticed I was serious she continued. "That should be fun—what time will you pick me up?" I told her I would try to get an eight o'clock reservation so thought we should leave no later than seven.

Telling her I would call if there were any changes, I mentioned that I would be on another job the rest of the week and that there would be another supervisor at Countryside.

"Where are you going to be?"

"What are you doing, Jan, gathering research for a book? I'm going to Wesleyan Hills, a job we're doing for the college in Middletown—a city-within-a-city concept. It was modeled after one in Virginia, another in Maryland. They've had tremendous luck with this model. The theory behind it was to preserve land and facilitate living in general—in this small 300-acre city. We're in the process of starting additional mini-neighborhoods. The company wants to finish there this year."

She asked if I would be leaving Countryside permanently, and I told her that while it was likely, I still wasn't sure. I told her that I'd be back to this site for occasional visits, asking if she was jealous that I was going elsewhere. She smirked.

Before she left for work I asked Jan to check the desk in the model condo. Sealed in a white envelope with her name on the back was only one of which would be many future surprises. It was a poem written to her, entitled *Friendship*:

our world together; drifting
in a sea of loneliness
distantly estranged—forgotten . . .

'twas tender barbs, yea a multitude,
slippery, fleeting on wings of strife
torn in slothful innuendo
frozen in wretched haze—
of fogged reverie

'til hope, lie the eternal smile
in sincere remembrance;
a handclasp loose
to grasp the rose
of a sealed kiss
true friendship . . .

On the bottom I signed it *Jan, will you be my friend?* When I called her two days later she didn't say anything about the poem; curious, I asked for her impression. The answer was apologetic, yet sincere: "I had to read it over so many times before I could understand. . . ." I told her that was okay, my English professor at the university had the same problem with my stuff. He claimed it was too obscure. Jan admitted, however, that once she figured out what I was trying to say, she realized it was profound.

We had several more dates after the Log Cabin, including movies, lunch, dinner, a picnic (same park), and a trip to the driving range. With each date we seemed to enjoy one another more. We had interesting conversation about likes and dislikes, sports, religion, politics, poetry, entertainment, entertainers, and our families. She told me her only sibling—a brother—got married young (nineteen) and her parents tried to discourage it but now found themselves admitting his was a good marriage of trust and love. In addition, she admitted to wishing she had a sister, for it would be nice to have had someone to relate to. She often lamented she was not enamored with her job, but it paid well so she endured it. She knew that I had come from a large family, although she did not know just how large until then, and told me word around her office was that all the brothers were millionaires. I chuckled at that, advising her not to believe everything she hears and reads, and only half of what she sees. She laughed.

Rumors were circulating about us. ("Did you hear that Lou has a girlfriend?" "Really? Who is she?" "I'm not sure, but word has it she works for the company—they say she's nice.") ("Do you know Lou's seeing. . . ." "No really! Who's the girl? How long has it been since his wife . . .") This talk took place on site, in the main office, and within family, until one Sunday while the kids and I were having dinner at my parents' home, my father, who incidentally had no inclination I was dating someone, reiterated that I should get married to give the kids a mother. With the old-timers a family was always Mother and Dad—there was no other way. While I respectfully restated my feelings that I was not interested in marriage again, his face showed a look of dismay.

In light of the abounding rumors, I told Jan it would be nice if she met my family, which she was receptive to. She thought it would be less stressful to meet the whole family at once, so I realized the easiest way would be at my parents' estate at Indiantown in Old Saybrook on the Fourth of July. There would be a reunion, including the usual cookout and other great food, water skiing, boating, fishing and family, family, family—some seventy or so members!! This didn't frighten her, so we agreed to make it a date.

I prepared the kids, telling them that Daddy's friend would join us to go to the beach and spend the day. I didn't want them to be surprised so I carefully I briefed them, yet they were so excited in anticipation of going to the beach to see Grandma and Grandpa, their cousins, aunts and uncles, that they never questioned me about Jan. When I picked her up I discovered something about kids' minds—Kids 101. And that is that they have good memories, and they will challenge you if they feel you are mistaken; secretly, they absorb everything like sponges. I had told the kids that Daddy's friend would accompany us to Indiantown, but when she got into the car, Little Louie looked her over, smiled, and blurted out, "Hey, Dad, wait a minute. She's not Daddy's friend, she's Daddy's work!"

What followed was jovial banter between Jan and Louie, but with Nancy it was another story. As we progressed to the shore Jan casually put her left arm across the back of the car seat, with part of her hand ending up on my right shoulder; when Nancy saw this she purposefully lifted Jan's arm, moving it forward until it was removed from my shoulder. She was not sharing her dad—whom she finally got to know and love—with (just) anyone. The behavior was not out of the ordinary; on the contrary, it reflected an intuition of insecurity, especially from the experience of a child missing the early bonding with her mother. It would be years before she would accept the reality of the situation—but I never pressed her, for it was something only an individual who has experienced such trauma could deal with.

When we arrived, the place was buzzing with people. My brother Frank was on the steering committee and decided to have the place decorated, and to this day I felt it was for Jan's welcoming. There were streamers and balloons, small American flags waving in the shoreline breeze, a LaCava coat of arms insignia hanging on a picnic umbrella, and music by Perry Como piped outside.

As we walked up the driveway everyone came to greet us and meet Jan. One by one they filed by, and the warm greeting showered upon her pleased both of us. She handled herself extremely well, albeit scared to death at first; what helped was her outgoing, gregarious personality. She would get in there with the best of them! And when the games started she was willing to participate—football, volleyball, badminton. The beach and the boat followed; there was even water skiing. She loved all these sports and activities, blending nicely with the huge, effervescent clan.

The most heartwarming moment came when I introduced her to my parents. They both immediately accepted and extended warm greetings, telling her to make herself at home. Jan smiled, for this definitely seemed to relax her. My father, the patriarch, was exceedingly pleased, not only because Jan was outgoing and attractive, but also because he didn't have to tease her to eat. Italians equate eating to a celebration, praising God for food, health, and every new day. They want to share the food, the fun, and the frivolity with everyone. Jan liked to eat, and Italian food was her favorite, which pleased my father immensely. Words could not describe adequately the joy that beamed from his face when he met her, and eventually they would become the best of "buddies." The day was a success, the kids had a lot of fun, the family was pleased that we came, and Jan and I were very content. The kids fell fast asleep and Jan cuddled up close on the ride home as I sang tender ballads to her; we were imperceptibly becoming an item.

The severe recession caused some variety with my job and additional stress in my life. Instead of one location, my schedule took me to several towns, a routine that lasted for three months before money loosened up again. Banks once reluctant to lend money now altered policy and selectively opened up to stable and loyal clients in the latter part of 1974. This in turn stimulated the local economy; a few men were put back on the payroll, which insignificantly affected the unemployment numbers, but lifted spirits and one could sense the cautious optimism. The company started two buildings at the condominium complex and I was back as the project manager. But this position would be short-lived, for in May of 1975 I would be transferred permanently to Wesleyan Hills in Middletown to stay until the development was completed.

Jan and I dated frequently over the next four months. Our dates were for the most part casual and unstructured; she would come over and we would play with the kids, bathe them, and put them to bed. After, we would play cards, Scrabble, or cribbage, or work on puzzles, and I would regularly play my guitar and sing. Sometimes I would get rambunctious and go into one of my loud operatic arias or Neapolitan numbers and she would reprimand me, afraid I would wake the kids. On occasion, I would augment our dating pattern by taking her to lunch or dinner, or to a movie, but that was a rarity.

I continually harbored a guilty feeling of neglecting the kids if I went out too often. Jan never complained about not going out, and often she would babysit when I had a night meeting or a business seminar. The quality time she went with the kids in this venue brought them closer together. She would read to them, tell them stories, watch television with them, play with them in the yard, and take them for ice cream cones when the Good Humor man came down the street, though they never told me about this, as I didn't allow the kids to eat sugar and sweets. Their confessions only came years later. Nevertheless, she would do everything for these kids, and more importantly, she was a good influence on their young minds. Needless to say, I was very pleased.

One day I called her at work and asked if she could come over that evening, as I had something special for her. But I told her to take a circuitous route by the model on the way over and to look under the sales journal, where there would be something for her. She queried me, "Is this another poem, Lou?"

"I'm not telling—just please do what I ask."

"How is this connected with me coming over tonight?"

"My lips are zipped tight."

"Why can't you tell me?"

"I can but I won't, but you'll be surprised!"

"And if I don't go?"

"I'll be disappointed."

She finally agreed to the home date after a zillion excuses and a million questions. I had bought her a beautiful gold watch, and with the presentation I wrote a poem; in addition, I had a single red rose, which I preferred over giving a dozen. A dozen roses to me was stereotyped, unimaginative, dull, and made one conform to a standard established by florists and merchants. It had nothing to do with how a person felt—a "disconnect." I wasn't giving the roses, the florist was; I was just paying for them. But the presentation of a single rose held great significance and meaning. I want to give you this because you're special, and it has nothing to do with volume—often volume has an underlying guilt attached—it means love has won, with tenderness, affection, endearment; heart speaks to heart, heart knows heart, sharing has begun and on and on and on. I felt so strongly about a single rose that I even wrote a song about it many years hence. The poem was written out in longhand with red pencil:

Soliloquy in Open Verse

existence; so clandestinely fragile
in thy vast vicissitude of struggle.
'tis heavily measured
in the very essence of time
weighted in forgiveness
thus, purified by the omnipotent healing power
of all eternity . . .

formerly drawn and empty
save for a legacy . . . children;
suddenly hope sanctified my spirit
thence, sweetly renewed
to its fullness of faith
by gifts blessed
through your
redemptive acquaintance. . . .

The phone rang at seven P.M. It was Jan, but it didn't sound anything like her. Since we met, she was usually loquacious, buoyant, scintillating, and charming; that night the converse was true. She was introspective, quiet, monotone, and reticent. She had just gotten home, was extremely tired, and wanted to go straight to bed. I asked her if she had a stressful day at work, or if something had disturbed her. She candidly informed me she didn't want to talk tonight and to call her tomorrow. I had taken the watch out of the drawer in anticipation of a nice evening planned and hid it under one of the pillows in the family room sofa. I put it back, took the rose out of the water, and set it on a shelf in the refrigerator.

One of my sisters had called the previous night to tell me she was preparing tomorrow night's dinner for us and brought over a huge, natural, unsmoked ham. I had intended to surprise Jan with a nice dinner. I fed the kids and they repeated over and over, "More, Dad. More, Dad." Although I wasn't hungry, and was not a ham fan, my curiosity got the best of me, so I cut a slice for myself. It was the most succulent, most delicious piece of meat I had every tasted—and ham to boot. I said to the kids that Dad's friend missed a real treat, and to this day the author never has tasted a ham as fine. I asked my sister where she purchased it but I could not replicate it. When we finished, I cleaned the kitchen, called my sister to thank her, put the kids to bed, and went to bed myself, hoping the next day Jan would be rested and in a better frame of mind. I wanted to reiterate the invite and present the watch and rose to her as a sign of appreciation of our friendship.

About eleven o'clock the next day I called her at work; she was taking dictation and couldn't talk. When I tried her several times in the evening there was no answer. I naturally became curious when she still wasn't home at eleven and was relieved to find out the next day that she had been at an anniversary celebration at her brother's house. I had no reason to doubt her.

We made a date for Friday. She was going to leave work early, go home to change into something comfortable, and be at my house at five. I alerted the kids that Daddy's friend was coming to visit tonight, and they were both very excited, hoping to play some games with her. I explained to the children that Dad had a surprise for his friend and agreed to tell them if they promised to keep it a secret. Kids always promise! But we had a lot of fun in anticipation of her arrival. I asked Little Louie if he wanted to play a harmless practical joke on Daddy's friend. He beamed, anxious to be in on the fun. Jan was going to drive her car into the garage and enter by the laundry room. I warned Louie he had to be careful not to laugh or he would give away our practical joke. He would greet her while I stayed behind the door. I directed him to close the door slowly when she stepped in, but it was important he position himself with his back to me, then commence to walk side by side with her quickly away from the door after it was closed. I cautioned him not to laugh or look guilty or he would divulge our little ruse.

As she walked in, Jan innocently asked, "Louie, where's Daddy?" Well I didn't rehearse the probable questions she would ask and this caught him off guard.

"Ooh—Dad, I don't . . ." Then he started to laugh and she caught on, but played along to Louie's delight, pressing him with the question of what was going on. In the meantime, Nancy came bouncing in toward me. I can still see her image. She always ran fast as a deer and had the bounce of a gazelle. With popcorn in one hand, and her little pink bunny in the other, she jumped up, sailing in the air toward me, something we always did. I would catch and swing her over my head, imitating pair skaters. But this time I grabbed her off balance, the bunny went flying at Jan and the popcorn in her hand and mouth bombarded me. I bumped Little Louie and fell over on Jan. Nancy let out a howl, and for a moment there was her mother, for it had the same timbre, cackle, and continuity. The four of us lay sprawled on the floor in front of a window in the laundry room. It was hilarious, and a grand start to a beautiful evening.

The kids finally settled down, and as Jan took off her jacket and put it on the dryer, I did a double take. "What do you have on?"

"Hip huggers—that's the style!" As far as I could see, they were jeans fit tight to her body with the top part missing. She also had on a short, light blue halter, exposing her midriff, and a sweater open down the front. She looked very sexy, absolutely smashing.

I responded, "Style? You look great, but aren't you cold? Don't you feel naked?"

An emphatic, "No, Lou, I'm not," followed, and she changed the subject. So since that was the end of that conversation, I put my arm around her and we walked with the kids down to the family room, where I had the single rose, with the ribbon-wrapped watch box tucked under a sofa pillow.

While the kids went out to the sunroom to play with their toys before dinner, I ushered Jan to sit down on the big divan next to me. I gave her the rose first, which she said was nice; then I took the box with the watch from under the pillow, hidden from the kids, and presented it to her. When she opened it, a poem could have been written by the expression on her face, then there were tears, then "Thank You!" and a kiss. After a few minutes, she wiped her face and the black mascara that had smudged down from her eyes. Then she reached in to her sweater and pulled out a crumpled piece of LaCava stationery that I recognized immediately as the poem I had written for her over a week ago to coincide with this occasion. Smoothing it out, she looked at me and said, "This was so nice, Lou." I told her simply that I was pleased she liked it.

We held hands and talked for several minutes before I said, "Come on—get the kids. Grandma cooked a nice meal and a special treat—vanilla pudding. I hope you're hungry." Admitting she was starved, she rounded up the kids and got them to the table in record time.

Three weeks after the presentation of the watch I had a serious flashback, which started after reflecting on a call I received from Dr. Fernandez of the Lahey Clinic in Boston just two months after Kathy died. While filing some documents I had received from probate regarding her estate, I came across a follow-up letter to the phone call, expressing regrets at Kathy's death. They had had no indication she died; Saint Francis Hospital never notified them. I held no animosity about the call, as it was just the aftermath of a long and bizarre tragedy, but reread-

227

ing the letter would have a prolonged and detrimental effect on me mentally and physically in the near future.

The following day I relived Kathy's illness in its entirety. Every aspect of her suffering, every phase of her treatment and maltreatment, the strange meeting with Dr. *** and her sadistic warning, the ensuing infection, images of seizures, breathing difficulty, her steroid-swollen face, the veteran nurse telling me to get her out of there, the sadness in her face from privation and loneliness brought on by isolation from her children . . .

Before me constantly were hospitals, doctors, nurses, visitors, priests, ministers, and more nurses and more doctors, the funeral home full of flowers, the church, the eulogy, the cemetery. I couldn't sleep, I couldn't concentrate at work, and I couldn't eat. My weight dropped fourteen pounds. My natural outgoing demeanor changed radically, and I would seldom talk unless it was necessary. I had periods of vertigo and fatigue similar to what I experienced in Boston during the apex of Kathy's illness. When I entered the house after work it was a ritual for the kids to dash to the back door and leap airplane-style toward me, and I would catch them and swing them under my legs and over my head. I no longer had the enthusiasm nor the desire to do even that. When the kids would ask me why, my nightly reply was always the same: "I'm tired."

The intensity of this flashback continued for three weeks, with an added dimension. I became overwhelmed with guilt over Kathy's death, and my lack of response to the kids' fatherly needs. I would read to them every night, like I always did, and play with them, but I wasn't really there. Once Little Louie asked me if I was sad, and my response was the same answer the mother gave her son in Elizabeth Park one lonely day: "He's not sad, just tired!"

Depression and guilt wouldn't leave me—night and day, day and night, hour after hour, and day after day, and during this mental anguish Jan didn't react. She was kind and understanding, but her visits were less frequent, and our phone conversations went from four daily to four weekly. The only time she let on that she was aware something was bothering me was in a call late one night. I had bathed the kids and put them to bed, and then had just started to work on a blueprint when the phone rang. We talked for a few minutes; she asked about the kids and how my day went. Then she asked if I wanted company, I replied she was always welcome, which seemed phlegmatic. She had to stop at the store first and would be over in about an hour. As an afterthought, she timidly added that she would come "only if I was up to it."

It was well over an hour before she arrived. I was weary and had to struggle to be pleasant. We talked about various and sundry things, with her basically initiating the conversation, and as the evening evolved she obviously surmised we weren't getting anywhere. She politely suggested that she should leave. I never intended to convey that message, but when a person is depressed it's usually apparent to others, especially close friends. Despite total fatigue, I felt I was being good company and as hospitable as possible under the circumstances. But I was now aware that she felt uncomfortable, which only exacerbated my depression. I reacted to her suggestion of leaving with, "Jan, that's entirely up to you. I have no problem with you here."

She was not going to let that go unanswered. "When are you going to snap out of it?" She had held this in for two weeks and could do so no longer.

"Out of what?"

"Can't you see the way you've been the last two weeks? What are you doing to yourself?"

"How's that?"

"Come on—let go of it," she said with her voice quivering.

"What are you talking . . . what do you mean?" This bothered me. I was tired and just wanted to sleep. I was not up to what I thought at the time was badgering. She then pulled up the sleeve on her sweater, exposing the watch I gave her, and started to fumble with the band, and while twisting her wrist, cried, "Lou, she's gone and won't come back." Removing the watch, she put it on the coffee table and walked out, crying.

The implication stuck with me throughout the night. I tried to sleep, but it would not come. I went down to get a glass of milk to quench my thirst. Before returning to my room, I went to check on the kids and found them both soundly sleeping. Returning a second time to Nancy's room, I gazed at her for several minutes, overcome by a tremendous feeling of thankfulness. I reflected on how fortunate I was, when a vision of Kathy screened before me, with her voice resounding in my ears, "Can't you see, Lou, you have a legacy left to you." "Is that not sense?" "I want you to get married again." "Lou, Lou! Please look at me."

Swiftly, the devastation from the terrible depression that had gripped my soul for over two weeks suddenly subsided. And a new force that caused it to release its vise of torment from my mind—and a river of peace and tranquillity—surged forward. This was emotion I hadn't felt for two years. It was a great transformation that would echo daily in my brain, releasing new energy and a sense of well-being. I wanted to do things and be with people. I began to write again in earnest, with many of my poems laced with scriptural meanings. I dusted off my guitar and was singing again, and I even had the desire to get back on skates, this time with two small protégés. I could not explain what caused the dramatic change—the return to my positive and optimistic old self; was it something that Jan said? Was it the answer to the many prayers that were said and continued to be said for the children and me? I'll never know, but I have to believe that it was caused by a higher power, spiritual and mysterious.

I called Jan early the next morning to express that it was unfortunate what had transpired the previous night, yet good had come out of it. I wanted her to come over that night for dinner and to watch a movie with me. Public television had scheduled *The Great Caruso*, starring Mario Lanza—one of my favorite tenors; I was anxious to see it and wanted her to share the experience with me.

Still hurt from the exchange we had, Jan was unsmiling when I greeted her at the door. I apologized and kissed her, and we walked down to the family room with the kids hanging on to both of us. Little Louie, in his own inimitable way said, "Hello, Daddy's friend." This broke the tension, and as she removed her jacket, putting it on the same couch we had sat on the night before, she noticed the watch—in the same spot where it had been when she stormed out. I went over, picked up the watch and said to her, "Jan, this doesn't fit me. Give me your arm." I fastened it around her wrist, suggesting she behave herself and never let that happen again. Her retort was in her typical jovial way—that it was entirely my fault.

We had a nice dinner and talked about many things, and after putting the kids to bed we began a game of gin rummy. I asked her, in a very general sense, her opinion of marriage (she looked at me surprised)—its advantages and disadvantages. Soon I turned on the television set, and we snuggled while watching the movie. It was a night of reconciliation.

The next few weeks were spent preparing for Christmas. Jan was very happy and a frequent fixture in our home once again. She was extremely helpful and facilitated the debate on whether we should have a real Christmas tree or use the artificial one my sister had given us the previous year. The kids and Jan were adamant, siding for a real one. I wanted to use the other, so when the votes were counted in their favor we decided to have two. The real tree would be set in the family room, the artificial one in the living room.

Saturday, the week before Christmas, the four of us went out to purchase a tree. To me, what should have taken—liberally speaking—half an hour, took two hours. There was more debate and discussion on the size (height, length, width, and type) than there was in the United Nations debate during the Cuban Missile Crisis! Finally, after chagrin from the proprietor and the loss of my forbearance, one was selected that pleased all.

When we got home I immediately built a sturdy stand, one that was fall and child pull-down proof, essential to me when there were small children to consider. I then sat back and watched the kids and Jan as they performed a stellar decorating job. She had purchased tinsel, bulbs, lights, garland, and a cover for the stand—and there was an angel for the top. Further, she encouraged and supervised the kids to make their own ornaments and paper chains using colored construction paper.

It was interesting to watch the three of them, filled with excitement and Christmas spirit. Jan unraveled the wires, laying them out on the floor until they were all attached together. She then stressed the importance of trying the lights before placing them on the branches. Once tested, she gave the middle of the loop to Louie and the end to Nancy, instructing them to march forward toward her as she circumvented the tree from the bottom to top, gently placing the wires in a spaced pattern, careful not to leave unsightly gaps. It was done with imagination and precision, so I complimented them not only for their dexterity, but also for their sense of creativity. When the lights shone bright, we all oohed and aahed, and I continued to congratulate them on a job well done as I sat back observing the scene before me.

The kids stopped for a popcorn break while Jan opened boxes that packaged bulbs in the traditional colors of red and green, as well as blue and white, and various combinations of colors, shapes, sizes, and designs. Removing each bulb from its packaging, she gently handed them to the kids, cautioning them to be very careful not to drop any while directing them to areas that needed an ornament. I watched her intently, amazed at the expertise and finesse she used in inculcating the children's activities. She was kind and tender, decisive in the plan she had laid out in her mind, while implementing the task with such aplomb it did not sacrifice the kids' spontaneity, individuality, and fun.

Decorating the tree took a long time, but it was such a pleasant experience. I relished the close-knit atmosphere the four of us created. The happy look on Jan's face made it evident she was enjoying the task, while the kids were spirited and focused on doing the job right. Bing Crosby's *White Christmas* was interrupted occasionally as I would try to sing my own songs, but this was thoroughly nixed when they all implored me to let them listen to "Bing."

When all was finished, Jan took her camera and snapped pictures to capture the fruits of their labor for posterity. And unbeknownst to me, Jan had purchased three long red hunting stockings, which she now presented to the kids, instructing both to hang them on the fireplace for Santa to fill on Christmas Eve. She cautioned them to make sure they hung them far enough over that Santa would have enough room to get into the family room from the chimney. I smiled to myself at her imagination and simplicity, and as she continued with the Christmas Eve plan to leave cookies and milk for Santa, she promised them we would make those cookies the following evening.

I was impressed. When they were finished, the kids were sent upstairs to get into their pajamas and then came back down to watch the *Peanuts* and *The Grinch* Christmas specials, which were just about to start. When they finally appeared, they looked so cute zipped into their red fleecy sleepers. We all snuggled together on the couch, and I felt so good about Jan, totally impressed with her competency, attitude, and talent.

Jan slept over on Christmas Eve to facilitate activities on Christmas morning. The kids were up by six, and Louie came in my bedroom to tell me that Santa Claus had come, excitedly exclaiming that there were "all these" presents. In his exuberance, his voice rose with every word—"And, Dad, there's this big—big—big box! And Dad—listen . . ." And then he stretched his arms wide to indicate to me how big it was. I had to shush him, for Jan was sleeping in the guest room and I didn't want him to wake her too early. Asking him to whisper was a measure in futility, and came too late, for he laughed loudly, telling me that Nancy was already talking to her. "Daddy's friend" was awake and downstairs ahead of me!!!

I had a slight setback the octave before the big holiday, one which would last through New Year's Day. I was retrospectively reliving the last Christmas home with Kathy. It had been brought on after I was looking through the bookcase and knocked over a picture of me in a chair holding Little Louie; Kathy was standing behind talking to him, with her head on my shoulder. And her words still buzzed clear through my mind: "You're the sweetest little boy in the whole wide world." As I gazed at the picture, every detail of that precious time and her last Christmas flooded back in vivid memory. How happy she was to be in her home once again, with the turkey dinner my siblings had prepared, and the jewelry I bought her—to be able to be with the kids again, if only for a few days—the fervent conversations we had renewing our love and commitment to one another . . . it had all been so special.

The change in my mental status caught me totally unprepared. I became morose and ambivalent. Christmas had lost its

233

meaning, but I had vowed to myself not to spoil or disrupt it for Jan and the kids. I had no desire or enthusiasm to shop. Jan had volunteered, and I recall what a marvelous job she did purchasing the kids' clothes, educational toys, and stuff to fill their stockings to the brim. I thanked her, commending her time and energy. In the large box was the "Big Wheel" that Louie had repeatedly asked for, his priority for the year 1974. And despite my lack of spirit, there was a big dollhouse for Nancy, which had several options for completion. I had applied tiny wood shingles to the roof, a very tedious time-consuming task, but I enjoyed the challenge. It became an obsession to get each course straight with equal space between, which took several evenings to complete and turned out to be good therapy. Upon finishing the roof, I stained it, and did other painting, and Jan and I papered some walls, then hinged one side of the roof so Nancy would have access to the "attic space" as well as the other rooms, from the open back. In addition Jan finished the interior with the purchase of a few pieces of furniture and accessories, being careful to leave some things undone so that Nancy could have a hand in adding to the house as she got older. We both took a lot of pride in a job well done, and today the house is a collector's item.

When I got downstairs Jan had started to get breakfast but suggested opening the gifts first, for the kids were extremely excited—which could be characterized as an understatement. She read the names on the packages that were wrapped with varied and colorful paper—it was evident she had taken great care to make each package special and unique. Then the packages were handed to Nancy, who was the "passer" for that year. She took her job very seriously, in between jumps and laughs so like her mother's. This would be the traditional system until the kids could read on their own, and then they would take turns reading and passing. But this year Jan did it to move things along, for breakfast was waiting and there was a long day ahead. And when all the gifts were distributed, everyone had something to open—but Jan. Well, she did have two large sheets of construction paper with a Christmas drawing to wish Daddy's friend a Merry Christmas.

Jan had bought several gifts for the children and several for me; I had not returned her thoughtful generosity and love in kind. Though she had spent many hours and expended so much energy in her planning to make this a happy Christmas for us, she was also cognizant of my mental state and didn't really expect anything in return; she did it for love. She was so empathetic at times, even overlooking some of my terse comments to her questions and days of unintentional rejection and reticence. In the true analysis, she was God sent, but I was too engrossed in a remote past to cope with the present and reality of tomorrow.

During breakfast the magnitude of my insensitivity became apparent to me. I could tell by her eyes that she was deeply hurt. There was a controlled sadness in her voice, yet she was still gracious and continued to shower the children with love and affection. Throughout the day she never mentioned a word about it. When the kids went in for their naps, Jan indicated she was going to visit her parents, which I thought was a change in the plans, for she always visited her family on Christmas night. Beyond that, she had asked me several days before Christmas to join her with the children. Now I casually said to her, "Jan, are we still going tonight?" It was the right question at the wrong time. She started to cry.

"I worked hard to make it a happy holiday for all of us, and I did it because I wanted to—out of love. I didn't want anything in return and didn't expect anything, but to think you couldn't even pick up a card for me that said Merry Christmas, Love, Lou!"

When she finished with me I felt like the villain in one of Alfred Hitchcock's movies, subdued and beaten. I apologized sincerely while rationalizing that I was going through a bad time around the holidays. We talked for over an hour and she forgave my lack of sensitivity, but I promised to give her something every day throughout the twelve days of Christmas. She had all the right to complain, but she never conveyed ill feelings or a belligerent attitude; the author was surely blessed.

Every day there was something: earrings, poems, cards, a sweater, a red rose, a yellow rose with a yellow ribbon, chocolates, dinner, and a pin. I missed the twelfth day of Christmas as I was at a banking seminar all day in Waterford, and when I returned it was eight-thirty. Tired as I was, I tried to call Jan after the babysitter left, but there was no answer, so I went to bed. The next day I bought a small box of candy with a single red rose, attached a poem to it and stuck it in her entryway. When she went home for lunch she immediately called me in Middletown, where I was working at the time, to insist it didn't count because it was the thirteenth day. She accepted it affably, scolding that I was "something else," which I took as a compliment and an expression of love. Atonement for my flagrant indiscretion!

Jan's relationship to me at the turn of the new year continued to grow from acquaintance and friend to the special lady in my life. Before, I was grateful that she was around for companionship—someone I could confide in and sound off to, as well as someone to help me attend to the children. But that had changed. Now when she was absent for a few days I would miss her, thinking about her often. The transformation in me that had begun only a few months prior did not soften, but rather crystallized into a shining star that lit up the horizon of my spirit.

Our relationship, characterized by many as platonic and nice (Jan's a nice girl, Lou's a nice guy, they're just good friends, he's ten years older than she is) abruptly took on new meaning for both of us. We quickly started to meld, forming a strong bond, so much so that I had decided, without reservation, to ask her to be my wife! This decision would surprise, even shock, those around me and in the family, only because many times I had openly vowed never to marry again.

I decided to propose to Jan on Saint Valentine's Day, which was four days away. Although she must have thought that some day it would come to this, regardless, I wanted the timing to be a complete surprise. I would write a poem, attach a single rose to it, and take her out to dinner. I was determined to make it simple, as Thoreau advised, and then give her the opportunity to select the ring—I felt that she deserved the best, and the sky was the limit.

I made dinner reservations for eight o'clock on Saint Valentine's Day. It was cloudy, overcast and raw, one of those days when the chill filters right through to your bones; but to my delight, the weather forecasters were also predicting light snow. When I heard this, I said to myself this was going to be a roman-

236

tic evening! Originally we had planned to watch a movie on television but I would use the old ruse of deceit, then surprise!

I called Jan shortly after six, suggesting we get something out to eat, for I was tired—to get ready and I would pick her up in fifteen minutes. She inquired about the babysitter. I told one of those harmless white lies that I had just talked to her and she could stay. (I had previously arranged with the babysitter for a long day.) The only time she got suspicious was when I asked her how she was dressed. We were going to Carbone's, and I was hoping she was still in her work clothes. When she replied that she hadn't changed yet since work but wanted to get into her jeans, I convinced her that would take too long.

Since it was Valentine's Day, the restaurant was filled to capacity, and even though we had a reservation it was twenty minutes before we were seated; but that did not disturb my plans nor cramp my style, for we joined my brother Rocco in the lounge, sitting with some friends. When Jan left to go to the powder room I told those about me that this was a surprise proposal dinner but that I was concerned that it wouldn't evolve the way I planned because Jan was too suspicious.

Once seated, we relaxed with a nice dinner of filet mignon and Chianti wine. After coffee, chocolate mousse dessert, and spirited romantic conversation, the scene was set. Jan was very happy, admitting she had no inclination we were going to Carbone's, but wondered why I was wearing a suit and tie. I smiled nonchalantly and pulled from my pocket a poem transcribed on red Valentine paper, sealed in a red envelope, and handed it to her.

"Oh, Lou, you didn't forget my Valentine!" She wanted to wait until she got home, but I beseeched her to read it now.

Parable of Love

the sparrows of life fly distance to hoard
largess; sustenance young ones that board
encounter great risk numerous abound
evil hate latent strife that surrounds
ah, the spirit of truth descends—from above
omnipresent tangible, white as a dove
never to cease sings ballads thereof
encased in one's heart sweet fire of love!

love all eternal shall never leave
dies inside who reject and deceive
I humbly plead for your open hand
forever to cherish this sacred gold band
for each it is written there's one and the same
for some, mysteriously, they are two in his name
thru toils and joys will you join in my life
to nourish and keep to be my fair wife?

I promise my love 'neath heaven's blue sky
thou fragile a world with you 'til I die
imperfect this human mistakes as we live
If God does so often we too can forgive
join me please, Jan, on a journey so fine . . .
kindle your love with this poor heart of mine!

With a tear streaking down her face she happily teased, "You rat. You could have at least given me the opportunity to dress up for the occasion."

"You didn't answer my poem's question."

"Of course!" I was relieved. As we held hands across the table, through the opening I noticed Rocky with the maitre d' approaching with champagne and a proposal toast. As the four of us lifted our glasses to the engagement, I happily reflected: fate, Kathy's dying plea for my remarriage and a mother for the kids. What I couldn't acknowledge at the time had won out.

New Vows

Beautiful June Bride

wane ancient moon—old silvery sky
doth true lover yearn espy
'tis your spell, tranquil and bright
soon fair damsel in waxing light . . .
shall I count the days of yore
thus, far beyond a distant shore
nay, nay . . . just to find you by my side
young sweet rapture!
beautiful June bride!

Our wedding would take place on Thursday, 12 June 1975, at three o'clock in the afternoon. While the initial planning of a life's commitment had commenced very well, the next step was to find the right time and date. As we looked at the calendar, it became apparent that we had very little lead time, and since the spring was a very busy season and most everyone and every place was booked on weekends, we settled on a mid-week wedding.

It was decided that the occasion would be for just immediate families and a few close friends—this totaled around 125 people. The site was established—The Red Coach Grill—which had a cozy, intimate room just perfect for our day. Keeping arrangements rather low key, we opted to only have a dinner; but close to the date Jan's father convinced us dancing would be in good taste and booked a live band.

Although Jan was not Roman Catholic, she had agreed to bring the children up in the faith. I took my vacation the week before the wedding and we spent Monday and Tuesday reviewing schedules, verifying the time for the band, delivery of flowers, etc. I had made arrangements with my mother-in-law to care for the kids while we were away and she was thrilled. Kathy's family was very happy that I had found someone like Jan to raise these children who were so precious to them. The kids were excited about the wedding, and Louie would tell everyone he came in contact with in the weeks before the wedding that his dad and friend were taking a honeymoon to Bermuda, pronouncing it Babuda.

I asked Kathy's mother to stay over the night before the nuptials, to help feed, bathe, and prepare the children's clothes for the next day. When the kids were tucked away in bed and her chores were complete, we had a long conversation that covered the gambit. She told me how deeply indebted she was to me for the care extended to Kathy and my efforts to search all avenues in the realm of medicine, noting that the time I spent in Boston was indicative of my deep and abiding love for her daughter. Tearfully, she reminisced about the brief periods Kathy was home, carefully recounting how I carried her up and down the stairs, and saying she would never forget my kindness and strong faith. She cried about my optimism to the very end, and always finished a thought and a sentence with the phrase, "God is good, Louie."

This was the first time since Kathy's death that we had talked for any length of time about her daughter, and then the conversation segued smoothly to Jan and how fond she was of her. She poured out her heart, telling me how lucky I was to find someone like her so soon, that she was intelligent, attractive, and loved the kids. It felt complete to have her affirmation.

The skies were very overcast when I rose at six A.M., though it wasn't raining. I was anxious to get an early start, for I wanted to go to the office to check my desk and see if anything came in during the week that I should attend to before returning from the honeymoon. I then planned to pick up a single rose for Jan—to give to her when we left for our honeymoon as a sign of my esteem and love.

While I was slipping on my bathrobe, Nancy bounced in and wanted to talk about the wedding. She was extremely bright and very sensitive to my upcoming marriage, and queried me in her almost-three-year-old way on every aspect of it, including the trip and the day we would return. After I answered all her questions, while she was snuggled up to me on the armchair, she asked in a sober, melancholy voice if I was coming back. I'll never forget the look on her face. The early years of bonding that she missed from her dad had produced such insecurity in her, and instilled in me a devastating guilt that would take many years to relinquish.

After reassuring Nancy we would return in eight days, I tickled her under the chin, picked her up over my head, to her delight, and swung her out as if I was throwing her into a jump, then quickly hauled her back, placed her on the floor, whacked her on the bottom, and told her to get back to her bed. She bounced out, giggling loudly, as I cautioned her not to disturb Grandma.

By the afternoon of June 12th in 1975, it was raining cats and dogs, but the service at the Church of the Incarnation happily came off without a glitch, although I later learned that my bride and her parents had locked themselves out of George and Dolly's house, where they had dressed, and were it not for an extra set of keys Jan's mother had thrown into her evening bag, I would have been left standing at the altar! I was comforted and very pleased by everyone's cooperation and precision, especially because it was a mixed marriage, officiated by Father Crawford, and Jan's minister and family friend, Reverend Joseph Zezzo. With my best man, brother George, I waited in the sacristy, and my curiosity got the best of me, whereby I stole a peek at Jan waiting at the end of the long center aisle in the back of the huge church. She was calm and smiling, looking absolutely gorgeous in her simple gown of white silk. Her hair, shorter than usual, was feathered onto her face, and flowers adorned her head. Even from where I stood so far away, I could see that she glowed.

The organ pump engaged and the first measure of Mendelssohn boomed out into the gabled cavernous edifice, and I could feel the beat of my heart speed up as we started slowly to the center aisle and the front of the altar. I saw Jan smiling brightly from my peripheral vision as she and her father made their way toward me, nodding to those in attendance, with happy faces now, though many of them had shed tears in this same church while listening to the same priest give a eulogy less than two years before. I looked straight ahead, and my eyes saw a priest, but it wasn't Father Crawford; it was a big barrel-chested Jesuit who was with Kathy throughout her stay in Boston. He was always a comfort to be with and made himself available whenever I needed someone to talk with, night or day. And now he was once again here by my side. Often he would say to me, "Lou, we can't explain or know the why of suffering, pain, or sorrow, especially for someone as young as your wife. It's all a mystery in faith, but someday you'll have an answer for what is happening now." The wisdom that he conveyed to me played out that day of 12 June 1975. Jan was now three-quarters of the way down the aisle when I said to myself, "She's the answer." I couldn't think of or explain anything else, but my thoughts scattered like wedding confetti.

A million memories from my early childhood to the present bleeped through the radar screen of my mind and finally stopped on some words from a poem by an obscure poet named Roy Croft that I had memorized in my school days. It was called "Love." It expressed my true feelings precisely at the time and was certainly apropos as my betrothed walked the last few yards before she would greet me and pledge her life for the balance of time. The organ's harmonic tones of surrender, commitment, and love were augmented by the poet's words:

I Love you,
Not only for what you are,
But for what I am
When I am with you.

I Love you,
Not only for what
You have made of yourself,
But for what
You are making of me.

I Love you
For the part of me
That you bring out;
I Love you. . . .

When the ceremony was over, the first person to be in the receiving line was Little Louie, dressed in the little navy jacket, white pants, and saddle shoes Jan had so lovingly gotten for him to wear. He stepped before her and on tiptoes looked up and said, matter-of-factly, "Daddy's friend—now I can call you Mommy!" This moment in time was captured by the photographer and remains Jan's favorite memory of the day. Some guests standing nearby could hear what Louie said and laughed; many had tears in their eyes.

Outside it continued to pour cats and dogs, but inside the band was softly playing "Moonlight and Roses," the waitresses were pouring champagne into long-stemmed glasses, and a photographer held his camera high above his head while standing on a chair to capture us as we arrived at our reception. Once everyone was settled, George stood up, clanged a glass lightly to get attention, then asked everyone to rise so Father Crawford could commence with the blessing, and to remain standing for the toast. Father started, "In the Name of the Father and the Son and of the Holy Spirit, Amen. Lord, grant Jan and Lou health and peace. . . ."

When he finished George prefaced his toast by telling a story about our first date, when I had called to ask if he and Dolly would join us on a double date. He graciously accepted without asking any questions, having no knowledge that I was dating, let alone the girl's identity. When I arrived to pick him up and he noticed Jan in the front seat, he was pleasantly surprised, for George had known Jan for quite some time. Raising his glass, he said, "I ask you all to join me by lifting your glass in a special toast to the best for my brother Lou and his lovely wife, Jan. I wish them, with your blessings and prayers, a long healthy future steeped with happiness and success. . . ." The invited guests raised glasses to our future, then applauded as the band struck a soft chord to commence with dinner.

The main course was complete, and before the dessert was to be served, George got up to ask the waitresses to stop while my father spoke. George Sr. had a great infectious and optimistic philosophy about life and all that it encompassed; moreover, he had accumulated a reservoir of wisdom throughout his long and illustrious years, and used it to its fullest when the need arose. He was so pleased the first time he met Jan it showed on his face, and now our marriage was the culmination of his wish and prayers that the kids have a mother and the author a wife. If there was any doubt that George Sr. was pleased with this out-come, one need only witness his dancing that day, especially with Jan before the celebration came to a close. He had a charis-matic ebullience about him that exuded great warmth and a con-tagious charm that fascinated people and commanded tremendous respect, not only from his huge family, but also from the community at large.

My father rose, and immediately you could have heard a pin drop. "Mama and I are very happy for Louie and Jan; in addition, I am exceptionally grateful, for she likes to eat, especially Italian food—(everyone laughed). I am not so much concerned with Louie's appetite with Jan's cooking . . . sure it will be satisfied. She'll fatten him up. You children have listened to my advice and feelings about life many times over—happiness on this earth is obtainable not by striving for it, rather through generosity—and Louie, you have heard me recite my 'Recipe for a Happy Mar-riage,' but there are people here who haven't. So today, perhaps, commemorating a marriage will not be an exception. Allow me, please."

I had listened to my father's advice and philosophy of life and heard him recite this poem for years. I knew it by heart and could easily have said it myself, but I was anxious to hear it again on our special day. He took a sip of water, adjusted his glasses, and started:

Recipe for Happy Marriage

First, preheat oven of desire to 1000 degrees and set it to life
Then take a big bowl adequate to hold all the main ingredients
    of energy, ingenuity, and creativity;
Start with a pound of patience
Slowly mix a full cup of perseverance
Sprinkle lightly a teaspoonful of persistence and forbearance
Blend three-quarters cup of endurance
Cover with tender arms and let sit for ten years
And after it has gracefully risen together
Pour a quart of kindness,
A full gallon of understanding
Sympathy
And forgiveness
Then generously combine with sunny and rainy days
And bake forever with
Hope
Faith and
Charity.
There are really only three ingredients for a happy marriage
They are
The Lover,
The Beloved,
And Love which is God. . . .

As long as I could remember, though some of the lines were added, this poem was always well received, and so it was on our happy marriage occasion.

The Baby, the Bottle, the Book

It was an extremely long and tiring day in early October, a day when I was very anxious for five o'clock to arrive so I could return home to my gorgeous wife and beautiful kids. Jan had been a little under the weather for the last week, so I wanted to be as much help to her as I could during the evening. Shortly before five, three potential buyers drove into the development, one after the other in the space of less than thirty minutes. It was the last "mini" neighborhood in Wesleyan Hills, and the company was gearing down to the finishing stages, anxious to move the operation from Middletown to a site in Cromwell, where sales were off the charts. Part of a super's job description was to stop everything, regardless of what he was doing, if a potential customer came to the site. I spent time showing them the models, patiently answering their questions. Subsequently it paid off, for an agreement to hold one of the lots was consummated immediately, and the other two the following day. When I left work that day it was close to eight o'clock.

I decided on my way out of the "little city" to stop at a diner and get a soda for my parched and dusty, dry mouth. As I was leaving, a friend I hadn't seen in months was entering, and we sat down at a booth at one end of the restaurant, where a spirited chat about the past commenced. I casually glanced at my watch and was surprised that another thirty minutes had elapsed. Before leaving I called Jan to tell her I was on my way home.

As I walked through the door the house was quiet, which meant the kids were in bed. There was soft music coming from the intercom system, and Jan met me at the door with a grin on her face. I knew something was up. She put her arms around me and said, "Hi. I know you must be tired, but I have something important to tell you." My first thought was that she was only being playful, yet her eyes were serious. The only other thing I could

246

think of was children problems, having become conditioned to expect the worst.

Jan put one of her arms around my waist, and with the other took my briefcase and ushered me to the family room couch. When I sat down she went up and returned with two small glasses filled to the brim with ice and mixed with a small amount of something bubbly. She placed them on the glass coffee table, sat down, and passionately kissed me, then softly whispered, "Congratulations, Daddy!" I was tired, famished, and sweaty, and despite my wife's desirable appearance, my fondest desire was to get onto my recliner, raise my feet, and relax. I had no inclination about what she was getting at until she noticed the confused look on my face. It was then that she shared the secret she had kept for two days. She thought the mood had to be just right. "We're going to have a baby!" Needless to say, that reinvigorated me.

"You're kidding!"

She smiled. "No, I'm due on our first wedding anniversary—June 12th! How's that for timing?!" I pulled her close to me and held her, elated—our family would be wholly enjoined by God's mysterious works—and I heard Kathy's words again: "Our dreams will be yours, your new wife's, and the children's dreams." As we walked up the four steps to the kitchen area for dinner, Jan asked what I was thinking. I seriously answered that I don't ever try to understand life to the fullest, but I was blessed to have unwavering faith with a realization that suffering has a significant role in spiritual power. I wondered often if mine was not strong enough.

Jan's pregnancy, after her first trimester of nausea, had gone well. She felt wonderful, and we all happily anticipated the new little person who would be the cement in our family. On May 30th, I had all six windows and the six-foot sliding doors open wide in the 10'x20' sun room area off of the family room, and a powerful fan helped create a cross ventilation. Jan was always involved in my projects, and although she was two weeks from delivery, she was insistent on participating in the application of beautiful new carpet squares to replace flooring that had been damaged by water. The squares were 16" x 16" and made of an easy-to-install synthetic material, but the negative aspect was the necessity to use adhesive called "blue glue," which derived its name from its color. The glue had to be spread with a toothed trowel until free of all lumps; moreover, it had to set for thirty minutes, slowing the completion of the project immeasurably.

Because of the strong fumes emitted, I told Jan that it would not be a good idea for her to help me spread the glue, promising that after it was set I would call her to supervise with laying down the pattern she wanted. I called to her for the time, and when she said it was two o'clock I knew that it was going to be a long day—never imagining just how long it would be! Everything was progressing rapidly and we were happy, for even with only half of the room complete, it was taking on a bright and more square effect, which we had hoped for. Jan had taken the opportunity to go upstairs in the bedroom to rest a bit, as she was feeling the fatigue of the final weeks of pregnancy.

Twenty minutes had passed, and as I started to call upstairs to see how Jan was doing and tell her we could start the carpet again, Little Louie came in. "Daddy, can you get me a drink of orange juice?" I told him he was a big guy and he could get it himself, as I wanted to see where Mom had gone. "Hey, Dad, did you finish with . . . the glue?" I had wanted the kids out of the house when we were working with it.

"Not quite, Louie; give us another hour and you guys can come inside if you want to." Louie gulped his juice and turned to leave when Jan came down with a concerned expression on her face.

"Lou, my water broke."

"Really?!"

Louie had finished his juice and heard Jan, and taking a stab at the meaning, asked, "Does that mean Nan and I are going to have a new baby today?" Jan looked at me and smiled, telling him that was very possible! He skipped out, bubbling over with joy, and as he opened the garage door we could hear him excitedly yell to Nancy Anne, "We're going to have a baby!!"

I smiled again at Jan, told her I needed another hour to finish with the blue glue, and asked if she could wait. She looked at me as if I had lost my senses, telling me she had just talked to the doctor and he had told her to come right in to the hospital. She had already called Dolly, who was on her way to stay with the kids. The plan was for Louie to go stay at her house and Nancy to go to Rosie and Paul's.

"Lou, how many do you have left—how long will it take? I don't want to deliver in the car—my contractions are already close and strong." When I told her fifteen or twenty minutes, she said even that was too long—she had to leave right away, but conceded she could probably last another ten minutes. I promised to be no longer, telling her to sit down and be calm!

Dolly, who lived behind us, came running through the yards with her daughters to fetch the kids as we were about to get into the car. She told us not to worry about anything—she would take care of the house and the children. While helping Jan into the car, I asked how she felt. When she replied she didn't know, I responded facetiously, "If it has to be delivered in the car, shouldn't we bring some boiling water?" I had always seen people call for boiling water in the movies, though I never really knew what the necessity was. We all smiled then Jan interposed, "Lou, that's not cute. Just get in and drive—fast!" It was just before four P.M.

Running most of the red lights on the way, we arrived at Hartford Hospital in a short time. A nurse met us at the door, alerted by the doctor that Jan was in very active labor, and hurried us right past the admitting desk up to the maternity floor. Jan had taken classes in the Lamaze method of childbirth, and was scheduled for natural delivery, so they hooked her up immediately to a monitor for the baby's vital signs, as well as its movement. It was found that the baby was in the "posterior position," so that meant it would take some extra time to get it turned facing properly for delivery. What could have been a very short time was going to take longer, so Jan was started on her measured Lamaze breathing to work through very strong contractions.

More than five hours later we were moved into the delivery room, Jan in the stirrups and me in my white gown, mask, and gloves. In the process, an anesthesiologist friend who was on the hospital staff poked his head in to see how things were progressing.

"Hey, Janet, what are you doing here?"

249

Jan replied, "Oh, Lou's having a baby! It's really nice to see you, Charlie, but not at this particular moment!" She laughed (but just barely), he laughed, and the nurses and doctor who were ready for the imminent delivery laughed, as he wished her good luck. And only a few minutes later, at 11:02 P.M. on May 30, 1976, I was holding a beautiful baby girl in my arms by the name of Courtney Lee LaCava.

The nurse took the baby from me, and I left the delivery room so they could finish their work. After removing the gown, mask, and gloves, I walked downstairs to see if the coffee shop or pharmacy was open to get a little something for Jan. After returning upstairs to the lounge, I noticed a nervous father-to-be, sitting and staring into space. He greeted me, asking if my wife was going to have a baby that night; I told him she had just delivered and I inquired about his status. Empathy welled up in me when he quietly revealed that his wife was having difficulty. I immediately felt sorrow for his trouble, identifying with him in the sense that we were brothers living in hope with the same God. I couldn't now feel his pain or anxiety, although I had surely known those emotions in the past and remembered how comforting it was to have someone benevolent and compassionate to talk with. As we conversed I tried to craft the right words to ease his anxiety, but it became evident to me that it would be better for him to be alone. His doctor came in shortly thereafter, which gave me an opening to leave. While I was walking down to see if Jan was back in her room, something that Mark Twain had said struck me: "Grief can take care of itself, but to get the full value of joy you must have somebody to divide it with." The first part, I thought, was paradoxical, though I totally agreed with the latter.

I made calls to spread the good news: On this day, 30 May 1976, at 11:02 P.M., a beautiful baby girl, Courtney Lee, was born to Lou and Jan LaCava.

Despite the wonder of the day, I would try to comprehend how any doctor or mother could kill an innocent baby in the womb. Conception and birth, in all their mysterious and wonderful aspects, were incredible miracles of vast proportions, and for anyone to frivolously destroy a baby was a horrific act of violence! If the objective moral balance became tilted too far, would there be a collective day of retribution? I was struck with this implausible question at a most inopportune time, yet I would not let the monumental joy of this moment be usurped by negative feelings. I wanted to jump from the rooftops proclaiming this blessed joy and clearly remembered something Kathy's mother always repeated: "God is good, Louie. God is good," and I had to agree that yes, He really is. And that goodness can only be recognized through strong faith. But did I have strong faith? Kathy's illness, grief, suffering, and sorrow could easily have had very little meaning and worth to the author, summarily dismissed as a waste of human potential. Yes, I prayed and received the Sacraments, and yet the question now was simply begged: did this frame of mind disavow all the gifts God bestowed upon me? The complexities of the issue were too much for me to digest while attending the birth of another daughter, notwithstanding the reality that a father's witness of his child's birth engulfs the heart, conjuring up a myriad of reflections.

A million questions that need answers are hidden from mere mortals like me; locked somewhere outside the fixed stars, hidden in our faith, the mystery of the Trinity—Father, Son, and Holy Ghost, is the great truth made known to us in part through tradition . . . revelation, and Scripture. It is this great, compelling preponderance of life that causes our minds to flounder in bewilderment. What determines diverse patterns of change from youth to maturity? Are matter and form, cause and effect, potentiality to actuality, less defined to govern habits of the human person, or are suffering, pain, joy, nirvana, and ecstasy so intertwined in the soul that these passions will only be understood at the end of time? There certainly was a plan and it all had meaning from the beginning of time. If that not be so, as Saint Paul said, this life would make no sense. Though the world was only apprised of pieces of information through revelation, there is clearly reason enough to believe these mysteries were never for man to fully untangle. What was revealed to the human person, however, was an understanding that truth and prayer are the essential ingredients for any happiness found in this domain.

How strange were my mental ramblings while waiting for

the doctor to finish with my wife and new child! I wondered what other fathers thought of while experiencing one of the most important events in life. I thought of the philosophy of Augustine, Aquinas, and even Sheen, then reasoned obstacles in life did not come as impediments to harm, but rather as a wedge or tool to facilitate growth and inspire the awesome thirst for understanding. My experience at Courtney's birth would start a process that took on a whole new spiritual dimension of understanding and total acceptance of His will, which the author would never doubt again.

I got to the end of the hall and noticed a phone, which I used to call and ask how the kids were doing. My niece said they had been very excited all evening in anticipation of the baby, but she had finally gotten them to bed and they were now sleeping soundly. I told her the "good news" and asked her to please call her mother and father to give them the word and tell them I would be home soon. She said it was fine, and if she got tired her mother would come to relieve her.

The nurse who was present at delivery walked toward me and said Jan was back in her room. She was sitting up, wide awake, anxious to have something to eat. She also wanted to make sure her parents had been told; I said I had called and they would be down as soon as visiting hours would allow them the next day. There was a small end table with a vase of artificial flowers in the room, and I pulled one out of the arrangement, being very careful not to damage anything. I presented it to Jan with a 3x5 card I pulled from my pocket, on which I had penned the following poem, entitled *Babe*. ("Boose," an affectionate nickname Louie had given Courtney at first sight, was added years later. It is strange how these names originate—it had nothing to do with size or characteristics, etc. It was just something he said when he first laid eyes on her "It's my baby, my Baby Boose." And it permanently stuck with her.) The flower image had nothing to do with the theme of the poem or its contents; nevertheless, it set a mood that would help draft the words in the fashion I wanted to express:

Baby (Boose)

from thy womb, mother's arms to rest
nestled close with suckling breast
sweetly, babe, doth thy beauty shine
once hidden from this heart of mine
where dreams had flown
in hope despairs
left alone ne'er to share
a burden of requited past
returned in you my angel hast . . .
a family whole, thy gift above
yea, fondness babe a father's love!

A nurse came in to ask about Jan's comfort. She said she was tired but wired and would like very much to have something to eat and drink. As it was very late, she told me to go home to the kids and get some rest. I kissed her and told her I loved her, then went home to see the rest of the family. God had surely blessed us!

Years of Growth . . . Research the LaCava Story

Years of growth—raising a family in the 70's and 80's, as in any decade, was a challenge filled with joy, disappointment, and reward. The 60's had been different, however, than any time in our history; society had been catapulted to a level of new and exciting technological advances that affected, favorably and negatively, every facet of industry, sports, and entertainment. A wave of hedonism spread throughout the land like an infectious disease, reflected in music, language, literature, and fashion. Boundaries and what was always sacred seemed to have little value in our culture. Government (our leaders), the collective role model, took on a liberal philosophy, obsequiously using the politics of "privacy" to gain power that even influenced our judicial system with "agendas" frightfully, to the degree of flagrant misinterpretation of parts of the Constitution one never dreamed could be defiled.

The thread that held the fabric of a society together with norms and civility wore thin, whereby efforts to repair the damaged filament tempering society's excesses were challenged in the universities, in Hollywood, and by the intelligentsia. We had left an age of "class," decorum, and heroes—the Eisenhowers, the DiMaggios, the Crosbys—and meshed into obscurities of abstracts—the Ginsbergs, Ferlinghettis, and Kerouacs. God was dead! Primacy of the ego—I have to identity myself, do my thing—the Kinsey reports, the "me generation" was the new God. And regretfully, this philosophy, so passionately espoused, would have confounding results for the respect of life and freedom as the nation once knew them. The trend would continue through the 90's, exacerbated by a culture of new age, henceforth debasing without shame or decorum in general. The whole pro-

254

cess would have a devastating effect, and it would ultimately take years before the start of redemption.

The prime hope and prayer of every parent at this time was that influence from this new manifesto would not indoctrinate or undermine their efforts in raising their children. Guidance, once essential—part and parcel—now became a mandatory daily ritual. The school curricula, the teachers' union, leaders, and outside organizations with monetary and political goals and collective humanistic motives, had to be monitored zealously. When Planned Parenthood became successful in its quest for "liberal" sex education as part of school curricula, even to the degree of dispensing condoms, great care had to be exercised to caution children not to participate in these classes. The argument they gave to legitimize their cause proved to be wrong. Teen pregnancy, instead of dropping, increased to great proportions, infectious disease skyrocketed, and basic human values deteriorated to such a degree that decency and respect for one another was the exception to the rule.

Television and movies took on a new dimension with the slogan "give them what they want"—more sex, more violence. A polarization and lack of regard for authority had turned the country to strife; violence through heinous crimes of serial and mass killings, abortion, murder for hire, and capital punishment all increased to mammoth proportions. Societal stress was etched on faces, people were frightened to go out alone at night, doors left unlocked at other times in history now had to be dead bolted, and alarms were installed in huge numbers of homes and businesses. A philosophy—a political norm that was "demagogued" to give the people more—in effect eroded their freedom.

Humanistic theories, whose sole purpose was indoctrination, were boldly expressed, and the use of carefully crafted phrases like "diverse pluralistic society," "empowerment of the masses," and "pro-choice" were slowly infiltrating churches and places of higher learning, creating a conformance to ignorance (boldly dumbing down the school systems). A drastic change took place in the secular mood of a country whose people were "endowed with certain rights." The lack of fortitude and courage from good people to speak out against this "purge" would pale in comparison to any other time in our history. The pattern started to feed it itself, broadcasting globally, whereby the Pope would term the radical shift of mores in the latter part of the twentieth century "The Culture of Death"!

Jan and I were very fortunate to have the same values and philosophies and a specific plan and direction to guide our children. The first ingredient was love, and it was a tough love, which meant being truthful and open to the children's needs, questions, and problems. I always made it a practice to have open debates with Jan if we were in disagreement or impasse. We didn't go into another room and whisper; we thought it was healthy for the kids to be part of our disagreements, not to choose sides, but to learn that it was all part of life. I didn't want the kids to find that we weren't honest or truthful, as was the norm in so many families, causing them to say we were phonies later in life. I'm convinced this is the most devastating situation a child can be in, especially during vulnerable and tender growth stages. Insincerity and lack of forthrightness were and are the cause of much unhappiness and many problems with children.

Through hard work and prayer, Louis Michael, Nancy Anne, and Courtney Lee grew in health and knowledge, and their resolve gave us reason to believe in the American dream—the American experience as it was, instituted in the Bill of Rights and the Constitution. We were very proud of their accomplishments, and time had come where I could commence with the writing of the LaCava story.

The children's maturity had lessened my responsibility, leaving me with extra time to continue research on a book many family members, as well as friends and close business associates, were encouraging me to write. The task was gigantic and awesome, for I wasn't a writer of stories, although some teachers had told me to pursue my poetry. But a book of this caliber was different. I had attended writing workshops and had a general knowledge of the fundamentals of the language, having learned that basic preparation was the catalyst for any successful author. I took the notes from these workshops under advisement, but one great maxim stuck in my head that would facilitate my initiative: Writing is not a science—just write!

Malaise—Midlife Crisis—Healing

I was engulfed with a chronic feeling of emptiness when the older children were gone and Courtney had started at Colgate University. The joyous years of bonding, togetherness, and sharing our lives in close active family surroundings suddenly came to pass and we were alone. A quiet private time that parents look forward to should have made me ecstatic, but for a type-A, its arrival struck me like a proverbial ton of bricks. The schedule and pace of my life previous to the children's departure was hectic, yet I thrived on it—coaching soccer, umpiring Little League, and attending dance recitals, swim meets, concerts, concerts, more performance, summer camp, and more, and then it was over—gone! It is a time in a parent's life that has no tutorial mechanism to prepare for. You're totally filled with life, and suddenly there's an indescribable void that penetrates, then violates, the basic structure of one's heart and soul.

As an antidote to boredom and malaise, I threw myself into my work. I was involved with the Home Builders' Association, having been on the Board and chaired the largest Home Show in the state, or New England for that matter, for four years. My poetry took on a new therapeutic necessity, and I delved into writing during every remaining opportunity left over from a bizarre, frenetic schedule. Returning to the ice after not skating for fourteen years, I found that I could still jump and spin, so I attacked it with vigor and purpose. I went to New York to be fitted for new skates and was encouraged to be tested again by a young coach; within a period of six months I found myself with five coaches, as a member of Yale Skating Club and was testing again. In addition, I started to work with a partner in pair skating, with the intention of senior competition.

When I wasn't working, writing, or skating, my guitar was in my arms, and I resumed with my music at a feverish pace, enthusiastically writing two to three songs a week. I became so entranced and inspired by some of the stuff I was turning out that when Louie was in town I asked him to arrange and record some of it for a demo at the sophisticated studio we had presented him upon his graduation. Louie did such an excellent job that I sent the demo to Charlie Rich and was encouraged when I was told they would evaluate the material, hopeful they would issue it on a single. But I lost concern for the demo route upon the sad news of his sudden death only a few weeks later.

While I tried to assuage the ennui experienced from this incredible pace, I found little time for home and my beautiful, patient, and understanding wife. Instead of time and dinner with her, it was dinner with other skaters, friends, poets, and musicians. Usually in a selfish relationship more than one person gets hurt, and this was no exception to that rule. My dad always counseled in a five-word axiom that today is cliché: What goes around comes around. Maybe my father originated it, for it was wisdom in its highest form—the natural order is based in the continuity of truth and always will prevail—it can never be reinvented. Finite can't change, enlarge, or enhance infinity! What is, is. . . .

My docket soon would come to closure with a thud when my electromagnetic field was interrupted by powerful contrasting forces that caused the rearrangement of a calendar cluttered with activity and a life wedded with incessant intensity.

I had felt minor sciatica pain when working with patch (ice figures to the circle) on a West Hartford rink one brisk but sunny February. I didn't think much of it, and after skating for an hour doing some jumps and spins, the pain subsided. It continued for a few days, then it vanished, but in another two weeks it returned, this time with increasing intensity. On the day a dance test was scheduled at Yale I was in such agony it was difficult to find a comfortable position. I was not inclined to cancel the test, as waiting for another month to retest was unthinkable. Moreover, my coach had already registered me; there was no way I was going to back down. In retrospect, this decision reflected extremely poor judgment. The test should have been postponed and it may have afforded better marks, plus saved me months of pain and agony.

The problem became progressively worse. A doctor examined me and said there was nothing that he could do, offering some "pain killers," which I couldn't take. I went to a chiropractor, who took X-rays and said if the X-ray was negative she could start me on treatments. I continued my brisk schedule, for I felt guilty to sit idle—I would not release my "tawdry" grip on the delicate gift of time, and to justify my thinking I wrote:

Time

Tick-tock, tick-tock—this brazen bold clock
swallows time with measured constancy and skill
and rapes the days that linger still . . .

did you try to slow those years
that did smitten through your fears
did you grasp and hold on tight
thru a myriad of suns' bright light?

just to find this force that trails,
wretched thief of time prevails . . .

should I counter or review
all the days it took anew
or simply acquiesce with tears and shame,
for life not lived—ne'er to reclaim!

Reluctance to refine my schedule would wreak havoc on my health, and on a trip to Puerto Rico with Jan, Courtney, and her classmate, the *coup de grace* would claim another victim. My daily five-mile jog around an asphalt track was shortened abruptly behind the eighteen-hole golf course and in front of Chi Chi Rodriguez's house when a sudden and excruciating pain exploded down my left side, forcing me to literally crawl back to our room. The next day would test my resolve and fortitude, and re-

259

align my focus with a message loud and clear: slow down to life's essentials, or pay a terrible price!

That next day was one of the longest of my life. The pain was sharp, constant, and unbearable. Our flight back to the mainland was scheduled for five P.M. and my physical condition was obviously not conducive to flying. I had spent most of the night with ice packs on my back and leg and would occasionally doze off for a few minutes, then fitfully wake up moaning and writhing in agonizing torture. Jan and the girls, who planned to take full advantage of their last day of sun, were up at eight, and after inquiring if they could do anything for me, went down for breakfast. The pain had sapped my appetite, yet I forced myself to nibble on what was left in a bag of mixed nuts. Taping the ice packs around my upper leg at the thigh, I struggled to put on a bathrobe, hobbled out onto the balcony, and carefully crunched into a plastic straightback sun chair. When I raised the right leg to support it on a round metal table up against the balcony railing, I was pleasantly surprised that the shooting pain from the leg to the back lessened.

The slight relief of pain afforded me the luxury to clearly think again; I opened my briefcase on the lounge chair next to me and started a first revision of a thirty-four-verse epic I had been inspired to write on our first day of vacation. Sitting on the balcony that day I was startled, delighted, and curious when a little golden-winged songbird flew under and perched on my shoulder. I said, "Hi, how are you today?" It tweeted as if to answer me, thence a colloquial gibberish ensued for what seemed like several minutes. It flew in and out several times, and each time we resumed our conversation. When he left I took pen to paper and "The Bird" was born.

The Bird

a little bird radiant as gold
soared from a tree
as I turned to my surprise
perched on my balcony. . . .

As I worked to complete revision of the next thirty-three verses, the girls came back, at noon. They poked their heads out on the balcony to ask how I was feeling and if they could do anything for me before they went to their room to clean up and pack. Not to concern them, I replied that I was a little better, but in reality and truth, I now felt worse.

The plane was at cruising altitude of 35,000 feet, the No Smoking sign was on, and the Fasten Seatbelt sign was off when a stewardess noticed I was in severe pain and asked, "Sir, are you alright?" I explained my dilemma and requested to move to the rear of the plane, where Jan had noticed several empty seats together. She kindly obliged; it was a move that was heaven-sent, for I draped my leg over the arm of the empty seat to the right of me, relieving lateral pressure from the sciatic nerve centers. I had spent many hours in the air and loved to fly, but this was the longest four-and-a-half-hour flight I had ever experienced in my life!

When we landed at Bradley International Airport in Hartford, the flight attendant asked me if I wanted a wheelchair. Too proud, I declined, which was a terrible mistake. Waiting until everyone departed, I slowly shuffled, dragging my right leg, down to the baggage claim area, fell onto a chair that was a distance from the bag rotary conveyer. In vain, I tried to position myself to lessen my anguish, and that's when I finally recognized the seriousness of the situation.

Despite the torture, I kept reminding myself to not display the pain on my face. I believed I was succeeding, until a young girl dressed in jeans and a yellow sun shirt with a white flower stuck in the left side of her hair, came over and said, "Sir, my dad told me to ask if you need help to get your luggage." I looked at her warmly, assuring her my family was taking care of it, and I asked her to thank her father anyway. But then I stopped her and asked why they had offered. She said, "We got on the plane with you in Puerto Rico, and my father told us you were hurt and in pain." Then she excitedly said, "Today is my birthday. I'm eleven, and this is the first trip I have ever taken by airplane. We had a good time—I hope you did, too." And she skipped away.

261

This little scenario brought to mind a story I had read about Bishop Fulton J. Sheen, who went through a period of discouragement at one time in his life that was so serious he contemplated discontinuing his teaching, lecturing, and television show, *Life Is Worth Living*. While praying at a shrine he told the Lord that if He wanted him to continue, to show him a sign. The Bishop requested that a thirteen-year-old girl, dressed in white, present him with a white rose before he left the garden. We all know His answer, but it was a moving story: he was just about to leave the fenced area when a little girl in a white dress came running down the incline and yelled for him to wait, for she had something to give him. She handed him the white rose, declaring that her father had said to go give the priest this rose, for he looked so sad. The little girl started to leave when he asked how old she was. She replied "thirteen." What this story had to do with me, my pain, and the little girl that offered me help, I don't know; moreover, I was left with a strange feeling about why this story would come to me, especially in my situation, when it was an effort to even remember my name. Curiously somber, I mentally recited as she walked away:

little one;
you grace the flower in your hair
sweet gesture so kind—
rare 'tis said a world so meek
gentle, mild . . . sublime. . . .

Three weeks of treatment with a chiropractor didn't help, and when she saw me start to drag my left leg while walking bent over, she urged me to get an MRI as soon as possible. The neurosurgeon called late at night the day the series was done and advised me to come to his office early in the afternoon of the following day. The film was hanging on a view box when we entered his office, and after niceties were complete he pointed to a black dot obvious on one image and said, "That's your problem." I asked what it was, and he explained, in doctor lingo, it was a fragmentation from a disc that was lodged against my spine, and that it would only get worse if not removed. "Mr. LaCava, this should be done as soon as possible; I am backed-up for three weeks, so I would ask my secretary to schedule you today."

I reluctantly agreed to the operation, but during the interim I was determined to explore every possible option to avoid surgery. The first was a second opinion, so I scheduled an appointment with my doctor in New York. Since a train ride would be impossible, Jan drove into the city, but we had parked in the wrong parking lot, and I had to walk two blocks to the clinic. The pain was so intense that I could only shuffle along leaning on Jan; the short distance took me twenty minutes.

When my personal doctor saw me slouch with my back bent nearly ninety degrees, dragging my left leg, he shook his head and said, "This is my figure skater? This is not good!" This doctor was a young, affable Yale graduate, and we got along famously. Every visit I would bring a list of questions pertaining to my health and the medical profession in general. He would invariably say, "This is like I was back in med school." Repeatedly, we both got a laugh out of it, but he always answered my questions. Throughout the years we had many discussions on figure skaters, as he was a big fan of the sport.

He reviewed the film and said that, indeed, I had to have surgery, and suggested the arthroscopic method, where they remove the fragment through a probe hole the size of a nail head. He informed me that a particular doctor who performed this type of surgery had worked on many sports figures with ultimately good results, and it was possible I could be home the same day. Responding quickly, I exclaimed that if I had to have surgery it would be done conventionally and in Hartford, primarily because my insurance company would not cover New York; moreover, the neurosurgeon I had seen was extremely reputable. I reminded him I was there for a second opinion only, and if he was telling me surgery was necessary, so be it. Wishing me well, he accompanied us—slowly—to the elevator.

The night before the operation, when the anesthesiologist came in to brief me on what to expect from the procedure in the morning, I was working on a poem, and I must confess when it was accepted for national publication I was totally surprised:

Suffering

from a smile a tear wells in one's eye,
curse the shame for me to cry
though my body wracked with pain
gone carefree days of power-lasting fame!

many pass me in the crowd
remember my name, shouted loud
now my beard has shades of gray
has so much talent they used to say

pompous, proud, aloof with greed
youth, charm, adulation; what does it breed?
only bitterness—capped with scorn;
shoulders stooped, a face forlorn.

to do it over I'd make amends
I'd love more people; I'd make true friends!
life is fickle and time is brief,
mistakes bring suffering and days of grief!

please! allow these autumn days—to reflect
some things of yesteryear would now reject
replace with sharing; others' mindful of
enkindle hope with God's sweet Love!

My last post-op visit to the surgeon was ten days after surgery. The young doctor noted that my superb physical condition had promoted rapid healing. As is typically done upon discharging the patient, relieving their responsibility, he counseled me using medical "jargon" to be careful and keep a healthy body. I listened respectfully, delighted when he gave me the green light to skate again, yet with restrictions, cautioning me not to jump for a while, and also not to swing a golf club. I thanked him for his superb job, and gave special thanks to the Hartford Hospital for their unending professionalism. Two weeks after the operation I was back on the ice, but my life and schedule would dramatically change.

I discussed with Jan the ramifications of my spinal operation and the fact that my job was not a challenge anymore—I was in burnout mode, and I was going to request an early retirement. We had a long, frank talk about our future. I said that never would I get into the hectic schedule again, articulating unequivocally that she could be sure of it. I apologized for my past transgressions, enthusiastically declaring my prime interests would be to finish writing the LaCava story, and to pursue my poetry, and my music. Skating would now only be exercise, which meant cutting ice time from twenty hours a week to three. She was pleased, and my life took on a new dimension more conducive to family and my health.

There were two places to visit that were essential in order to commence collating the data compiled over the previous two years—Ellis Island, where the author would spend many hours on two visits, and Italy to research my father's birthplace. In the meantime, I was writing vigorously and with passion, with some of my work being praised locally; moreover, I was encouraged when one of my poems was accepted for publication in a national anthology. This turn of events could not have enhanced my zeal or eagerness any more; it motivated me to join literary clubs, attend workshops where readings were required and critiqued, and also jump into writing competitions. Although I never thought "Tapestry" was one of my better poems, I was thrilled by the attention it received; in addition, I was ingratiated when it was published.

Tapestry

woven cloth, oh! Renaissance
textile history speak to me
you kings and queens of ages past,
skilled fingers capture destiny.

so delicate your features form
of yarn through hue and tinge,
tender woven authority
bound within a fringe.

astute, embroidered majesty,
incarcerated past,
great artisan of yesteryear
preserve, emblazon cast!

One year after retirement, I was asked to participate in an international symposium in Washington, D.C. It was a competition of forty lines or less on any subject and any style of poem, including cowboy. This was a very interesting competition, exhibiting a tremendous amount of talent from forty countries around the world. We had the opportunity before individual adjudication to read at several diverse venues, including coffee houses, libraries, and hotel lobbies. Adjudications were comprised of forty poets. It was a positive event, which left me satisfied with my showing, but the highlight of the symposium was during a reading room the first night.

There were many reading rooms that could accommodate between fifty and 100 poets, where they had an opportunity to practice reading in front of a large audience. The author had made the rounds, where he'd read and listened to the many talented writers at this symposium, when there came about a very moving experience. I had just finished reciting three of my poems, and out of respect always returned to my seat to listen to several other poets before moving on to a different venue.

An Afro-American male of about seventy, distinguished with gray hair, got up and said that he had worked in restrooms in very famous hotels all his life. He had the opportunity to meet people of all walks of life, some who would occasionally read his work in awe and encourage him to pursue it. So here he was. After introducing himself, he meekly beseeched his colleagues to open with a joke, for this worked in calming his nerves. He went on: A boy ran into the house, scared out of his wits, telling his mother that Dad was going to kill him and his friend John, for

266

they had rolled the outhouse down the rather steep back hill. His mother assured him that it was not a big deal and that when Dad returned to just tell him what they had done. "I am sure he will be proud of you for telling him the truth," she said, and then went on recounting George Washington's righteous deed when he told his father about the cherry tree incident. His mother's counsel didn't relieve his fears, so she finally asked him why he couldn't take any comfort from George Washington's story. He excitedly spit out, "Well, his father wasn't in the tree when he chopped it down!"

This story and the way he presented it not only "brought the house down," but made him relaxed and ready to recite his poems. He started to read, and I was utterly moved—some poems were about his childhood and growing up; those and many others were, I thought, absolutely brilliant. The images, enjambment, word selection and arrangement were skillfully crafted—he had the entire attention of everyone in that room. He had conveyed his messages loud and clear, and when he finished I choked up, and said to myself, then to the lady next to me, "Why didn't someone recognize this guy when he was young?" She replied, "It's never too late—remember Grandma Moses?" Nodding, I thought to myself there has to be something or someone to get this type of talent out and heard in its early stages so the world can appreciate the true depth of our cultures in America.

I thought about the fact that there are so many literary, creative writing and poetry clubs and organizations, yet they draw mostly people who had guidance, encouragement, and established self-confidence when they were growing up. Or perhaps these people have the prestige of self-esteem garnered from academia and are involved in these groups, for the most part politically unencumbered; but there was nothing out there for naturally talented neophytes—poets who have much to share. It occurred to me that all the education in the world a poet will not make, and I realized we were losing some great and gifted people.

As the plane home from Washington was climbing to altitude, it came to me—why not form a gathering of "closet poets"—people who were keeping their work to themselves? The

267

sole criteria, the objective, would be to get the novice, the tyro, out to a place where he or she could read, learn, participate, or just listen—at least they would be out, and would perhaps eventually present their work. The most important requisite or epistle of this organization would be that there would not be one. It would basically be non-structured—no dues, no by-laws, no plaques, no awards, no log, no formal critique—because I wanted it as devoid of stress and tension as possible—totally unintimidating.

Upon my return, I asked for a meeting with the town of Wethersfield librarian, seeking her input. In addition, promotion was needed at a neutral, apolitical venue. I ran my idea by her, and she was very supportive—and The Closet Poet Gathering was born!

The first night we had sixteen poets. From my experience with the initiation of clubs, these numbers are statistically rare. We arranged the chairs in a circle, the age group ranged from sixteen to seventy, and the author facilitated. I didn't necessarily want to read, but the librarian was not involved in poetry at that time, so I came prepared with about fifty of my poems to distribute among the group, to "jump start" the evening if the group was reticent or reluctant to read their own material. I had learned a long time ago that poets will always be willing to read someone else's work—so that was my ruse, my stratagem to bring people out of themselves. I didn't know what to expect—our promotional material stated that all amateur, published, and non-published poets were welcome, and included the mission statement above. Little did I fathom the delightful surprise in store.

Luckily, a high school English teacher who brought two of his most talented students started the ball rolling. The first to read was a boy of about sixteen; he presented two works that were rhyme and very good. I was extremely thrilled that there was so much response when he finished. Everyone that attended that night read—some more than once—and when the session that was only supposed be to an hour and a half went on for two, I knew there was a great need for this type of venue. In addition, my belief that great talent was out there had been confirmed.

The first year of the Closet Poet Gathering was an overwhelming success by any standard, far surpassing my expectations, with large numbers of new people attending the meetings held every other Thursday night. Unimaginable at the inception, it made all efforts worthwhile, and the caliber of writers it was drawing renewed my belief that the greatest talent is not what is in front of us, but rather the latent. The reason why this talent never comes to the forefront is because it seemed beyond the control of those so blessed—they needed a venue free from intimidation.

I had a dream that the Closet Poet Gathering would mushroom across the nation, establishing chapters, weeding out for America the "hidden gifted." This would benefit people in diverse areas, bringing pleasure to many, and advancing the arts. When I saw another local library advertise a "closet poetry gathering," I was thrilled to think that maybe the idea had caught on.

But the highlight and most satisfaction came to me one night, when a lady came up to the author before a meeting and asked if her eleven-year-old son could read. She confided that they had taken him out of school after being informed he had a severe learning disability, although they questioned this because of the poems he wrote. His talent had convinced her to seek private testing, which revealed he was merely hard of hearing. The boy read a poem that night in front of twelve adults; it was very good and read with unusual poise. I realized this was a fantastic opportunity for building self-esteem. His mother thanked me profusely, and that one night made all the effort and time putting this group together worth it. As of this writing, the group is still in existence and as strong as ever.

My life settled into a pattern of poetry, music, and compiling information for the book I had intended to write for so long. My greatest hope was that the manuscript could be started by the end of the year 1996, but first it was extremely important that I go abroad; it could not commence without the help of the catalyst, the early history of the great one, the patriarch. It would start via Madrid, Rome, Naples, Sorrento, and Corleto: The LaCava Story, Act 1—*Egidio, Ora et Labora.*